MEDITATION

MEDITATION

by
Dr. Mohan Makkar Ph.D. (A.M.)
Dr. Geeta (Naturopathy)

Winsome Books India

ISBN: 81-88043-49-4

Edition 2007

Published by
WINSOME BOOKS INDIA
209, F-17, Harsha Complex, Subhash Chowk,
Laxmi Nagar, Delhi-110 092
Email: winsomebooks@rediffmail.com

CONTENTS :

The Fundamentals Of Meditation

By

Phra Acharn Plien Panyapatipo

The Fundamentals Of Meditation

- The Mind is thinking carefully about thinking and thinking: pondering about this, wondering about that, turning over assorted problems. Indulging in these suppositions and notions gives the mind no rest.
- Being aware of the thinking mind is defined (by the Lord Buddha) as mindfulness (sati).
- The knowledge of the mind occupied in thinking about something is clear comprehension (sampajañña) and judgment.
- We need to train mindfulness and clear comprehension so that they become swift enough to keep up with the mind. If mindfulness is still weak it will be unable to match up against the speed of the mind, and samadhi can't then progress. The mind can't be brought together with the selected meditation object; it can't concentrate on the in-and out-breathing.
- Instead it continues on its own way with mindful awareness lagging behind, unable to catch up. We almost manage to bring it in but it then slips away to (thoughts of) 'America', and upon following it we find it's already back in 'Thailand'....or 'Germany' and so on. We can but chase after yet never catch up because mindfulness remains undeveloped and immature. It can't match the mind. This is the source of problem in the development of our meditation practice. It is therefore essential to improve and cultivate mindfulness.

The Cultivation of mindfulness starts from being aware of the current bodily posture. If standing, be mindful of that. Walking, sitting or lying down – be present with that movement and posture. Bathing, eating or excreting be fully aware of what is going on. This constant awareness of bodily actions brings mindfulness and clear comprehension to the forefront.

Once this skill is developed you will become aware of changing postures as different activities occur: working on the job, washing clothes or dishes, reading or writing, sewing or knitting. Whatever you are involved with be present with that activity while you are doing it. Don't allow the mind to wander away. This is how mindfulness develops in daily life.

You will now find mindfulness becoming swifter and sharper, able to recognize and catch the fleeting mind. Wherever your mind may go mindfulness will follow and return with it to the object of meditation. Being more practiced you will now succeed in concentrating on the in-and out-breath. Whenever the mind wanders away you will catch up with it and bring it back together with the breathing.

Now skilful and sharp endowed with mindfulness, you will bring the mind and its wayward thinking to reflect on the breathing until it comes into view. At the time the breath is actually seen, the mind is present there together with the breath. Without such vision the mind must be elsewhere and yet if you bring them together again you should be able to understand about this. Whatever, if the mind isn't with the breath it's off rambling and concocting.

Those who can bring the mind to reflect on the breath with relative ease will find that it becomes still quiet with the breath going in and out. There is awareness of a heavier or softer, longer or shorter inhalation and exhalation, as breath succeeds breath. This knowledge and awareness indicate the mind is together with the breath. It should be understood in this way. If it only happens a litter and briefly before separating, then this is defined as momentary concentration (khanika-samadhi).

You should then pull the mind back to reflect again on the breath. Together again for a longer period the breath seems much more refined, almost as if there isn't any at all. You can't find it! It's at this point that people fear death: "*Where's my breath gone*?" "*It was here just now….*" And so they come out of samadhi. They withdraw being afraid they will die.

Don't go and be so afraid. The breathing is still there only it's extremely subtle and refined. But there's no need to go searching for it. Direct you mindfulness and discernment to the mind and return it to the meditation object. Go and examine: exactly where does the heart or mind have its origin? Where does its thinking arise?

What is the feeling of happiness and contentment currently been experience like? At that moment you have found the heat. Now direct it to the chest area or some such point. Place the pleasant feeling which the heart is experiencing there, and support it with your mindfulness and discernment. Keep your reflection there, let that be where any 'thinking' occurs. In this way a deeper, more profound tranquility will develop until the level of access concentration (upacara samadhi) is reached.

At this point some people may experience a bright radiance. But if nothing happens for you, don't feel discouragement. The practice of meditation is not concern with the desire to see any manifestations. Don't fabricate any expectations about seeing a bright light or any such thing.

Do not speculate about what may be going to happen. The state of tranquility will develop in its own way and whatever happens, happens. Never crave for a vision of heaven and hell for that type of wishful thinking will itself block any approach to tranquility.

Anyone who finds concentration easy to manage will certainly experience ease and happiness as soon as the heart is still and tranquil. You will realize for the first time what happiness is all about.

This state must also include rapture (piti) though it may manifest in a different manner for different people. Your hair may tingle all over and 'stand on end'; or a sense of coolness refreshes the heart; or you may feel as if enveloped in soft cotton wool; or as though a flash of lighting precedes the coolness; or the body seems so light and buoyant that it might float away.

The meditation teacher can't order or control this sort of experience. They are termed 'the buoyant body and the buoyant mind.'. Why should the calm mind be so light and buoyant? It's because it has released the hindrances (nirvana) and is free of such burdens. Endeavor to support and sustain this state of mind.

I would like you to bypass the affair of voices heard in this state. They sound a bit indistinct like over long distance telephone lines. You may actually seem to see and hear both local and distant conversations concerning yourself. However they cut off when the mind either goes deeper or withdraw from that particular level of calm.

The mind just happened to be properly tuned in, so don't go around boasting of your clairaudience or Clairvision. Some people may not want to experience such images but whatever appears depends on the nature of the concentrated mind itself.

On leaving these things behind, the tranquility deepens, by the hour, the physical body will seem to drop completely away. No arms or legs: you don't notice your hands or body. Wherever are they? There's the temptation to open your eyes to check but don't bother about doing that. Never mind about those things. Come and look closely at your heart to check what object it rests with, and sustain it there. Tremendous happiness is prominent and vividly present. This is attainment concentration (apanã samadhi) where the mind is enraptured and engrossed in that buoyant state, free from all hindrances.

There is no hunger or thirst, no wanting of any external object only the desire to stay with that happiness, never experienced before. This spiritual happiness attained through samadhi puts all gross worldly affairs and desires out of mind; business and work concerns are completely thrown out.

Should attainment concentration continue in sublime happiness letting go of all else, then it is called absorption (jhãna) . This serenity is only a litter different from the state of equanimity (upekkhã).

At this point, the question of other people comes up: *'has anyone else experienced what I have?' 'How can they manage to do so? '* this is the time to be extra careful so that you don't start flaunting your knowledge. It's all too easy to become sidetracked here so stay prepared and alert to this matter.

Many people go off the rails and become crazy, telling all and sundry, "*It's such real happiness...You must do this! ....You should do that!....*" Forestall this with mindfulness and discernment. Don't go around preaching --- you're not enlightened yet.

Examine and remember the sequence of steps you have taken to achieve this level of samadhi. Next time you will then be able to retrace the way with ease and greater skill. Notice how you establish mindfulness and clear comprehension right from the beginning of your practice. How was the mind placed? What was developed and what disregarded? When the deeper level of samadhi was reached, how was the mind sustained in attainment concentration?

When coming again to the practice you will immediately be able to deal with anything that intrudes. Such things are disposed of in the same way as before and the previous state becomes established again. A person skilled in this way will be proficient in doing this under any circumstances; traveling by car, ship or plane, wherever he might be sitting. Whichever country, it's all the same. Once expert in entering and withdrawing from meditation it all seems easily and swiftly accomplished. The hindrances no longer come into the picture at all.

There are some people though who find it difficult to concentrate their minds. No matter how they try, the mind always seems to wander away. They should keep mindfulness on the mind's trail until it tires. It really can't escape for it is stuck on thinking about money or a car, or a house, or the children or grandchildren and near friends.

As soon as it fastens onto some such object, mindfulness and discernment must follow and catch it there. Interrogate it immediately about its possessiveness; *"Why be so grasping and attached to this (for example) house ? Is it even yours? "* The answer will come back, *"certainly, it's mine."*

Mindfulness and wisdom must then probe and examine the mind with, "*Then when you die will you take it with you?"* If it should admit the impossibility of that, then follow up with, *"Then why be so preoccupied with it; it's solidly built and isn't going to run away."*

The mind must be reprimanded and when necessary brought to order by intimidation. Such threats will leave the mind baffled and dazed and it can then be led back to the meditation object, concentrating on the breathing. This is the way of wisdom developing samadhi, for those who find concentration difficult. It means using the right and most appropriate tactic, the best skilful means that accords with the situation.

Once the mind is together with the meditation object it is time to curb and restrain it there. Sustain it without allowing it to break away. On occasion though, the mind will also deserve approval and praise. For instance the wish to go and meditate arise even in the midst of unfinished work. Try to nourish that intention by speedily tying up any work which left undone might remain a cause of uneasiness. However as no task is ever completely settled, as soon as the right pause or lull appears rewards the mind's desire by quickly going away.

Take the break sitting samadhi in your room or think of a way to get away, like escaping via the bathroom. For it's when the mind wants to concentrate that the calm and tranquility will develop with special facility, backed by the full force of faith. Any preoccupation will automatically be cut aside.

The stilled mind brings happiness without any drawbacks or anxieties. It is content in itself. It's as if one likes the climate and atmosphere of some cave, forest or shady spot. The cool breeze blows and one feels relaxed and quickly becomes at ease.

So the praise worthy state of mind wishing to meditate must be encouraged to do so. If at nighttime the mind is very tranquil then continue on with the practice until midnight. And if it still progresses then don't quit but develop it further to perfect serenity. It will deepen and establish itself more and more firmly, on a more and more profound level. Don't stop now. This is the time when you'll recognize how far your meditation has developed.

With this accomplishment you can now go to bed. After offering respect to the Lord Buddha lie down and recollect the steps you have taken to tranquility and sleep together with that. On awakening the mind will immediate go to the meditation object and that level of samadhi. I myself practice in this way.

The mind will automatically be drawn and concentrated deeper and deeper at the place it knows. With constant development and with genuine samadhi there will absolutely no dreaming during sleep. Once awake again the mind knows its duty and this is what we call mindfulness and clear comprehension. They are there to unremitting uphold and care for the heart.

You have to understand about the trained mind. When it needs to be chided, you must chide it. When it needs disciplining then do so and sustain it when it needs supporting. And when it's commendable then applaud it. It's like confronting one's disobedient children. One takes hold of their arm without releasing until they accept.

When they listen to one, are good and study diligently then they should be rewarded with praise. The mind is similar in that it resists if one continually uses force, so you must also soothe and coax it along. Being bullied, it might refuse to study, to work; it becomes weak and lazy. But with praise and encouragement it will work all day, our employees need this treatment too.

The assistant in our shop sells our merchandise for us, helps us with our work and to earn our livelihood. We can't simply bully and be on their back all the time. They also need care and attention, kind and solicitous words. However, if a mistake is made they will still need telling and correcting.

The child is quiet and still because of wise handling on the part of the parents. They don't solely punish and bully for otherwise the child may fail in his studies or even have a nervous breakdown. The serene mind also needs similar treatment with mindfulness and wisdom carefully watching over and correcting it. Mindful discernment this is the resource to use. The more the better.

Mindfulness also supervises speech. Defilement's come in many forms so we need to be aware of what we are saying. By talking in such a way, is it beneficial ? Is it well justified? For example, is what I am saying right now useful to anyone? Does it offer happiness and is it worthwhile? Holding forth without mindfulness supervising means you will blunder and go astray. In the beginning we all have to make mistakes so the first thing is to recognize that and then it can be corrected.

After dealing with speech you come to your thought. Be aware of unwholesome thinking and know when it's good. Thoughts going in a bad direction must be held back; you must keep them on the right track. The mental process need to be supervised and cut off when necessary. Let go of evil thoughts. Fix your mind on skilful thinking in every posture standing, walking, sitting, and lying down.

Then happiness will arise. Once you realize this mind will diligently apply itself in the wholesome direction and accumulate virtue. Comparing this with something on the strictly material plane, it's similar to making roads, cars, aircraft, ship or clothes etc. Careful and skilful thoughts will result in good, favorable products which will sell well and make your fortune.

So with the mind. Good thoughts make your mind buoyant and happy, whereas evil thoughts will result in suffering. If you do not produce good products they will not sell. If you say bad things, you will soon be quarreling and fighting. Then suffering will certainly appear for anger and hatred can only bring distress.

The meditation of everyday life will bring happiness when you are continually aware of whatever activity you're engaged in. Watch; while standing, walking, sitting, lying down, eating, going to the bathroom, washing your hands. Notice the mind thinking and see with what topic it calms down. No matter what you do be conscious of doing it. People like this meditate all the time. Cooking or washing dishes it's the practice of samadhi. They concentrate their mind while walking to the bathroom, while using the toilet.

Contemplating and being aware of the mind this is unfailing meditation. There's no need to lock yourself away to meditate, the wise person will be able to do so at any time. This is what I would also advise you to do. Don't continually wait for the appointed time, develop samadhi as you read this book, as you write or sew or even while you cut your fingernails.

Be mindful and concentrate on the thing in hand and rest your mind with it. But keep away from unwholesome things for such thinking will bring distress instead. People who diligently watch over their mind in this way, who are aware of the mind at every moment except when in sleep - - will always be serene and at peace.

The enlightened being (ariya) and our venerable teachers (acharn) practice in this way. Their minds are always concentrated. They converse and it's still samadhi because their heart doesn't go out to take issue or bother anybody. Mindfulness and wisdom supervises the whole process so that even a chat together becomes samadhi. Those venerable acharns who recently were killed in a plane crash were prepared for death.

Their minds were endowed with samadhi and ready to die without fear at any moment. Wisdom was always composed and present to sustain the mind through any eventually. They were prepared to die at any time, and being always aware of the potential for death they could simply abandon their bodies at the actual time without any distress.

Those people who have never practiced meditation or developed samadhi may find such things hard to believe. If they don't know what their own minds are truly like through meditation, then they can't be expected to comprehend things anyway. To them it is impossible for anyone to train his mind because it keeps changing all the time. When the mind grasps onto suffering, we suffer; when it holds to happiness, we're content. For those acharns the mind was released and serene.

If the mind dwells in samadhi then we meditate all the time. I've been contemplating this and really consider the teaching of the Lord Buddha to be very deep and profound, so subtle and intricate. It becomes clear how the purity of mind of those perfectly practiced and accomplished acharns might even suffuse their bones too.

Dear Readers,

Thank you for purchasing a book of "Magic Series"

"The Meditation Magic".

What is so Magical about Meditation? Try for a few months, and you will know the Magic of Magic's, "Meditation Magic."

Remember to keep the same time, same place and prefer to wear the same clothes. Start meditation with ten minutes a day, increasing it to 30 minutes over a period of one month.

We will be talking about a lot of meditations, so, do not get confused. Peace is where the heart is. Travel inwards. An exact world exists inside you, I would say, a better world, a complete universe indeed.

I have extended my hands, take them in yours, and, let's meditate together, for an out of this world experience.

With love and light

Dr. Mohan Makkar Ph.D. (A.M.)

SECTION - I

MEDITATION
Groups

Know Your Cults / Foundations / Groups

INDEX Section - I

<u>CHAPTER 1</u>

ABOUT 3HO - KUNDALINI

Yogi Bhajan

Healthy, Happy, Holy Organization (3HO) is a worldwide association of people dedicated to the excellence of the individual. The basic philosophy of 3HO affirms that you as a human being are so perfectly created that by using exercise, breath and meditation you can balance and revitalize the physical body, nervous and glandular systems and bring balance and peace to your life.

3HO brings to the public the ancient science of Kundalini Yoga. It offers complete lifestyle guidelines on nutrition and health, interpersonal relations, child rearing and human behavior. You may choose from a wealth of knowledge to find the exact techniques you are looking for to become healthy, happy and holy.

The Concept of Healthy, Happy, Holy You Can Be Healthy. Enjoy greater strength and flexibility, enhance your respiratory and circulatory systems, improve your digestive system, invigorate your glandular system, build up your immune system, and maintain a youthful appearance.

You Can Be Happy. Increase your mental energy and heighten your concentration. Give yourself the experience of a deeper inner calm. Increase your connection to yourself, and clarify the direction of your life.

You Can Be Holy Yoga creates union. The experience of unity through yoga brings you into contact with your infinity, your link to the universe.

Founded by Yogi Bhajan in 1969, the 3HO Foundation revolves around the simple belief that to be healthy, happy and holy is the essence of a fulfilled life. The focus is on kundalini yoga, as taught by Yogi Bhajan, who is credited with bringing kundalini teaching to the West. Today, 3HO operates more than 300 centers in 35 countries.

CHAPTER 2

ANANDA

Ananda was founded in 1968 by J. Donald Walters (Swami Kriyananda) a direct disciple of Paramahansa Yogananda. Although not affiliated with Yogananda's Self-realization Fellowship, the focus is on Yogananda's Kriya yoga.

Swami Kriyananda says “"Forgiveness is the sword of victory! When we forgive those who seek to hurt us, we rob them of the very power to do us harm."

The Thailand Meditation Group was created and dedicated for all those that are inspired and lead to begin their journey in learning the silence within. In addition, for those that has an interest in learning a technique to realize God and the manifestations of love from within.

Thailand Meditation Group is also affiliated with Ananda Church of Self-Realization(founded by Swami Kriyananda, living disciple of master) and its world mission in "helping others how to positively guide their lives through the priceless teachings of Paramhansa Yogananda."

"When you practice truth whether you call yourself a Christian, a Hindu, a Buddhist, or a devotee of any other religion, Christ will claim you, and so will Krishna, Buddha, and all other divine incarnations of truth." - Paramhansa Yogananda.

A Pranayama technique such as Kriya Yoga is a scientific route or method that leads one to self-realization. Anyone that practices a certain religion can keep that religion along with practicing the scientific techniques of Pranayama Kriya Yoga. This can only enhance ones particular understanding of his or her religion on a much deeper level. Eventually we realize that all paths lead to the same destination and that is the truth we all must learn to accept in the world today.

Yoga can be traced back 5,000 years as the science of realization developed as scientific techniques, not just a religion. Many throughout the world since the 1800's have been practicing the ancient science of Kriya Yoga. The Pranayama Kriya Yoga technique that is mentioned in the Bhagavad Gita and by the leading exponent of Yoga science Patanjali, in the Patanjali Sutras was revived by the great Babaji in the 1800's which had been lost in the dark ages. Lahiri Mahasaya was the first modern Yogi that Babaji picked to disseminate the Pranayama teachings. Paramhansa Yogananda was chosen to bring this highest science to the west in the 1920's.

There have come to be many groups around the world that teach Kriya Yoga, that have been lead by different directions or teachers. Just as God picked several instruments to help spread the teaching of all great techniques, this technique is not kept in the dark as a secret but given out to those devotees that really want to know God.

When one is ready the teachings will be presented to them. God is in all things not just a body or a group that is in charge of the dissemination.

Only when we are given the proper tools to quiet our restless minds, can we begin to understand and learn that pure joy and happiness is within all of us. Master (Paramhansa Yogananda) has often said, "Kriya Yoga is said to be the Airplane route to self-realization." While there are many rivers that lead to the one ocean, there are also faster routes, which are better suited for ones consciousness.

CHAPTER 3

AUM SHINRIKYO

Aleph, Aum Shin Rikyo

What is Aum Shinrikyo?

Aum Shnrikyo is a religious sect founded by the 'Venerated Master,' Shoko Asahara (born Chizuo Matsumoto on March 2, 1955).

In 1984, the forerunner of Aum Shinrikyo, 'Aum Divine Wizard Association,' was established in Shibuya, Tokyo. Mr. Asahara is said to have attained final salvation in the Himalayas in 1986. In 1987, the samgha-system was introduced. In this, followers undergo religious training while living as a group. It was at this time that the headquarters of the group was transferred to Setagaya Ward, Tokyo.

In 1989, the sect was recognized by the City of Tokyo as a religious corporation, and in 1990, Mr. Asahara and a number of other top ranking officials of the sect announced their candidacies as Supreme Truth Party representatives for the House of Representatives. (None of them won.)

The group reveres Shiva as their chief god, and is involved in ancient yoga, primitive Buddhism and Mahayanist Buddhist teachings. The group's ultimate aim is to 'save all living things from transmigration.' The group is often referred to as a new Buddhist sect, but it also claims to be an original religion based on

Hinduism and created by Mr. Asahara.

Mr. Asahara had prophesied that because of increasing evil the world is heading for a catastrophe at the end of the century. He said that in 1999 a nuclear war will erupt that will cause the end of the world. In order to prevent this, 30-thousand people must attain salvation, since only by spiritual awakening will holy energy be created to avert the coming crisis.

Based on the four main areas of doctrine, meditation, religious austerity, and initiation, there are three training systems called the yoga tantric course, siddhi course, and the bodha course. Through salvation and enlightenment ultimate happiness can be obtained. Followers aiming for salvation renounce the world and donate their personal wealth to the sect.

<u>CHAPTER 4</u>

THE BAHAIFAITH

"THE WELL BEING OF MANKIND, ITS PEACE AND SECURITY ARE UNATTAINABLE UNLESS AND UNTIL ITS UNITY IS FIRMLY ESTABLISHED."

-Bahá'u'lláh-

Bahá'u'lláh is the Prophet-Founder of the Bahá'í Faith, the youngest independent world religion. There are over 6 million followers spread in over 235 countries and territories.

What is the Bahá'í Faith?

"The Bahá'í Faith upholds the unity of God, recognizes the unity of His Prophets, and inculcates the principle of the oneness and wholeness of the entire human race. It proclaims the necessity and the inevitability of the unification of mankind."

Who is Bahá'u'lláh?

Bahá'u'lláh is the Messenger of God for this age and the Promised

One of all religions. He suffered 40 years of imprisonment and was exiled from Tihrán in Iran over Constantinople/Istanbul in Turkey and Adrianople/Edirne in Turkey to 'Akká in the Holy Land, where He passed away in 1892. Bahá'u'lláh means "The Glory of God".

"This is the Day in which mankind can behold the Face, and hear the Voice, of the Promised One ... Great indeed is this Day! The allusions made to it in all the sacred Scriptures as the Day of God attest its greatness. The soul of every Prophet of God, of every Divine Messenger, hath thirsted for this wondrous Day."

The Báb is the Forerunner of Bahá'u'lláh. He is the Messenger of God Who prepared the people for the coming of Bahá'u'lláh. He declared His Mission in 1844 in Shíráz in Iran. After six years of suffering and imprisonment, He was martyred. His followers were persecuted and over 20,000 were executed. The Báb means "The Gate".

'Abdu'l-Bahá, the eldest son of Bahá'u'lláh, was the Exemplar of the teachings of Bahá'u'lláh and was appointed as the sole Interpreter of His Writings. He also suffered with Bahá'u'lláh in prison. 'Abdu'l-Bahá means "Servant of God".

What are the teachings of the Bahá'í Faith?

Oneness of God

"There can be no doubt whatever that the peoples of the world, of whatever race or religion, derive their inspiration from one heavenly Source, and are the subjects of one God."

Oneness of Religion

"The purpose of religion as revealed from the heaven of God's holy Will is to establish unity and concord amongst the peoples of the world."

"Every Divine Revelation hath been sent down in a manner that befitted the circumstances of the age in which it hath appeared."

"Know of a certainty that in every Dispensation the light of Divine Revelation hath been vouchsafed unto men in direct proportion to their spiritual capacity."

"Know thou assuredly that the essence of all the Prophets of God is one and the same. Their unity is absolute. God, the Creator, saith: There is no distinction whatsoever among the Bearers of My Message."

Oneness of Mankind

"O Children Of Men! Know ye not why We created you all from the same dust? That no one should exalt himself over the other ... Since We have created you all from one same substance it is incumbent on you to be even as one soul ... that from your inmost being, by your deeds and actions, the signs of oneness and the essence of detachment may be made manifest."

"Ye are all the leaves of one tree and the drops of one ocean."

"Be ye as the fingers of one hand, the members of one body."

Religion should be the Cause of Love and Affection

"Religion should unite all hearts and cause wars and disputes to vanish from the face of the earth, give birth to spirituality, and bring life and light to each heart. If religion becomes a cause of dislike, hatred and division, it were better to be without it, and to withdraw from such a religion would be a truly religious act."

Elimination of Prejudices

"... religious, racial, national, and political prejudices, all are subversive of the foundation of human society, all lead to bloodshed, all heap ruin upon mankind. So long as these remain, the dread of war will continue."

The Purpose of Life

"All men have been created to carry forward an ever-advancing civilization ... To act like the beasts of the field is unworthy of man. Those virtues that befit his dignity are forbearance, mercy, compassion and loving-kindness towards all the peoples and kindred's of the earth."

The Potential of Man and the Importance of Education

"Regard man as a mine rich in gems of inestimable value. Education can, alone, cause it to reveal its treasures, and enable mankind to benefit there from."

Self-Education

"How couldst thou forget thine own faults and busy thyself with the faults of others? ... magnify not the faults of others that thine own faults may not appear great."

"The holy Manifestations of God were sent to make visible the oneness of humanity. For this did They endure unnumbered ills and tribulations, that a community from amongst mankind's divergent peoples could gather within the shadow of the Word of God and live as one, and could, with delight and grace, demonstrate on earth the unity of humankind."

Bahá'u'lláh has revealed spiritual and social teachings and laws that mankind needs to solve the problems of this age. In the Bahá'í community there is no clergy or priesthood. Instead, there are institutions at the local, national and international levels, each consisting of nine elected Bahá'ís.

If in your heart you agree with what you have read, then you can consider yourself a Bahá'í and can be linked with the world-embracing Bahá'í family.

CHAPTER 5

BRAHMAKUMARIS

Founder : Dada Lekhraj

Brahma Kumaris World Spiritual Organization
As a worldwide family of individuals from all walks of life, the Brahma Kumaris World Spiritual Organization offers an education in human, moral and spiritual values. To meet the challenge of change, it initiates dialogue and presents a fresh vision of the future. It recognizes the intrinsic goodness of all human beings and teaches meditation to help each one rediscover their inner resources and strengths. Details on free meditation classes and locations near you can be found on their website.

Perhaps few organizations have stimulated as much change and discussion at the time of their inception, or have undergone such expansion in the course of 60 years, as the Brahma Kumaris World Spiritual University. And yet, from its beginnings the BKWSO has managed to remain steadfast in maintaining its original principles and in adhering to its original purpose.

The University came into being under the name "Om Mandali" and consisted of only a handful of men, women and children living in Hyderabad (now part of Pakistan, but at that time part of colonial India). These spiritual pioneers were inspired to transform their lives after a respected and wealthy member of their community; Dada Lekhraj experienced a series of profound visions in 1936.

The visions revealed spiritual truths about the nature of the soul and God, the Supreme Soul. These concepts were simple in their expression but their meaning so deep that they awakened a powerful sense of recognition in those with whom the visions were shared.

A year after its establishment, the organization moved from Hyderabad to Karachi. For fourteen years, until after the partition of India and Pakistan, the founding group of 300 individuals, lived as a self-sufficient community spending their time in intense spiritual study, meditation and self-transformation.

In 1950, the community moved to Mount Abu, a quiet place reputed for its ancient spiritual heritage. Nestled high up in the Aravali Mountains of Rajasthan, it provided an ideal location for reflection and contemplation. Brij-Kothi was their first home. This building was located in a vast expanse of bare rocks, uninhabited except for a few recluses living in small caves. A few years later, the community moved to another site which remains the University's world headquarters - Madhuban (meaning 'Forest of Honey').

The potential of the place did not go unnoticed as the location offered opportunities for expansion. The courtyard of Madhuban, which serves as a meeting place for students from around the world, was once two large stables. These structures were the first to be transformed into classrooms and living quarters. With every I year, there came an addition in the form of an extension or new building.

In 1952, Brahma Baba, as Dada Lekhraj had become known, felt that it was time to reach out to the rest of India and share this knowledge, as he was aware of the devastating scars the troubled independence process and partition had left on peoples' lives.

A few sisters left their haven and moved to Bombay and Delhi 'on service'. Their task was to establish study centers where the knowledge of Raja Yoga would be taught. Today, there is scarcely a town in India where the name of Brahma Kumaris has not been heard.

From its modest beginnings, the organization kept progressing in leaps and bounds to reach by early 1996, about 3,200 meditation centers in 70 countries with over 450,000 students. Madhuban serves as the nucleus of the Brahma Kumaris' centers worldwide and Mt. Abu, 'the Father's mountain' is regarded as a pilgrimage place by many who are in search of spiritual rejuvenation.

Together they attract over a quarter of a million individuals from all ethnic and religious backgrounds every year. From classes in the stables, the organization has come a long way and has just inaugurated 'The Academy for a Better World' as part of the celebration of its 60th anniversary. This Academy is a place of international endeavor -- a place where men, women and children can reach their unique human potential and cultivate the values of our common humanity.

On a physical level, he was a man of stature, with soft white hair, a well-formed forehead and prominent cheekbones. On a spiritual level, his presence was soothing and gentle, and from his eyes emanated wisdom, understanding, compassion and strength.

Born in 1876 into a humble home, and the son of a village schoolmaster, Brahma Baba was brought up within the disciplines of the hindu tradition. He, however did not follow in his father's footsteps and instead entered the jewelry business, earning a considerable fortune as a diamond trader. As a businessman, he maintained a highly respectable position within the local community and was known for his philanthropic acts.

He had an inherent ability to cope with change. At the age of 60, when most of his colleagues were planning their retirement, Brahma Baba entered into the most active and fascinating phase of his life.

In 1936, over a period of several months, he felt the need to invest more time in quiet reflection and solitude. Then one day, while in a meditative state, he felt a warm flow of energy surrounding him, filling him with light and exposing him to a series of powerful visions. These visions continued periodically over several months giving new insights into the innate qualities of human souls, revealing the mysterious entity of God and describing the process of world transformation.

The intensity of the message they conveyed was such that

Brahma Baba felt impelled to wind up his business and devote himself to understanding the significance and application of this revealed knowledge. The sound of the words ringing in his mind seemed new, yet they felt so true and real.

60 years have passed since Prajapita Brahma received the series of visions. Who could have guessed -- besides those touched by the same visionary experiences -- that the young women he placed at the fore of the institution would now be on the world stage, sharing platforms with political and religious leaders at the highest level, and leading a lifestyle revolution followed by over 450,000 people from all backgrounds of culture and religion, race and society? Or that millions of others would be taking benefit from the teachings, finding empowerment in the present and hope for the future, when loss of integrity in human hearts and minds has plunged so many into despair?

The living skills that he taught have stood the test of time. The young women that he put to the fore, now in their seventies and eighties, have become beacons of love, peace and happiness, in a world increasingly troubled by disordered relationships, greed, addiction, anger and violence.

Brahma Baba left his body in 1969 at the age of 93. The Tower of Peace stands as a tribute to the invincible spirit of an ordinary human being who achieved greatness by rising up to the challenge of the deeper truths.

<u>CHAPTER 6</u>

BUBBA FREE JOHN

Da Free John

Franklin Jones, born in Boston, 1939, changed his name to Bubba Free John, and claims to be nothing less that an incarnation of God, a guru to be worship... the first American-born SIDDHA, with headquarters in New York City.

"Da Free John" is the name by which Avatar Adi Da Samraj was known publicly from 1979 until 1986.

"Free John" is a rendering of the root-meanings of Avatar Adi Da's born name, "Franklin Jones". "Da" means "to give", or "the Giver". The Name is hidden in the Upanishads, the venerable scriptures of India, in which "Da" is the syllable uttered by the Divine Voice in thunder, and the central syllable of "hr-da-yam", which means "the Heart", "the Divine Condition of all". The Name "Da" also appears in the Tibetan Buddhist tradition, where it is defined as "the one who bestows great charity", "the very personification of the great Way of Liberation".

When He revealed the Name "Da" to His devotees in 1979, a new period of Avatar Adi Da's Work began. He no longer related to devotees socially as "Bubba", or Divine Friend. He began to be acknowledged by His devotees in a more traditional and sacred manner as the Divine Giver of Grace and Blessings. The Name "Da" has been Avatar Adi Da's primary name since 1979.

He went to India, had apparitions of the Virgin Mary, and founded the "Free Primitive Church of Divine Communion", the "Free Community Order", and the "Laughing Man Institute".

- The Doctrine, is Hinduism, specially the Advaita Vedanta, with salvation coming through total devotion to the guru, namely, Bubba John!

... But he also performs miracles, causing violent thunderstorms, and amazing supernatural phenomena, similar to those in demonism, and classical spiritualism.

CHAPTER 7

DHARMARAJ SIDDHI SADHANA

Dharmaraaj Yamaraaj Namo Namah

The Lord of death, Yamaraj, is also called Dharmaraaj or the Lord of justice. It is Yamaraj who decides the amount of pain, suffering, fear and sorrow that one would suffer in life. In the face of these negative influences no human being can make progress in life.

Mental disturbances lead to loss of vital life energy. To balance this situation one not only needs to pray to all deities, rather one also needs to worship Yamaraj.

The cause of mental and physical affliction in a person's life are his past life Karmas and the Karmas of the present life.

One can surely control and change the present Karmas or worldly actions but how can one neutralize the adverse effect of the Karmas of the past life due to which one might be suffering from obstacles, pain and misfortune in the present life?

The famous ancient text Mantra Mahodadhi states -

"I pray to Lord Yamaraj who has a complexion like a dark rain-laden cloud, who is the son of Sun, who blesses good action with boons, who punishes bad action, who travels on a he-buffalo, who wears so many ornaments, who is the ruler of spirits and hell and who wields a mace".

It is clear from this verse that Yamaraj is the son of Sun. Hence by worshipping Yamaraj one also gets the blessings of Sun. Sun represents one's personality and all other planets revolve around him. The above verse is actually the Dhyan Mantra of Lord Yamaraj.

Dharmraj Sadhana

As explained earlier the basic cause of all problems in human life are past Karmas and it is Lord Dharmaraj or Yamaraj who decides how to punish a person for his bad actions. Thus through the Sadhana of Dharmaraaj one gains totality - physically, in one's mind and at work. Through this Sadhana one is able to control all diseases.

All one's actions effect not only the individual but also his family. Hence Dharmaraaj Sadhana is very essential for the protection of all family members. It is stated in the Rahasya Tantram text -

i.e. A person who chants the Dharmaraaj Mantra that has been prefixed and suffixed with the Mrityunjay Mantra is freed of all problems and all his wishes are fulfilled.

More painful than physical illness is mental trouble. Due to disturbance of mind a person becomes prey to worries and he cannot make any progress in his life.

The cause of mental disturbance are problems in family life, trouble from the state side, obstacles in tasks and physical illness. By making the mind pure and tension free the physique could also be made fit. And for this the best Sadhana is Dharmaraj Sadhana.

Due to this Sadhana one is not only able to find solutions to the problems of the present rather one is also able to prevent problems from occurring in the future.

The person who attains victory over fear is able to win the whole world. Through Dharmaraj Sadhana this very thing is possible provided one has faith, devotion and patience.

Special time and days are designated for all Sadhanas so that one could attain to success in the very first attempt by trying the Sadhana in auspicious moments. One can try any Sadhana any time in the whole year.

But if particular Sadhanas are started or accomplished in auspicious moments then the result gets magnified several folds.

As Lord Yamaraj is the son of Sun hence try this Sadhana on a Sunday.

The Sadhana Process.

For this Sadhana one needs special Sadhana articles. These are 11 Gomti Chakras, 11 Hakeek stones and a seasonal fruit (water melon would be best). One also needs lamp black, incense, sweets, vermilion, red sandalwood paste and flowers.

At night have a bath and wear fresh clothes. Cover a wooden seat with a red cloth. On it with lamp black draw a triangle large enough so that a watermelon or the chosen fruit can be placed in it. Arrange 9 Hakeek stones and 9 Gomti Chakras in a way so that each arm of the triangle has four Chakras and stones. Then at the base of the triangle place two stones and two Chakras. In the center place the fruit.

Accomplish this Sadhana at night only. Light an oil lamp and incense. First of all worship the Guru and then having arranged the Sadhana articles as indicated before start the Sadhana.

First of all take water in the right palm and chant the following Mantra once. Let the water flow to the ground. Then chant the Dhyan Mantra given earlier 21 times. Each time place your hand on a different Gomti Chakra.

Thus each Gomti Chakra has to be energized with the Dhyan Mantra.

Each time also wish for riddance from your problems. Speak out the problems one at a time clearly in your mind. Think of one problem only at a time as you chant 21 times. Thereafter with a black Hakeek rosary chant 11 rounds of the Mantra.

Do the Sadhana daily for seven days and surely you shall have the desired result.

On first day after the Sadhana cut the melon and offer it to the Lord. Then eat it seated at the same place.

After completion of Sadhana tie all articles in the cloth and leave it under a Peepul tree or drop in a river.

It is said in Uddees Tantra -

"The person who chants Dharmaraaj Mantra daily is freed of all pains and afflictions and he attains to longevity. Dharmaraaj is the son of Sun and the brother of Venus."

Hence through the Sadhana of Dharmaraaj the boons of Venus Sadhana are also obtained. It is when all problems are neutralized that happiness in life is attained.

In the present age this Sadhana is very fruitful and divine and it surely produces the desired result. For success in life and in one's tasks one should surely try this Sadhana. If possible daily chant the Mantra before going to sleep each night.

CHAPTER 8

DIVINE LIGHT MISSION

-Founded in 1970 by the guru Maharaj Ji, born in Hardwar, India: The only pathway to God is by submission to an "avatar", a "guru who is god"... this "Perfect Master" is Maharaj Ji, who sits in his throne with the crown of Krishna, and replaced Jesus... Ji is the Holy Spirit... but now he has "duodenal ulcer", living in the placid splendor of a large mansion in Malibu, California.

The way:

Is the "Four-fold Procedure":

- Blinding light: Seeing God with the "third eye", when the guru presses the temples and eyes of the initiate.
- Hearing celestial music: Hearing God with the "third ear", when the guru presses the ears.
- Tasting the divine nectar of God: When the guru puts its finger into the initiate throat.
- Sensing the vibrations of God: When the initiate is left almost unconscious after severe hyperventilation... rhythmic breathing for hours!
- And all this, after the initiate had listened to long sermons for extended hours, and being manipulated by auto-suggestive hypnosis.

"Festivals or lilas", are organized where audiences are doused with water and red paint, like the one in the Astrodome in 1973. In the USA: -In the seventies was one the largest imported cults in the USA, with 480 DLM centers, and 35,000 members. The "Divine Times" magazine was distributed in 66 countries. Today, there are 3,000 members in the USA, with 80 centers.

<u>CHAPTER 9</u>

ECKANKAR

"Eckankar", means "co-worker with God" founded by John Paul Twitchell in 1965, with 50,000 followers, or 3 million. Twitchell suddenly died in 1971 of heart attack, and the leader now is Sri Darwin Gross. Address: Box 3100, Menlo Park, CA 94024.

Based on Hindu teachings of karma and reincarnation, plus the experiences of Twitchell with the occult, and as a staff member in the Church of Scientology.

The promotional pamphlets you may pick up in a local grocery store offer the intriguing "ancient science of soul-travel", the "everlasting gospel", and the "one true source of all religions"... False!

CHAPTER 10

HANUMAN FOUNDATION

Another American!... the Jewish Bostonian Psychiatry Professor at Harvard, Dr. Richard Alpert, tries in 1961 LSD with his friend, Professor Timothy Leary. He went to India, and became a guru, with the name Baba Ram Dass.

In 1974 he founded "Hanuman", after the monkey-god of the Ramayana. He wrote "Be Here Now"; emphasizes "to live each moment meaningfully" ... but a guru is needed!... Baba!... because each person needs a special treatment :

CHAPTER 11

HIMALAYAN INSTITUTE OF YOGA SCIENCE AND PHILOSOPHY

Biofeedback

- "Biofeedback" owes its development to the expertise of Swami Rami, the founder of the Himalayan Institute: 5,000 students a month flock the Institute on Glenview, Illinois, to learn Raja Yoga, to "exhale all problems", and "inhale energy" to become a wave of bliss in the ocean of the universe.

- Swami, can stop the heart-beat for 17 seconds, move an aluminum knitting needle while sitting 5 feet away... and this was used by Dr. Green of the prestigious Topeka, Kansas-based Menninger Foundation to develop the principles of biofeedback.

- As a monk and as an American Guru, Swami has dedicated his life to create a bridge between East and West. He feels his mission is to combine Indian religious philosophy and psychological therapeutic techniques.

CHAPTER 12

ISKCON

The Founder-Acarya of ISKCON is
His Divine Grace A.C. Bhaktivedanta
Swami Prabhupada

The International Society for Krishna Consciousness (ISKCON) was established in 1966 by His Divine Grace A.C. Bhaktivedanta Swami Prabhupada (Srila Prabhupada). ISKCON has since developed into a worldwide confederation of 10,000 temple devotees and 250,000 congregational devotees.

Better known as the Hare Krishna movement, ISKCON is comprised of more than 350 centers, 60 rural communities, 50 schools and 60 restaurants worldwide.

The mission of this nonsectarian, monotheistic movement is to promote the well being of society by teaching the science of Krishna consciousness according to Bhagavad-gita and other ancient scriptures.

The seven aims that Srila Prabhupada set out for ISKCON.

1. To systematic

2. ally propagate spiritual knowledge to society at large and to educate all people in the techniques of spiritual life in order to check the imbalance of values in life and to achieve real unity and peace in the world.

3. To propagate a consciousness of Krishna (God), as it is revealed in the great scriptures of India, Bhagavad-gita and Srimad-Bhagavatam.

4. To bring the members of the Society together with each other and nearer to Krishna, the prime entity, thus developing the idea within the members, and humanity at large, that each soul is part and parcel of the quality of Godhead (Krishna).

5. To teach and encourage the sankirtana movement, congregational chanting of the holy name of God, as revealed in the teachings of Lord Sri Caitanya Mahaprabhu.

6. To erect for the members and for society at large a holy place of transcendental pastimes dedicated to the personality of Krishna.

7. To bring the members closer together for the purpose of teaching a simpler, more natural way of life.

8. distribute periodicals, magazines, books and other writings.

HISTORY

The International Society for Krishna Consciousness was founded by His Divine Grace A.C. Bhaktivedanta Swami Prabhupada in 1966. It belongs to the Gaudiya Vaisnava tradition, a devotional tradition based on the teachings of Bhagavad-gita and Srimad-Bhagavatam.

The precepts and practices of ISKCON were taught and codified by the 15th century saint and religious reformer Sri Caitanya Mahaprabhu and his principle associates, the Six Goswamis of Vrindavana.

Sri Caitanya, whom devotees revere as a direct incarnation of Krishna, gave a powerful impetus for a massive bhakti (devotional) movement throughout India. Under his direction hundreds of volumes on the philosophy of Krishna consciousness were compiled.

Many devotees have followed in the line of Sri Caitanya Mahaprabhu including, in the 19th century, an outstanding Vaisnava theologian, Bhaktivinoda Thakura who brought Krishna consciousness to a modern audience.

Bhaktivinoda's son, Bhaktisiddhanta Sarasvati Goswami, became the guru of Srila Prabhupada and instructed him to spread Krishna consciousness in the West.

Vaisnava Philosophy

The Vedic scriptures state that spiritual life begins when one inquires into the nature of the absolute truth, the Supreme

Godhead. Gaudiya Vaisnavas are monotheists and know the personality of Godhead as Krishna, the All-attractive. But it is also recognized that the Supreme has unlimited names such as Rama, Buddha, Vishnu, Jehovah, Allah, etc. The ultimate goal of Gaudiya Vaisnavism is to develop a loving relationship with the Supreme Godhead.

The Vedas also tell us that the understanding of the self, as being non-material or spiritual by nature, is the preliminary stage of realization of the absolute truth. To understand knowledge of self-realization one must approach a genuine spiritual master, just as one. The congregational chanting of the maha-mantra, Hare Krishna, Hare Krishna, Krishna Krishna, Hare Hare, Hare Rama, Hare Rama, Rama Rama, Hare Hare, as promoted by Sri Caitanya, is accepted by the Vedas as the most effective means of self-purification in this age. The Vedas describe the mantra as a prayer to the Lord, "Please Lord, engage me in Your service".

Devotees may accept formal initiation into the chanting of the Holy Name vowing to abstain from intoxication, gambling, illicit sexual connections and the eating of meat, fish or eggs. ISKCON members believe indulgence in the aforementioned activities disrupts physical, mental and spiritual well-being, and increases anxiety and conflict in society.

At the time of initiation devotees also agree to chant a prescribed number of mantras each day. learns the essence of any subject from a perfected practitioner.

CHAPTER 13

THE KARMA KAGYU TRADITION

Chenrezik

The Karma Kagyu school forms part of the Dakpo Kagyu tradition of Tibetan Buddhism, which was established in the eleventh and twelfth centuries C.E. by the three masters, Marpa the translator (1012 - 1097), student of the Indian siddhas Naropa and Maitripa, his disciple Milarepa (1040 - 1123) and the latter's disciple Gampopa (1079 - 1153) who was heir to both the tantric teachings of Marpa and Milarepa's lineage and the sutra teachings of the Kadam school. After Gampopa's death, the tradition split into four principal branches; Karma, Baram, Tshalpa and Phakmo Dru, from the last of which eight sub-sects subsequently emerged. Under the leadership of seventeen incarnations of the Karmapa Lama, the Karma Kagyu has been the most powerful of the four chief lines of the Kagyu.

His Holiness 16th Gyalwa Karmapa

The most prized teachings of the Karma Kagyu tradition have been the cycles of mahamudra ('great seal'), derived principally from Maitripa, and the 'six doctrines' derived from Naropa. Although the Kagyu tradition is especially famed for its emphasis on meditation, it has also produced talented scholars such as the third Karmapa, Ranjung Dorje (1284 - 1339), the eighth Karmapa, Mikyo Dorje (1507 - 1554) and Jamgon Kongtrul (1811 - 1899). This last master is particularly renowned for his propagation of the Zhentong Madhyamaka philosophical view, which has found many exponents in the Karma Kagyu school.

The head of the Karma Kagyu tradition, His Holiness the sixteenth Gyalwa Karmapa, Rigpé Dorje (1923 - 1981) visited our centre Kagyu Ling in Manchester in 1977 at the invitation of Karma Thinley Rinpoche and Lama Jampa Thaye.

A number of other eminent Kagyu and Nyingma masters have also visited Kagyu Ling including Jamgon Kongtrul Rinpoche, Taisitu Rinpoche, Gyaltsab Rinpoche, Kalu Rinpoche, Dingo Chentze Rinpoche, Thrangu Rinpoche, Ato Rinpoche, Chime Rinpoche, Khenpo Tsultrim Rinpoche and Bokar Rinpoche.

<u>CHAPTER 14</u>

KRISHNAMURTI FOUNDATION OF AMERICA

It was not founded by Krishnamurti, but by the Theosophy leader Annie Besant when she proclaimed on 1907 that Krishnamurti was the reincarnation of Jesus Christ, and the Messiah the world was waiting for... the "Order of the Star of the East" was created, with a periodical, "Herald of the Star"... with 100,000 members.

- Krishnamurti rejected all these claims, and the essence of his massage is that "all problems could be solved when human beings achieve a "right relationship" with each other.... just look within for the incorruptibility of self". He disdains devotees, but still conducts world tours, sponsored mainly by the Theosophists and New Age groups.

CHAPTER 15

KUNDALINI MAHA YOGA

Shri Dhyanyogi Madhusudandas ji
(1878 - 1994)

Shri Dhyanyogi Madhusudandasji was a great saint, whose search for spiritual enlightenment took place during another era, in an India that no longer exists. He walked barefoot across India, in the 1890's and early 1900's, through what were then jungles, but are now cleared and settled lands, meeting saints living in seclusion, completely detached from the mundane world.

Born in Bihar, India, Shri Dhyanyogiji was a very spiritual child. Prior to his birth, his mother had a vision of Lord Krishna, indicating the coming of a great being. His spiritual quest began in earnest at age 7 when he left home in search of God. Although he was quickly found by his parents, he left home again for good at age 13.

The next 30 years were spent traveling all over India learning whatever the saints and yogis would teach him. He mastered

Mantra, Yantra, Hatha, Raja and Jnana Yogas, and became adept at yogic philosophies and scriptures. Yet after 30 years of austerities and intense searching, he still had not attained his highest goal, the ultimate encounter with God. Finally, in 1921 on Mt. Abu, he came into the presence of his final teacher, a great master named Shri Yogiraj Parameshwardasji,who gave him Shaktipat initiation. He immediately went into the hightest stage of Meditation.

Shri Anandi Ma is Shri Dhyanyogiji's spiritual heir and was known for many years as Asha Ma or Ashadevi. In January 1993, Shri Dhyanyogiji gave her the spiritual name, Anandi Ma, which means, "One who is in Bliss and keeps others in Bliss." Her early years passed in a quiet and uneventful manner, in an environment rich with spiritual practice and energy. One day in 1972, at the age of fourteen, she spontaneously entered a very deep, meditative state. In her own words, she saw "the light of a million suns," and in the same moment, had a vision of the Divine Mother, and merged with Her.

Shri Anandi Ma's father went to Shri Dhyanyogiji and asked him to come, meet her, and provide guidance and assistance. Shri

Dhyanyogiji went to their home and woke her. Later that day he asked her to describe her vision of the Divine Mother. "Did you see her as a picture, a statue, a living being?" Shri Anandi Ma answered, "Just as I see you now." Later that day, Shri Dhyanyogiji said that Shri Anandi Ma was the most spiritually advanced person, for her age, he had ever met. With her parents' consent, she left home shortly after receiving Shaktipat to stay permanently with Shri Dhyanyogiji.

He took her under his wing and trained her to control and radiate her energies for the welfare of humanity, especially by giving Shaktipat. He said, "I have been asked by my Guru to hand over the powers of this lineage to her," and put aside all his major activities to work almost exclusively with her, day and night, for four years.

During this period Shri Anandi Ma would enter profound states of meditation for hours or days at a time. From the beginning, Shri Anandi Ma worked alongside Shri Dhyanyogiji wherever he traveled, and accompanied him when he came to America in 1976. When Shri Dhyanyogiji returned to India in 1980, he told Shri Anandi Ma and Dileepji to marry and continue his work together.

Today, Shri Anandi Ma and Dileepji travel extensively in India, the United States and Europe, conducting meditation programs and yoga retreats. They provide spiritual guidance and Shaktipat initiation to sincere seekers. As part of her role as Shri Dhyanyogiji's spiritual heir, Shri Anandi Ma has also assumed the responsibility for continuing the humanitarian works begun during Shri Dhyanyogiji's lifetime.

These include operating a hospital, sponsoring eye surgery camps, and providing food for the poor. In all these works, she continues to spread the love and light of her lineage and of her beloved sadaguru, Shri Dhyanyogi Madhusudandasji.

The Path of Kundalini Maha Yoga
By Shri Dhyanyogi Madhusudandasji

For the past several decades, yoga, which is a spiritual discipline from India, has been a subject of interest to the people of America. I would like to introduce a form of yoga known as *Kundalini Maha Yoga*. Kundalini Maha Yoga is an ancient universal science, perfected over thousands of years. It is not a religion, but a spiritual practice that brings the experience of lasting inner peace and happiness to individuals of any belief or religious affiliation.

Kundalini Maha Yoga is based on a very simple principle: in every human being there is a source of divine energy. The Sanskrit word for this source of energy is *Kundalini*. Kundalini is in two states: the dormant state, and the active, aroused, or awakened state. When this source is dormant, a person leads an incomplete, unfulfilled life. One's understanding of the universe is restricted, and everything is perceived and interpreted according to a limited capacity.

On the other hand, when the source is active, progress is rapid on the path of spiritual evolution. One realizes the full potential of body and mind, attains inner peace, harmony and integration, and ultimately experiences the sublime truth of unity in diversity -- the fact that all life is one and is bound by that divine power called love. The purpose of Kundalini Maha Yoga is to awaken this source of energy if it is dormant, or to intensify the activity if it is already awakened. Thus, Kundalini Maha Yoga is a direct method for spiritual evolution.

A powerful yogi awakens the aspirant's Kundalini by a transfer of his or her energy to the aspirant. This process, known as *Shaktipat*, activates the dormant Kundalini and is like lighting a candle with one that is already lit and glowing. *Shakti* means power or energy in Sanskrit, and *pat* means transfer. Thus Shaktipat is transfer of energy.

Some people may have fears about working with the Kundalini, but it is absolutely safe to practice Kundalini Maha Yoga under the guidance of a realized teacher. By the grace and advice of my Guru, I have given Shaktipat to thousands of people who have derived immense benefits.

During the past decades, scientific developments have taken place at a staggering rate. It is both a joy and surprise to watch the progress of science. However, the storehouse of nature is limitless, and the more we know, the more remains to be known. It is obvious that no one can understand nature fully. We clearly feel the need to increase the power of the intellect, the capacity to comprehend, and generally to develop the potential of the mind to such an extent that capabilities previously unknown become active.

It is also clear that much remains to be accomplished in the area of physical health and the necessity for sound mental health must not be overlooked. Many serious diseases threaten mankind today, and a strong body and mind by themselves do not provide adequate protection.

In spite of our developments, scientific and otherwise, there is much fear, hatred, disharmony, distrust and discrimination among individuals communities and nations. This has led to the build-up of destructive weapons and the grave possibility of war. The peace we all desire so much has not yet been attained. The basic cause of these problems is that the general level of conscience, consciousness and other spiritual qualities has not evolved to the extent that science has.

We are in a state of unbalanced development, lacking on the spiritual side. Therefore, to attain what is missing -- peace, harmony and brotherhood -- it is necessary to realize that the entire universe is the creation of God, that all life is one, and that all are children of love. This realization is spiritual; it is not intellectual comprehension of an ideal.

Spiritual realization and evolution are the only solution to all the problems facing us. Kundalini Maha Yoga is a path for spiritual evolution and a significant tool to help mankind develop on the spiritual plane. It is a way to peace, prosperity, brotherhood and love.

Kundalini, Creation and Spiritual Evolution

Kundalini is the divine energy. She manifests both in the cosmic form, encompassing all of creation, and in the personal form. God creates the universe by producing subtle energies in an act of divine will. This can be compared to the process wherein sparks are generated from a single source of fire. The individual manifestation of Kundalini is like a spark of cosmic Kundalini.

This personal form of Kundalini is responsible for the creation of the individual. In the physiological process of development of the fetus in the mother's womb, the head and brain are formed first. Next, the spinal cord is formed from the nerves that branch from the brain, and at the same time, the trunk is formed. Then the extremities, the hands, and the feet are formed. The totality of the nerve centers in the brain is referred to as the *sahasrar chakra*. This is the root of the process of creation.

There are six different *chakras*, nerve centers, in the spinal column. The first center, located at the base of the brain, is the *ajna* chakra or the spiritual eye. This center is formed immediately after the sahasrara. Then five different centers which represent five different elements, or *tatvas*, are formed. The last center formed, the *mooladhara* chakra, is the furthest from the brain, located near the lower end of the spinal column. The Kundalini thus starts creation at the brain center, progresses downward along the spinal column, and completes Her work near the lower end of the spine. After the completion of Her work, She lies dormant there.

Spiritual evolution is the result of the awakening of the Kundalini and Her upward travel from the bottom of the spinal column to the brain center. As She travels upward, the individual develops deeper and deeper spiritual insight and life becomes more fulfilling. When the Kundalini completes Her travel to the brain, the individual attains liberation, understands his or her true identity, and is established in eternal happiness. Thus, an individual's spiritual knowledge is directly dependent on the upward progress of the Kundalini.

Many religions accept the concept of a cycle of the universe. Each cycle consists of the creation, preservation and destruction of the universe.

When one cycle of the universe is completed, the individual attains liberation. However, with the awakening of the Kundalini, the individual does not have to wait until the end of the cycle to attain liberation. This fact alone underscores the importance of Kundalini Maha Yoga. Spiritual evolution cannot take place unless the Kundalini is awakened.

There are many spiritual disciplines and techniques which do not directly aim at awakening the Kundalini. However, the Kundalini must be aroused if there is to be any degree of spiritual progress. Therefore, if a spiritual discipline is successful, it means the Kundalini has been awakened in at least an indirect way.

The practitioner may not be aware that the progress and

experiences are the result of the active Kundalini unless, of course, the discipline aims directly at awakening the Kundalini. However, the Kundalini does keep working and is the source of enlightenment.

Once the Kundalini is awakened through Shaktipat initiation, She does not become dormant except in some very special circumstances. The Kundalini will always try to make Her upward passage. She will try to keep the aspirant on the spiritual path by providing the necessary encouragement and protection.

Kundalini can be awakened by attaining perfection of certain hatha yoga postures called *asanas*, by certain breathing exercises aimed at controlling the breath called *pranayama*, by God's grace, by meditation or by intense devotion. Another technique of great importance is Shaktipat, the transmission of energy. A powerful yogi can transmit energy to an aspirant and awaken the Kundalini. This is accomplished in one of four ways: by touch, gaze, sound or thought.

The yogi may touch the disciple and transmit energy through physical contact, or gaze at the disciple and energy flows from the yogi's eyes. The yogi may utter words which carry energy or, more subtly, energy can be transferred directly by the yogi's thought or will. The process of Shaktipat can be performed only by those yogis who have gained complete control over the life force, which in Sanskrit is called *prana*.

Once the Kundalini is awakened, the student may have a variety of experiences: seeing flashes of light or colors, hearing internal sounds of bells ringing or bees humming, spontaneous vibrations or movements of the body, and greater mental peace, to name a few. Different individuals will have different experiences -- there is no definite pattern applicable to everyone.

Once the Kundalini is awakened, this fact becomes known through the student's own experiences. If at this stage the student persists in spiritual practices like meditation, then the Kundalini will travel upward from the base of the spinal column where She lay dormant before.

During Her upward journey through the spinal column, She pierces all the chakras in succession and ultimately reaches the sahasrara. When this happens, the student attains a state of transcendental consciousness called *samadhi*, understands one's true identity, and is thereby liberated.

During the student's spiritual efforts, the Guru's help is of immense value. Shaktipat initiation creates a subtle bond between the teacher and student that allows the teacher to give fresh impetus to his or her student's Kundalini and eliminate obstructions that may arise.

By the grace of God and according to the power and instructions given by my Guru, I have given Shaktipat to a large number of people in India, the United States and around the world. Their Kundalini has been awakened. They have attained peace of mind and good health. They have been led on the spiritual path.

Meditation is the practice of turning the attention from outer awareness to inner concentration. In the practice of Kundalini Maha Yoga, meditation is much more than a relaxation technique.

It is a way of easing resistance to the ascent of the Kundalini energy by quieting the fluctuations of the mind. Of all the forms of meditation, meditation through attention on the breath is the simplest and most direct way to Self-realization.

The aspirant can coordinate and integrate various energies of the nervous system by performing breathing exercises called *pranayama* in conjunction with meditation. Once this is accomplished, the student easily gains control over the life supporting vital air, the prana, which in turn leads to control over the mind.

When the student gains complete control of the mind there is an experience of unique peace and joy. The student realizes the entire world is the creation of one God. When this happens on a large scale, the miseries of the world will end and there will be peace and happiness everywhere.

Self-realization is the ultimate and the most desirable state to be attained, and the awakened Kundalini leads to this state. However, even when the Kundalini is aroused and spiritual evolution is substantially hastened, there is no guarantee that Self-realization will be attained in the current lifetime. Therefore, it is encouraging to know many tangible benefits are gained even during the early states of the awakening and upward travel of the Kundalini.

Awakening the Kundalini has a general purifying effect on the body and mind. For example, the aspirant's health often improves; the student often feels light and energetic; the mind becomes restful. Diseases of the body and mind are caused by irregularities in the functioning of the prana, which can be gradually eliminated once the Kundalini is awakened.

At more advanced levels of the Kundalini's progress the benefits are intensified and encompass more subtle realms. The student can achieve peace and mental control, can become more creative, can develop a profound understanding of nature and experience inner joy. The aspirant becomes a stronger individual, a more complete person who can function in adverse circumstances with great poise, and is able to consciously absorb prana from the universe and direct it for physical and mental well-being. Ultimately, the student encounters total reality, the absolute truth, knowledge of the Self.

CHAPTER 16

MAITREYA

- "Maitreya", the Lord Master expected by the Buddhists, is, in fact, a fiction created by the New Ager Benjamin Creme... he says it is not a religion, but he advises people to meet weekly in "Maitreya Groups" to create good Energy...

- Benjamin Creme, born in Glasgow, Scotland in 1922, is a co-editor of the New Age magazine "Share International", and considers himself to be like another John the Baptist, the precursor of "Maitreya", "to make the initial approach to the public, to help create a climate of hope and expectancy".

- "Maitreya", the "Master", in Creme's fiction, is supposed to be the "Christ" expected by the Christians, the "Messiah" expected by the Jews, the reincarnation of Krishna expected by the Hindus, the "Iman Mahdi" expected by the Muslims, the "Lord Maitreya" expected by the Buddhists.

- Creme attracted much attention in the early 1980s announcing the coming of the Lord Maitreya by 1982; when Maitreya failed to appear, Creme's popularity quickly died.

- However, Creme says that Maitreya is already alive, emerged from the Himalayas in 1977, and is living in London, in the Pakistani-Indian community as an ordinary man... but on the "Day of Declaration" the international television networks will be linked together, and Maitreya will be invited to speak to the world; we will see his face on television, but each of us will hear his words telepathically.

- Creme says that Maitreya is already making unexpected apparitions in different countries, like in Kenya in 1991, in Uganda with the healing of 400 patients with AIDS, and the healing waters in Tlacote (Mexico), Nordenau (Germany), Nadana (India) ... but all of them unsubstantiated... he appears and disappears, without anybody's notice, claims the fiction story of Creme!

- Creme claims Maitreya predicted the fall of Communism and dozens of world social and political events, but all unsubstantiated, predicted after they had happened!.

- A major event predicted by Maitreya, through Creme, in 1988, was "an international stock market crash"... but now, in 1997, still did not happened!

- Creme calls him "the Master of all Masters", including the Master of Jesus Christ... "the Head of the Spiritual Hierarchy of Masters", "the World Teacher", "the Lord Maitreya"... though Maitreya calls himself the "Teacher".

- For Creme, "Maitreya" means "the Lord of Joy and Gladness", dedicated to the reunification of all religions and humanity, and for the economic, social, and political welfare of the whole world.

- For me, Maitreya is another Hindu-Buddhist cult, a false Messiah... Maitreya is not God, as Creme claims... the face of Maitreya exists, a good looking Hindu or Buddhist man, as given by the fiction story of Creme.

CHAPTER 17

OSHO

OSHO, FORMERLY KNOWN AS BHAGWAN SHREE RAJNEESH

Early History of the Movement:

Bhagwan Shree Rajneesh (1931-1990) was born Rajneesh Chandra Mohan in Kuchwara, a town in central India. One source states that "Bhagwan" means "The Blessed One" and that "Shree" means "Master". At the end of his life, he changed his name to Osho.

His parents' religion was Jainism. However, Osho never subscribed to any religious faith during his lifetime. He received "samadhi" (enlightenment in which his soul became one with the universe) on 1953-MAR-21 at the age of 21. Rajneesh obtained a masters degree in philosophy from the University of Saugar. He taught philosophy at the University of Jabalpur for nine years and concurrently worked as a religious leader.

In 1966, he left his teaching post and gave his full attention to teaching his sannyasins (disciples) while pursuing a speaking career. He had an apartment in Bombay where he often met individuals and small groups, where acting as spiritual teacher, guide and friend. Most of his Sannyasins came from Europe and India in the early years.

In 1974, Osho moved from Bombay southward to Pune, India. Some anti-cult groups have claimed that this decision was made because of local opposition from the public in Bombay.

In reality, it was to establish an ashram (place of teaching) which would provide larger and more comfortable facilities for his disciples. The ashram consisted of two adjoining properties covering six acres in an affluent suburb of Pune called Koregaon Park. Some estimate as many as 50,000 Westerners spent time seeking enlightenment there with the guru. In 1979, he saw his movement as the route to the preservation of the human race. He said: If we cannot create the 'new man' in the coming 20 years, then humanity has no future. The holocaust of a global suicide can only be avoided if a new kind of man can be created."

He taught a syncretistic spiritual path that combined elements from Hinduism, Jainism, Zen Buddhism, Taoism, Christianity, ancient Greek philosophy, many other religious and philosophic traditions, humanistic psychology, new forms of therapy and meditation, etc.

In 1980, he was the victim of a knife attack by a Hindu fundamentalist during his morning discourse. Because of police incompetence, the charges against the terrorist were dropped.

In 1981 he left India reluctantly because of health problems. He went to the United States in order to obtain advanced treatment. There have been rumors of income tax evasion, and insurance fraud; it is not known whether these have any validity. The group settled on the 65,000 acre "Big Muddy Ranch" near Antelope, Oregon, which his sannyasins had bought for six million dollars. The ranch was renamed Rajneeshpuram ("Essence of Rajneesh").

This "small, desolate valley twelve miles from Antelope, Oregon was transformed into a thriving town of 3,000 residents, with a 4,500 foot paved airstrip, a 44 acre reservoir, an 88,000 square foot meeting hall..." [8] Many of the local folks were intolerant of the new group in their midst, because of religious and cultural differences.

One manifestation of this intolerance was the town's denial of building permits to the followers of Rajneesh. Some buildings were erected on the ranch without planning board approval. When officials attempted to stop the construction, their office was firebombed by unknown person(s). When the local city council repeatedly refused to issue permits for their businesses, some sannyasins elected themselves to the city council.

The town of Antelope was renamed City of Rajneesh. Top aides of Osho were charged with a number of crimes, including the attempted murder of Osho's personal physician. There were stories of a hit list. Some fled the country for Switzerland where they had control over the group's bank accounts. Two were eventually convicted of conspiracy to murder local lawyer Charles Turner in an attempt to prevent closure of the ranch.

In 1983, Osho's secretary Sheela Silverman predicted on behalf of Osho that there would be massive destruction on earth, between 1984 and 1999. This would include both natural disasters and man-made catastrophes. Floods larger than any since Noah, extreme earthquakes, very destructive volcano eruptions, nuclear wars etc. would be experienced. Tokyo, New York, San Francisco, Los Angeles, Bombay were all expected to disappear. There is doubt that these predictions actually came from Osho; they are not representative of his other teachings.

Fearing a raid of the type that later happened in Waco, several of Osho's disciples arranged for him to be flown to Charlotte for safety. In North Carolina, he ran afoul of US immigration law. He allegedly arranged a number of phony marriages between some of his Indian followers and American citizens so that the former could obtain clearance to stay in the country. He was also charged with lying on his immigration papers.

He entered an "Alford Plea," commonly called a no-contest plea. His lawyers suggested that he do this because of concerns over his health and safety if he had to spend more time in prison. He was given a suspended sentence on condition that he leave the country. He returned to Pune, India in 1987, where his health began to fail. Here, he abandoned the name of Rajneesh and adopted "Osho".

Osho was derived from the expression "oceanic experience" by William James. He died in Pune in 1990. Various rumors spread that he had been poisoned with thallium by the CIA, had been exposed to damaging doses of radiation by the U.S. authorities, or had heart failure.

It is obvious that he did not experience thallium poisoning, because he died with a full beard, and only male-pattern baldness on the top of his head. A person suffering from thallium poisoning suffers a dramatic loss of hair with a week of exposure. [6] His death certificate lists heart failure as the cause of his death.

At its peak, they had about 200,000 members and 600 centers around the world. They were targeted by many anti-cult groups as an evil, mind control cult. One source, in a masterful stroke of religious disinformation, claimed that "Bhagwan" means "Master of the Vagina." He has been called the "sex guru."

Beliefs and Practices

Osho developed new forms of active meditation. The best known is Dynamic Meditation which often starts with strenuous physical activity followed by silence and celebration. These were expected to lead the individual to overcome repression, lower their personal inhibitions, develop a "state of emptiness", and attain enlightenment. The person then would have "no past, no future, no attachment, no mind, no ego, no self." Prior to 1985, the disciples wore red robes, and a necklace of 108 beads which had an attached picture of Rajneesh.

Osho assigned a new name to each of the disciples. Men were given the title "Swami"; women were called "Ma". Although most members lived a frugal, simple lifestyle, Rajneesh himself lived in luxury. His collection 27 Rolls Royce, given to him by his followers, was well known. (Some sources say he had as many as

100 cars).

Recent Developments

Osho repeatedly stated that he would not appoint a successor to replace him after his death. He viewed each disciple as his successor. However, before his death, he appointed an inner circle of 21 individuals to look after the functioning of the meditation resort at Pune and handle administrative affairs relating to his work.

They now operate about 20 meditation centers worldwide. Rajneesh's main influence now is through his voluminous writings; they are read by many New Agers as well as followers of Osho.

Osho Commune International administers the center in Pune, India. Since it was established it has been expanded from 6 to 32 acres. The group has a Global Connections department that provides information about centers and activities worldwide. Osho International in New York, NY, administers the rights to Osho's works.

Some of Osho's aides who were imprisoned because of crimes committed in Oregon were released from prison in mid-1998 and deported to England.

CHAPTER 18

RADHA SOAMI

Radhasoami well known as "Radha Soami (Sant Mat)" and their teachings.

"Seth Shiv Dayal Singh, well known as Yogi Huzur Swamiji Maharaj (1818-1878) created his own cosmology and spiritual path from the Tantric, Hindu, Sikh and Sufi traditions. In due course his teachings took the shape of a new religion, called "Sant Mat" (Teachings of Saints) or "Radha Soami" (Lord of the Soul), which currently has several million follows in Northern India.

"As per the teachings of Huzur Swamiji there were six lower worlds, which associated with six lower chakras and six higher worlds. The lowest of which was associated with the Crown Chakra, which according to Indian Tantrism is the highest centre. In other words, Huzur Swamiji claims to have gone further, and hence attained a more developed occult teaching.

"The lower worlds constitute the material and lower spiritual universe, called Pinda, "body"; the higher ones, each associated with a divine melody or vibration (shabda or nada), were the higher spiritual worlds, the worlds of Universal Mind (Brahmandi).

"Each world is a heavenly region, ruled over by a particular god. And each world appears to be the highest, until one goes beyond it to the next world. By attuning oneself to the vibrations of the higher or "heavenly" worlds, one can ascend through the various planes, until one reaches the level of God, beyond all the worlds.

“A table constituting Huzur Swamiji's cosmology is shown below for your quick reference.”

1. Radha Swami Godhead
2. (Intermediate region)
3. (Intermediate region)
4. 1st Heavenly region - Sat Nam or Sat Lok; Divine World
5. 2nd Heavenly region - Banwar Gupha (an intermediate region)
6. 3rd Heavenly region - Mahasunna Great Void
7. 4th Heavenly region - Daswan Dwar - liberated souls Void
8. 5th Heavenly region - Trikuti - region of Gods Heaven
9. 6th Heavenly region - Sahasdal Kamal, Crown chakra; Lower Heaven
10. 1st ganglion Ajna - abode of soul Lowest Heaven
11. 2nd ganglion Vishuddha - prana - dreaming
12. 3rd ganglion Anahata - Shiva - subtle body
13. 4th ganglion Manipura - Vishnu - gross prana
14. 5th ganglion Swadishthana - Brahma - physical
15. 6th ganglion Muladhara - Ganesha

The Radha Soami cosmology [Heavenly region = Heavenly regions]

“These terms have been borrowed from various sources and sometimes taken out of context. Dashama-dwara for example (here, "Daswan Dwar", the 7th region from the top) was originally a term in Natha tantra for a small hole or vacuum at the root of the palate chakra (talu chakra), meditation upon which brings about a transcendent state of consciousness, but it is below the Sahasrara chakra, rather than above it, as the Radha Soami cosmology implies.

“So the five chakras above the crown chakra do not necessarily represent higher states of consciousness beyond the traditional enlightenment state. It may be that what Huzur Swamiji called "Sat Lok" (or Satya-loka in Sanskrit) is actually the Sahasrara of other Indian systems (the traditional equivalence of Satya-loka with the Sahasrara), and his other five higher chakras are intermediate chakras. In the thirteen-chakra model for example, there are a number of intermediate chakras and spiritual power points in the head-axis, between the Ajna or brow-chakra and the highest part of the Sahasrara or crown chakra.

<u>CHAPTER 19</u>

SAHAJ MARG

SHRI RAM CHANDRAJI MAHARAJ
"Babuji" (1899 - 1983)

Babuji was born in the north Indian town of Shahjahanpur, in the state of Uttar Pradesh, on 30 April 1899. He was named Ram Chandra after one of the great figures of Indian history. His father was a lawyer and noted scholar who educated his son extensively in English, Urdu and Persian, perhaps hoping that he would follow in his father's footsteps. But from an early age Ram Chandra displayed a craving for spiritual realization which overshadowed all other interests.

Ram Chandra became a babu, which in his native tongue designates a clerk, and it was from this profession that his affectionate nickname arose. (The suffix "ji" is an honorific, an expression of respect often appended to names or titles in India.) He held the position of court clerk in the district court of Shahjahanpur for more than thirty years.

He was married at the age of nineteen and his wife, Bhagwati, bore him two daughters and four sons before her death in 1949. Babuji's life was that of an ordinary householder, never that of a renunciate or sannyasi. He considered the home and family to be the very finest training ground for spirituality, and it was in this light that he approached his familial responsibilities.

He began his spiritual education on his own, experimenting with the forms of devotion available in the Hindu religion and with certain yogic practices such as pranayama (the control of the breath). In June of 1922, at the comparatively young age of twenty-two, he first met his Master, a man with the same name as himself who lived in the town of Fatehgarh, not far from Shahjahanpur.

Ram Chandra of Fatehgarh, affectionately known as Lalaji, was a saint of the highest caliber. He recognized Babuji as the man who had appeared to him in a dream years before, the one who was destined to succeed him as the leader of the great spiritual renaissance which he, Lalaji, had already initiated.

Though teacher and disciple met only a few times before Lalaji's death in 1931, Lalaji became the sole centre and purpose of Babuji's existence. The thought of his Master remained constant in Babuji's mind and heart from their first meeting until he himself passed on to the brighter world in April 1983. His conversation was punctuated by Lalaji's name, and no honor that Babuji could show his Master was enough to express the great love that existed between them.

"I went on with it regardless of all other things," wrote Babuji in his autobiography, “till I reached the level expressed by my Master in the following words in a dream when he left the mortal frame: I became 'Thee' and Thou 'I'. Now none can say that I am other than thee or that thou art other than me.”

Babuji was by nature the humblest of men, yet moved by a vast pride in his great Master. The communication established between them after Lalaji's transition continued throughout Babuji's life and filled his diaries with both astonishing visions into the nature of reality and practical instruction on how to lead a spiritual life.

He was perpetually striving for balance, to be neither pleased by good words nor displeased by bad, to maintain a temperament of humility but to avoid the habit of excessive modesty. It was his conviction that the ego, being the production of God, cannot be annihilated. Rather, through utter surrender and devotion to his Master, he was able to modify the ego, identifying it not with the body but with the soul.

Of his spiritual condition he wrote, “There seems to be uniformity in love. Ties of relationship seem to have been severed. I have as much respect for my servant as for my respected father. I have as much love for the sons of other people as I feel for my own son. I have as much regard for a dog as I have for my own person, as if my own existence and that of a dog are identical. I also consider gold and earth to be the same. I see the pious and the wicked with one eye.”

Following Lalaji's death, Babuji began to use the gift of transmission, or pranahuti (a yogic technique rediscovered by

Lalaji and passed on to his successor as the basis for the Sahaj Marg system of raja yoga) all over India. He would travel alone to places where he had no friends or acquaintances, tour the city or town transmitting divine energy, and leave without a word. The fruits of this labor are now visible in the widespread network of Sahaj Marg centers throughout India.

In 1945, Babuji founded the Shri Ram Chandra Mission in honor of his Master. Convinced that God is simple and can be arrived at by simple means, he began traveling outside of India to bring the method of the Sahaj Marg (the natural path) to the cultures of Europe and America in 1972.

He was accompanied on these travels by his attendant and long-time general secretary of the Mission, Shri Parthasarathi Rajagopalachari of Madras. Parthasarathi, known by his associates as Chariji, was chosen by Babuji to be his spiritual representative and to carry on the work he had started.

Sahaj Marg is a living practice, and as such it has been adapted by each successive Master to suit the times in which we live. At its core, however, it remains unchanged, with an intent that is both pragmatic and divine, described by Babuji in this way:

"We have set up a tiny creation of our own, in the form of our individual material existence, having layers after layers of grossness and opacity. What is now to be done is to shatter off those layers of opacity one by one and assume the absolute state as we had at the time of creation. This is all the gist of the philosophy of our system, Sahaj Marg. We are, so to say, to dissolve this tiny creation of our making or to unfold ourselves."

Shri Parthasarathi Rajagopalachari
Born July 24, 1927

Shri Parthasarathi Rajagopalachari was born on July 24, 1927, in the village of Vayalur near Chennai (Madras), in the south of India. Known to his family and close friends as Parthasarathi, he is affectionately called Chari, or Chariji, by his associates. His mother died when he was five years old, and his father never remarried, choosing instead to devote himself entirely to his responsibilities as a parent and provider.

Because his father's work as a railway executive required frequent relocation of the family, Chariji and his two younger brothers spent their early years in many different parts of India. In his autobiography, Chariji remembers his childhood and youth with great nostalgia and writes with much love and affection about the extended family that surrounded him during those years.

After earning a Bachelor's Degree from Banaras Hindu University, he took his first job with Indian Plastics Limited in chemical engineering.

He traveled abroad in this capacity and spent two years in

Yugoslavia studying plastics manufacturing techniques. He and his wife, Sulochana, were married in 1955 and two years later had their first and only child, a son, Krishna. It was also in 1955 that Chariji joined the T. T. Krishnamachari group of companies in Bombay, thereafter rising to the position of Executive Director of the Indian Textile Paper Tube Company. His work required him to travel extensively outside of Indiain Europe, the Middle East, and Africaand he represented India at the International Standards Organization Conference held in Burgenstock, Switzerland, in 1957.

Chariji's conscious spiritual aspirations were awakened at the age of 18 after hearing a lecture on the Bhagavad Gita. He took up a detailed study of this book as well as other religious and spiritual texts. At the age of 30, he began Vaishnava traditional instruction in the Hindu religion. Seven years later, in 1964, he met his Master, Shri Ram Chandra of Shahjahanpur (Babuji) and started the practice of Sahaj Marg.

While continuing to fulfill his familial and business responsibilities, Chariji was vigilant in his spiritual practice and dedicated to the work of Shri Ram Chandra Mission. As General Secretary of the Mission, he contributed greatly to the publication of Sahaj Marg literature and to the strengthening of the organization as a whole. Over the years he became Babuji's most devoted disciple, accompanying him on travels abroad and ably assisting him in his spiritual work.

Babuji characterized the ideal human being as a person having "a Western mind and an Eastern heart," adding that such a person would be needed to guide the Mission successfully into the future. In Chariji he saw this blend of qualities as well as the crucial ability to instill discipline in others. Babuji passed away in 1983, leaving instructions that Chariji should succeed him as spiritual representative and President of the Mission.

Chariji's labors have resulted in remarkable growth and expansion in the Mission's activities all over the world. In recent years he has traveled extensively worldwide, conducting seminars and giving instruction on the Sahaj Marg system of meditation. His book My Master is a monumental tribute to Babuji. His other books include diaries of his overseas travels with Babuji, an autobiography and numerous volumes of his talks in India and abroad, interpreting, amplifying, and representing his Master's teachings.

In Sahaj Marg it is understood that the Master is the greatest servant. Observing Chariji, one sees this principle in action. His entire existence is presently devoted to the cause of spirituality in the service of others.

Cultivation of Non-Attachment Sahaja Marg.

We can never be free from maya unless we cultivate non-attachment.

It is true that we can never be free from maya unless we cultivate non-attachment. But it does not mean severing our connection from home, family and all worldly concerns and taking up the life of a religious mendicant. I do not agree with those who hold the view that the only means of cultivating non-attachment is to get away from home and family and retire to a solitary corner discarding all worldly ties.

Renunciation effected by such forced means is seldom found to be genuine, for it is just possible that in spite of their apparent forced detachment from the world, they may still inwardly be clinging to it. No doubt, as a householders we have to look after many things; we have to support our family; we have to provide for the education of our children; we have to look to their wants and necessities; we have to protect them from heat and cold; and so on. For these necessities we earn and possess money and property.

The real evil is only our undue attachment to the things which we are associated with. This is the main cause of our suffering. But if we are able to do everything in life thinking it to be our duty without any feeling of attraction or repulsion, we are in a way free from worldly ties and have renounced the world in the true sense, although we possess and make use of many things. Everything we possess shall then seem to be a sacred trust from the Supreme Master, for the discharge of the duties entrusted to us. Renunciation truly means non-attachment with worldly objects and not the non-possession of things.

Thus, a householder's life in which possession of things and worldly ties are indispensable is no impediment in the way of renunciation and consequently of realization, only if one is not unduly attached to the objects he is connected with. There are numerous examples of saints having attained the highest degree of perfection leading a householder's life all through.

Renunciation is, in fact, a condition or an inner state of mind which brings to view the transitory and changing character of things and creates a feeling of non-attachment to such objects.

His eyes are fixed every moment on Reality which is unchanging and eternal and he is free from the feeling of attraction and repulsion. This is *aviary* (renunciation) in the true sense of the term. When we have achieved this state of mind, we are free from desires. We feel contented with what is available to us. The end of desire means stopping of the formation of *samskaras* (impressions).

What remains now is only to undergo the effect (*bhog*) of the previously formed *samskaras* (impressions) which are to be worn out during the course of our life. Nature too helps us in the process by creating a field for *bhog* in order to remove the impressions of our thoughts and actions from the causal body. When these coverings melt away we begin to assume finer forms of existence.

The man who is born in this world is sure to taste miseries. One cannot escape these. When I see the world, I find it very troublesome. Some are groaning with pain, a few are suffering from the loss of their dear ones and a great number are anxious to achieve success at each step.

We try to get rid of these by going into penance, and *rishis* (sages) have devoted themselves thoroughly to it. All that is born of attachment is misery. Pleasure and pain both contribute to misery. There is no remedy for overcoming these miseries except devoting ourselves towards Godly thought of the purest nature.

We need not renounce the world and go for penance in the forest. Let the material world and spiritual world go side by side, glittering equally. One cannot be a loser in any way, if doing his household duties, he brings himself up to the realization of God as well. We should soar with both wings if we want to succeed. It is a vague idea of the people in general that God is to be searched for in the forests. My idea is that He should be searched for in the heart.

One is performing the household duties and at the same time is equally busy with Godly devotion. You may say that these two things are incompatible and are contradictory to each other, but it is not the case. In the long run, Godly wisdom begins to work and one does his duty from the mind beyond.

Thus, *vairagya* (renunciation or non-attachment) can be attained only when one is wholly diverted towards the Divine. When it is so, one naturally becomes disinterested in his own self including everything connected with it. Thus he loses not only the body-consciousness but subsequently the soul-consciousness as well. What remains then is nothing but the "being in dead form or a living dead".

2. Observance of Preliminaries to Meditation

A natural posture (asan) ***paves our way to the Ultimate.***

When the thought of going back to the original was stirred up in man, it became essential for him to bring activity, which had sprung up in him, into a latent state as far as it was possible. He began to seek out means for it. At last it came to his understanding that just as the latent motion was grosser in comparison to the

Absolute with which it was connected, even so he must take up something grosser for the purpose, to enable him to attain the desired ideal of Reality.

This led him to the conclusion that he must create in him a form of contraction or withdrawal similar to that at the time of *pralaya*. Now Self is all pervading in man just as it is in the whole universe, taking the universe in a collective sense. The state of *pralaya* comes in when contraction begins to take place. Similar contraction in man leads to his individual *pralaya*. That means that he begins to proceed from his state of grossness to the real state. The contraction always starts from below and proceeds gradually upwards because of its upward tendency.

Therefore, in order to go upwards he must start contracting from below. The form of contraction could be only to bring his legs and allied parts to one pose and to keep them steady. In whatever way it might be done, the form will finally be that of the *asan*. It is essential because it paves our way to the Ultimate. This posture must always be the same. The reason is that in this way he gets himself associated with the great power, the very thing he takes up in the beginning for the attainment of his particular objective. Thus the form which is associated with Reality helps him a good deal in his primary initiation.

The upright position of the back-bone, neck and head in an erect straight line during meditation has been thought to be most advantageous from very ancient times, because the flow of Divine grace is believed to descend straight upon the abhyasi in that posture.

In our way of practice, however, this is not insisted upon. I advise the abhyasis generally to sit in a natural easy posture. Moreover, even those who assume a tight straight pose, are found to give way automatically to a suppliant, slightly forward drooping posture, as the state of blissful absorbency sets in. As such, it may be considered to be more natural even for the purpose of an ascent into higher states of consciousness. In fact, a controversy over a point of comparatively lesser significance seems irrelevant.

It is better to sit in the gray of the morning for meditation, or when that is not possible, at any fixed hour convenient to the abhyasi. Do not feel disturbed with the outer things but remain engaged with your own work thinking that they are in a way helping you to feel the necessity for greater absorption in your practice.

B. PRACTICAL

3. Meditation

When we meditate, the Central Power we have remains in force.

Under the Sahaj Marg system of training we start from *dhyan*, the seventh step of Patanjali yoga, fixing our mind on one point in order to practice meditation. The previous steps are not taken up separately but they automatically come into practice as we proceed on with meditation. Thus much of our time and labor are saved. In certain *sansthas* the usual routine followed for practice is often kept confidential. It is released and revealed only to those who undertake to join them formally. What their purpose at the bottom may be, is not quite understandable. Nature has no secrets and I think that one professing to follow the divine path must also have none.

The practice followed in our Mission is meditation on the heart. The same method has been recommended by Patanjali. There is a great philosophy underlying it. We find ourselves all the time busy with worldly things. If we are not doing anything, our thoughts seem to have wings in the leisure hours. We are always in tumult and disorder. Our individual mind has become used to such a characteristic activity, and thus we have made every thing topsy-turvy.

Our actions and thoughts count much in our wrong doing. When we remain in contact with ideas and thoughts of different kinds, they leave impressions upon our emotive feelings and senses. All the senses are spoiled and adopt a wrong course. The marks we thus make upon the senses and *indriyas* turn them solid like rock, having no *bodh* or wisdom. Soul is, no doubt, not acted upon, but we create such obstacles and coverings as to keep it enwrapped all round like a cocoon.

We cannot even peep into the soul, let alone realizing it. By the effect of our vicious thoughts and actions we spoil our sense of discrimination and right cognition. Those who have reached this state of solidity do not like to come under the training course of raja yoga. This is why people turn a deaf ear to what we say. No practice of hatha yoga can bring out true realization as it fails after the *ajna chakra* and there still remain very many states still to pass after it. Therefore raja yoga is the only thing that can lead to the end. There is no other means of approaching the Centre. We have got within us the same central force, though marred by our wrong doings.

We take work from the same force during meditation. This is how we proceed naturally with nature's force, so to say. When we meditate, the central power we have, remains in force. It disperses the overwhelming clouds which are greatly fried up by its force. It cannot be expressed in words, only an abhyasi can feel it. This can only be known practically. You will soon find yourself swimming in everlasting peace and happiness. Everything ends here. There remains no attachment with the world.

The mind is disciplined, it is regulated automatically. Senses begin to come under control and you gain mastery over them. To master yourself means to master Nature. When the passage becomes clear you find Nature's work within your bounds and limits: rather you begin to work yourself.

In our system the abhyasi is advised to meditate on the heart thinking of the divine light there. But he is directed not to view light in any form or shape like that of an electric bulb or a candle, etc. In that case the light appearing therein will not be real, but one projected by his own creative speculation. An abhyasi is advised to proceed with a mere supposition of light with the thought of Divinity at the bottom. What happens then is that we meditate upon the subtlest which is to be attained.

The method of meditation on the heart is to think of Godly light within it. When you begin meditating in this way please think only that Godly light within is attracting you. Do not mind if extraneous ideas haunt you during meditation. Let them come but go on with your own work. Treat your thoughts and ideas as uninvited guests. If even then they trouble you think they are Master's, not yours.

This process of meditation is very effective, and can never fail in bringing about the desired result. Sit in an easy posture for an hour in the morning in quite a natural way. You should only meditate. You should not struggle with your ideas which generally come during meditation. Concentration is the automatic and natural result of meditation. Those who insist on concentration in place of meditation, and force their mind to it, generally meet with failure.

Every saint has used the word 'light' and I too cannot avoid it because that is the best expression for Reality. But that creates some complications, because, when we talk of light the idea of luminosity becomes prominent and we begin to take it as glittering. The real light carries with it no such idea. Under our system, the abhyasi, no doubt, sometimes sees light. But the glittering light appears only in the beginning, when matter comes into contact with energy.

In other words it is only a clue that energy has begun to work. The real light has the dawn color or a faint reflection of colorlessness. Although light is not the exact translation of the thing (because light is really far more heavy a thing than what that actually is) it has been expressed so merely for the sake of understanding.

If the abhyasi begins to feel himself lighter and lighter, it means he is progressing, because in that case he is going into the state that God is in. Light means the loss of the weight of one's own thoughts. Thus the real Light refers only to the real substance, or more appropriately, substanceless substance.

All artificiality and misdirected emphasis guided by the abhyasi's own desires and preconceived notions prove injurious, very often irrevocably. As such the visions of light, etc., are not to be artificially created or insisted upon. These may only be noted, when they do arise, without any feeling of personal attachment to any of them. The only object of personal attachment should be the Ultimate goal, viz., realization, which is to be firmly held in view throughout; and this is to constitute the most reliable guarantee against any and every irrelevant diversion.

One example of harmful misdirected emphasis, as already pointed out, is the insistence on concentration of consciousness, expected anxiously during every session of meditation practice by most raja yogic abhyasis. This has played havoc in the history of yogic *sadhana* in India and elsewhere. Methods of ascetic austerities, penances and physical mortification usually applied for keeping the mind under control, do not relieve it of its misdirected trends. On the other hand, they only serve to keep the evil subdued within and it might at any time burst forth, when, by chance, the control is somehow relaxed. The real solution of the problem lies, not in controlling the mind artificially by suppression, restraint or mortification, but in its gradual molding which is to relieve it of its misdirected trends.

In this, and every other matter therefore, having the attitude of a sincere student, grasping and allowing everything to work and develop in a natural way, is to ensure the most speedy progress.

Generally I advise meditation on the heart at the point where you feel its beats. Meditation on other points can also be undertaken such as fixing the attention on the point of the nose or between the eye-brows, etc., but in my opinion, meditation on the heart is the easiest and most beneficial. There is a great philosophy underlying meditation on the heart. The heart is the pumping station of blood. It sends out purified blood to all parts of the body and to the smallest cells. Now we have taken the heart as the centre for meditation. The blood that runs through our system is affected.

The solidity due to our own thoughts and actions begins to melt away. This is the first thing that we begin to gain from the first day by this method of meditation on the heart. It is the nucleus and creates the vibrant motion, wherever it is directed. This is the field for the mind to work and this is the instrument by which we develop the discriminating faculty. The subtle force works in this place for the descent of divine energy.

If somehow our thinking conjoins with it, or we train it so that it may percolate the right thing and direct it towards Reality, the problem is solved. People may ask why it is necessary to proceed with meditation. The answer is quite plain and simple, that by meditation we gather ourselves at one point so that our individual mind may leave its habit of wandering about, which it has formed. By this practice we set our individual mind on the right path because it is now metamorphosing its habits. When this is done, our thoughts naturally do not go astray. The heart is the only point at which the connecting link between the animate and the inanimate is most clearly felt..

This is the reason why meditation on the heart is very useful. Further, heart is the field for the action of mind. Mind is always as it is. It is the heart which, as the field of action of the mind, is to be set right. Hence the most appropriate point for meditation can be only that wherefrom the current flows on, either upwards or downwards.

It can only be the heart and nothing else. *Trikuti* (centre of the eye-brows) can also be taken for the purpose but that is not an easy job for common people as it requires more labor from the abhyasi. It may also give birth to many complications in due course if the meditation is not properly practiced by the abhyasi. Meditation on the navel point has no spiritual value except that it causes a tickling sensation which finally makes the mind and passions all the more powerful.

At a certain stage of the development of faith in an abhyasi, we generally lay stress upon meditation apparently on human form. Critics may perhaps consider it suicidal to spiritual advancement. The case is not so, provided the man meditated upon is one of special caliber, who has come down from the Immaterial Absolute for spiritual training, or has attained the spiritual standard of evolution required for the purpose by supreme self-exertion.

4. Cleaning

The process of cleaning uses the original power of thought in the form of human will for the refinement of the individual soul to enable it to ascend the steep and slippery path of realization of the subtlest essence of identity.

In the evening again sit in the same posture, at least for half an hour and think that the complexities, the network of your previous thoughts and grossness or solidity in your constitution are all melting away, or evaporating in the form of smoke, from your back. It will help you in purging your mind and will make you receptive of the efficacious influence of our great Master.

As soon as I find that you are free from foreign matter I will either change it in some other way or ask you to stop, as the case may be. In this way, we soar up high by awakening and cleaning the chakras and the sub-points thereof, taking up *Kundalini* at the end, with which the abhyasi has nothing to do himself. It is exclusively the outlook of the Master. But it must be remembered that while practicing these methods one should not force his mind too much but only sit in a normal way.

This process of cleaning is to be repeated for about five minutes before meditational practice in the morning as well. Other ways of cleaning may also be advised according to the needs of individual abhyasis, and need not be mentioned here in detail. Suffice it to say, that the process of cleaning uses the original power of thought in the form of human will for the refinement of the individual soul to enable it to ascend the steep and slippery path of realization of the subtlest Essence of Identity.

5. Prayer

Prayer remains the most important and unfailing means of success.

O, MASTER!

Thou are the real goal of human life.

We are yet but slaves of wishes
Putting bar to our advancement.
Thou art the only God and Power
To bring us up to that stage.

One thing more by way of practice is to offer daily the brief prayer at bed time in the most suppliant mood with a heart overflowing with divine love. Repeat the prayer in your mind once or twice and begin to meditate over it for a few moments.

The prayer must be offered in a way as if some most miserable man is laying down his miseries with a deeply afflicted heart before the Supreme Master imploring for his mercy and grace, with tearful eyes. Then alone can he become a deserving aspirant. There are many methods of loving God and many '*bhavas*' are resorted to, e.g., paternal sentiment (*pitr bhava*), friendly sentiment (*sakhya bhava*), etc.

In my opinion there can be no relation better than that of the lover and the beloved. If an abhyasi thinks himself to be lover and takes God to be beloved and proceeds with the same sentiment the result will be that God himself will become the lover and the abhyasi the beloved in the long run. But if one thinks that one has realized the goal at this stage it will be a serious blunder. What remains further cannot be stated, for it is related to practice only.

Prayer remains the most important and unfailing means of success. Through it we have established our link with the Holy Divine. The reason why prayer should be offered with a heart full of love and devotion, is that one should create within oneself a state of vacuity so that the flow of Divine grace may be diverted towards him. When the world emerged into the present form, the central point was already rooted deep in all the beings.

This central point rooted in us being a part of the Supreme, turns our attention towards the source. In prayer we try to reach up to the same central point. This is possible only when we create a similar state within. This requires practice. It can be attained by resigning ourselves to the Divine Will, which is absolutely simple and tranquil. Apparently it seems to be very difficult, but in fact it is not so, though only for those who aspire for it.

When a man creates in him a strong craving for the Absolute, he is indeed in a state of prayer, and it is for every one to strive for. Whenever a man enters into that state even for a moment, his prayer is granted.

But it requires continued practice to accomplish it. People should be exhorted to offer such a type of prayer. If one achieves and settles down in it, what else remains for him to do except remembrance; and that too in a way that it never comes into consciousness even.

C. ADDITIONAL REQUISITES FOR RAPID PROGRESS

6. Constant Remembrance

We must remain in touch with the idea of God in all phases of our mental and physical activities.

Constant remembrance of God is of course, a special feature in spirituality. The method for cultivating constant remembrance is to think with firm conviction during your leisure hours whether in office or at home, in the street or in the market that God is pervading all over and everywhere and you are thinking of Him. Try to remain in the same thought as long as you can.

The minds of people are absorbed every moment in thinking about the various problems of their material life and their attention is seldom diverted towards God except when they are in deep distress and misery. The reason is that they attach primary importance to their worldly interests alone which constantly remain in their view. Thus they remain entangled within *maya* without ever thinking of getting out of it at any stage.

Frequent remembrance of God, though greatly helpful, is not all that we need for our final success in realization. We generally begin an important thing in the name of God and it is customary almost in every religion to do so. But that is only a matter of formality and has no significance. We never dedicate the thing to God in the real sense and at heart we are in fact quite away from the idea of God. Remembrance of God thus is of no avail.

The real significance of the custom is that we must remain in touch with the idea of God in all phases of our mental and physical activities. We must feel ourselves connected with the Supreme Power every moment with an unbroken chain of thought during all our activities. It can be easily accomplished if we treat all our actions and work to be a part of divine duty, entrusted to us by the Great Master whom we are to serve as best as we can.

Some people think that constant remembrance or even frequent remembrance of God is not practicable when a man in life is surrounded by numerous worries and anxieties caused by worldly attachments and responsibilities. But practice and experience will prove to them that it is a very easy process and can be followed by any and every one in spite of all worries and engagements only if they learn to divert their attention towards God in the real sense.

The idea of guru as the Supreme Divine force is very helpful in spiritual pursuit, if the guru himself happens to be merged in the Ultimate State of realization. You depend upon his guidance thinking him to be a super-human being. If you go on with your busy routine of life dedicating everything to your Master, imagine what good will it bring to you in the long run. While doing a thing think that you are not doing it for yourself but for your Master, rather think that Master himself is doing it for himself.

While at the breakfast table, you must think that your master is breaking his fast. When you go to the office, think that your Master is doing it all. While returning from the office, suppose you see an attractive dance on the way. Your eyes are caught by the charming appearance of the dancer. Then also think that your Master, and not you, is seeing the dance. You will at once lose curiosity for it because your Master's power will begin to flow in to relieve you of the temptation.

When you come back from office, your children rejoice to see you after so many hours. You too enjoy the merriment and it is but natural. Your attention for a while is diverted towards them, and you feel a bit away from the sacred thought. What you are to do then is to think that your Master within is himself enjoying and you shall be in touch with the same sacred thought again. If you are chatting with your friend, think that your Master, not you, is talking to him.

While walking, think that your Master himself is walking. Even during your meditation, if you entertain the idea that not you but your Master himself is meditating on his own form, it shall bring about excellent results. Similarly you can adjust yourself in all your routine of work. If you cultivate this feeling and maintain the outlook that your Master is doing every thing in your place, you shall not only be in constant remembrance all the while, but your actions will cause no impression whatsoever, and so you will cease making further *samskaras*.

7. Devotion

Constant remembrance acquires efficiency when the abhyasi has become devoted to the object of meditation or constant remembrance.

Constant remembrance, in fact, is a natural development of meditational practice and it acquires efficiency when the abhyasi has become devoted to the object of meditation or constant remembrance. It then ceases to be dry *abhyas* and becomes a luscious all-absorbing engagement. The fire of love and devotion alone burns down trivial trash, and wins the gold from the dross. The burning of love may, however, have three stages. The first is the suppressed smoldering giving out thick smoke.

The second has occasional sparks in it; and the last one gives the bright burning flame, capable of reducing everything to ashes in a moment's time. The first two states are subject to their exposure to the combustible matter in the air.

When the solidity which hampers combustion is removed by the effect of inner heating, the final action starts with full force. But then there is the electric fire as well, which bypasses the first two stages, and appears only in the final state, free from smoke and vapor. If you can light up such a fire within you, your progress shall be by leaps and bounds.

Devotion and love, of course, remain so easy and yet so difficult of achievement at once. Real devotion has no tinge of affection in it and goes hand in glove with enlightenment. In the initial stages the devotee may be conscious of his feeling towards the object of his love; but at higher stages the foam and fury is dimmed to the extent of an almost total loss of its awareness at the Ultimate stage.

The superfine level of devotion may be spoken of as total self-surrender, from which the awareness of surrender has entirely been withdrawn by the grace of the Supreme Master Himself.

The problem of practicing devotion, surrender, etc., in a natural way is there. For this purpose it is said that one can love another person of his own species best. So the guru is taken into account as the personification of the Supreme. In my case my Master was the only object of my love. I was not a lover of freedom or peace or perfection or any thing, but only of Him and Him alone.

My Master was no doubt worthy of it, being the fittest man to be meditated upon and be devoted to. He was altogether free from egoistic feelings, desires and worldly entanglements, and devoted wholly to his 'own self'. This phrase refers to a spiritual state of a high order not commonly bestowed upon man. That was the reason why I loved him as best as I could. I tried heart and soul to get myself merged in him in toto, and this had been the life pursuit for me.

It was because I got a Master who was unparalleled and matchless. For the results achieved there from, I have no words to express. In a word He is the infinite ocean of Grace in which we have all to merge. May it be accessible to all earnest seekers!

8. Surrender

Self-surrender has great importance for an abhyasi in his pursuit.

The easiest and surest means to achieve the goal is to surrender yourself to the great Master and become a 'living dead' yourself. This feeling of surrender, if cultivated by forced or mechanical means, seldom proves to be genuine. It must develop automatically within you without least strain or pressure upon the mind. If the knowledge of self is retained, even then it is not true surrender.

What remains to be done when you have surrendered yourself in the true sense? Nothing. I believe that in this state an abhyasi will be in close touch with Reality all the time and the current of divine effulgence will continue its flow to him without any break. In this way you can solve your problem of life in the easiest and most efficacious way in the shortest possible time. Therefore, if one can give away his heart, i.e., make a gift of it to the Divine Master, hardly anything more remains to be done.

This shall naturally bring him to the state of absorption in Absolute Reality. The adoption of this simple and easy technique makes the very beginning to be the end of it. What except a tiny heart can be the fittest offering for the achievement of the dearest object of life?

One thing more. To effect the surrender of heart in the easiest way, only an act of will is required. Besides, the lighter and finer the will, the more effective shall be its working. The adoption of this method is sure to bring in an attitude of renunciation from the very first day. A courageous start is all that is needed for the purpose.

Self-surrender is nothing but a state of complete resignation to the will of the Master, with total disregard of self. A permanent stay in this condition leads to the beginning of the state of negation. When we surrender ourselves to the great Master we begin to attract a constant flow of highest divine force from Him. In this state a man thinks or does only that which his Master's will ordains. He feels nothing in the world to be his belonging, but everything as a sacred trust from the Master and he does everything thinking it to be his Master's bidding.

His will becomes completely subservient to the will of the Master. Surrender is not an ordinary thing to be achieved easily. It begins after complete negation of all senses and faculties for which we proceed by elementary rules of devotion. We submit to our Master, thinking him to be a super-human being. We love him with devotion and faith and reverence trying by all means to attract his attention and favor.

Sages have classified disciples under two main heads: the *manmat* and the *gurumat*. The former are those who approach the guru with some particular worldly end in view such as relief from misery, desire for wealth, etc. They submit to him only so long as they are hopeful of satisfaction of their desires. When they meet disappointment in this respect they are off. For such disciples the question of obedience or submission does not arise, what to say of surrender.

Gurumat disciples are those who obey the commands of the Master in all matters and try to submit to his will in all possible ways. Submission begins with obedience. When we are deeply impressed by the great powers of a Master of higher attainments in spirituality we feel inwardly inclined to follow his biddings.

A beautiful example of surrender is presented to us by Bharat, the son of Dasharath when he went to the forest along with the people of Ayodhya to induce his brother Ram to return.

In reply to the entreaties of the people Ram gravely replied that he would be quite willing to return to the capital provided Bharat asked him to do so. All eyes were turned towards Bharat, who was himself there to induce him to return. But he calmly replied, "It is not for me to command but only to follow". Therefore self-surrender has great importance for an abhyasi in his pursuit.

CHAPTER 20

SAHAJA YOGA

Shri Mataji Nirmala Devi, the founder of Sahaja Yoga, was born on March 21, 1923 to a Christian family in Chindawara, near the city of Nagpur in Central India

She is a direct descendant of the royal Shalivahana dynasty. Sri Mataji was born with her complete Self Realization and knew from a very young age that she had a unique gift which had to be made available to all mankind. Both She and Her parents played a key role in India's Liberation Movement from under British rule. Her father, a close associate of Mahatma Gandhi, was a member of the Constituent Assembly of India and helped write free India's first constitution. He was a renowned scholar, master of 14 languages, and translated the Koran in Marathi. Her mother was the first woman in India to receive an Honors Degree in Mathematics.

As a child, Shri Mataji lived with her parents in the ashram of Mahatma Gandhi. Gandhi saw the wisdom of this child and used to appreciate her immensely, affectionately calling her Nepali due to the Nepali features of her face.Even at a young age, her deep understanding was evident to Gandhi, who frequently sought her advice on spiritual matters.

Shri Mataji's involvement in the freedom struggle is extremely remarkable. She was very courageous and played a daring role as a youth leader of this campaign. In the 1942 "Quit India Movement" announced by Gandhi, she was even arrested, put in jail and tortured along with other freedom fighters for actively participating in this movement.

Shri Mataji was born with a complete understanding of the human nervous system and its energy centers. In order to become acquainted with the scientific vocabulary attached to these subjects, she studied medicine and psychology at the Christian Medical College in Lahore.

In 1970, Shri Mataji, after half a lifetime of meditation and experimentation, succeeded in developing a method by which the residual spiritual energy in man could be awakened en masse. This method of self realization has become known as Sahaja Yoga.

Shri Mataji has introduced the practice of Sahaja Yoga in over 80 countries transforming the lives of thousands. These people who live a normal life, tap to their inner spiritual power through daily Sahaja Yoga meditation and have achieved greater balance in their lives on the physical, emotional, mental and spiritual levels.

Shri Mataji travels the world offering Her teachings free of charge. She has delivered thousands of lectures, given many television and radio interviews, and been the subject of hundreds of newspaper articles around the world.

She is an articulate and very humorous speaker, Shri Mataji is the founder and sole director of Sahaja Yoga or "Vishwa Nirmala Dharma", which is an established non-profit organization in the United States.

CHAPTER 21

THE SAKHYA TRADITION

His Holiness Sakhya Trizin

The Sakhya tradition of Tibetan Buddhism takes its name from the monastery founded at Sakhya in south-western Tibet in 1073 by Konchog Gyalpo of the Khön clan, an influential family that had previously been affiliated to the Nyingma tradition. Konchog Gyalpo studied the 'new tantras' with the translator Drokmi Lotsava.

The most important of the 'new tantra' transmissions that the Sakhya school subsequently preserved was the Hevajra Tantra with its associated instructions known as 'The Path and its Fruit' (Lam-Dré), which had been developed by the ninth century Indian yogi, Virupa. Other key transmissions that form part of the Sakhya spiritual curriculum include the cycles of Vajrayogini, Vajrakilaya, Mahakala and Guhyasamaja.The Sakhya sect was given its definite shape by the works of the 'five venerable masters', Sachen Kunga Nyingpo (1092 - 1158); Sonam Tsemo

(1142 - 1182); Dragpa Gyaltsen (1147 - 1216); Sakya Pandita (1182 - 1251) and Chogyal Phakpa (1235 - 1280). Since that time the tradition and its two sub-sects, Ngor, founded by Ngorchen Kunga Zangpo (b.1382) and Tsar, founded by Tsarchen Losal Gyamtso (1496 - 1560), have been adorned by many eminent yogins and scholars.

The head of the Sakya school, known as Sakya Trizin ("holder of the Sakya throne"), is always drawn from the male line of the Khön family. The present Sakya Trizin, Ngawang Kunga Tegchen Palbar Samphel Wanggi Gyalpo, born in Tsedong in 1945, is the forty-first to hold that office. His Holiness' principal masters, from whom he received all the transmissions of the Sakya tradition, include Ngawang Lodro Shenphen Nyingpo, Jampal Zangpo, Jamyang Chentze Chokyi Lodro, Appey Khen Rinpoche and Chogay Trichen Rinpoche. In 1974, His Holiness married Lady Tashi Lhakyi and since that time they have had two sons, Ratna Vajra Rinpoche (b. 1974) and Jnana Vajra Rinpoche (b. 1979)

CHAPTER 22

SELF - REALIZATION

Self-Realization Fellowship

Self-Realization Fellowship, the international nonprofit society founded by Paramahansa Yogananda, widely revered as one of the pre-eminent spiritual figures of our time. His Autobiography of a Yogi has introduced truth-seekers all over the world to India's age-old philosophy of Yoga and its time-honored tradition of meditation.

The universal teachings of Paramahansa Yogananda offer a science of spiritual exploration one that enables us to create for ourselves spiritually harmonious lives, and to contribute to a more compassionate and peaceful world.

"We are all part of the One Spirit. When you experience the true meaning of religion, which is to know God, you will realize that He is your Self, and that He exists equally and impartially in all beings."

Paramahansa Yogananda

Paramahansa Yogananda founded Self-Realization Fellowship in 1920 to make available the universal teachings of *Kriya Yoga*, a sacred spiritual science originating millenniums ago in India. The society publishes Paramahansa Yogananda's writings, lectures, and recorded talks; oversees temples, retreats, meditation centers, and the monastic communities of the Self-Realization Order; and guides the work of the Worldwide Prayer Circle, a network of groups and individuals dedicated to praying for those in need of physical, mental, or spiritual aid and for world peace and harmony.

Yoga Meditation Methods Taught by Paramahansa Yogananda

Central to Paramahansa Yogananda's teachings, which embody a complete philosophy and way of life, are scientific techniques of concentration and meditation that lead to the direct personal experience of God. These yoga methods quiet body and mind, and make it possible to withdraw one's energy and attention from the usual turbulence of thoughts, emotions, and sensory perceptions. In the clarity of that inner stillness, one comes to experience a deepening interior peace and awareness of God's presence.

Home-Study Lesson Series

Instruction in the practice of the techniques taught by Paramahansa Yogananda is presented in the *Self-Realization Fellowship Lessons*, a comprehensive home-study series compiled from his lectures and writings. Covering a wide range of topics, the *Lessons* offer his inspiring and practical guidance for achieving balanced physical, mental, and spiritual well-being.

Leadership of the Society

The activities of Self-Realization Fellowship are coordinated by members of our monastic order, under the direction of disciples personally trained by Paramahansa Yogananda. Serving as president of the society since 1955 is Sri Daya Mata, one of his earliest and closest disciples and one of the first women in modern history to be appointed as the leader of a worldwide religious movement.

Monks and nuns of the Order serve in many capacities in the society's ashram centers; travel to cities around the world to conduct lectures and classes and to lead retreats; and provide spiritual counsel and guidance in person and through correspondence to students of the Self-Realization Fellowship teachings.

In India (Yogoda Satsanga Society)

Paramahansa Yogananda's society is known in India as Yogoda Satsanga Society. Founded by him in 1917, and headquartered in Dakshineswar (near Calcutta), Yogoda Satsanga Society oversees 90 meditation centers, 21 educational institutions, and a variety of charitable facilities.

Temples and Meditation Centers

At Self-Realization Fellowship's temples and nearly 500 meditation centers, located in 54 countries, students of

Paramahansa Yogananda's teachings meet for inspirational and prayer services, meditation, and spiritual fellowship. The meetings include readings from Yogananda's writings, as well as periods of meditation and devotional chanting.

Several of our temples were established by Yogananda during his lifetime and have become places of pilgrimage for visitors from all parts of the world. Services at the temples are generally conducted by monks of the Self-Realization Order.

Retreats and Lecture Tours

At our Self-Realization Fellowship Retreats, and during our lecture tours and retreat programs in cities throughout the United States and other countries, we offer in-depth classes on the meditation techniques and spiritual way of life taught by Paramahansa Yogananda. For three quarters of a century, Self-Realization Fellowship, a worldwide religious organization with international headquarters in Los Angeles, has been dedicated to carrying on the spiritual and humanitarian work of Paramahansa Yogananda.

Through our worldwide service, we seek to foster a spirit of greater understanding and goodwill among the diverse people and nations of our global family, and to help those of all cultures and creeds to realize and express more fully in their lives the beauty, nobility, and divinity of the human spirit. To Donate

Annual Convocation

Each year, Self-Realization Fellowship hosts an international convocation in Los Angeles presenting Paramahansa Yogananda's teachings. This weeklong program includes classes, meditations, film and video presentations, guided tours to the ashram centers where he lived and worked, and other activities. The annual event attracts up to 6,000 participants from around the world.

CHAPTER 23

SHAMBALA MEDITATION

According to the Shambhala tradition, there is a natural source of radiance and brilliance in the world, which is the innate wakefulness of human beings. This is the basis, in myth and inspiration, of the Kingdom of Shambhala, an enlightened society of fearlessness, dignity and compassion.

About Shambhala

Throughout history, men and women have aspired to create societies that enable them to express the dignity of human existence and to lead meaningful lives within a flourishing culture. This is the vision of Shambhala.

At the heart of this wisdom tradition is the view that a dignified life based on meditative understanding is accessible to everyone and can blossom into an enlightened society. Contemplative practices bring into our ordinary lives a natural sense of goodness, fearlessness, and humor.

The Shambhala and Buddhist teachings can be studied and explored in the worldwide association of meditation centers founded by Vidyadhara the Venerable Chögyam Trungpa Rinpoche and now directed by his son and spiritual heir, Sakyong Mipham Rinpoche.

Shambhala Meditation Centers welcome anyone interested in the practice of meditation and anyone who aspires to expand the experience of gentleness and nonaggression into all areas of life.

A contemplative community

The Shambhala community draws on a wide variety of contemplative traditions. The core practice is mindfulness-awareness meditation. Instruction follows the tradition of oral transmission from teacher to student-an unbroken lineage that goes back twenty-five hundred years.

At each Shambhala Meditation Center, senior members teach meditation and work with their students in how to join the view and experience of meditation with everyday life. Meditation instruction is available free of charge at all Shambhala Meditation Centers.

A comprehensive path of Buddhist practice and study is offered through the network of local centers. The Buddhist tradition provides a well-defined, graduated method of developing skillful action and wisdom through meditation practice and study of the dharma.

Shambhala Training is a nonsectarian path of spiritual training that emphasizes the cultivation of fearless, gentle, and intelligent action in the world. This action arises out of trust in innate human goodness and the inherent power and sacredness of the world, connecting with both through meditation practice as well as mindful activity in everyday life. Shambhala Training welcomes people of all religious traditions as well as those who follow no particular spiritual path.

Nalanda programs bring the contemplative perspective to the arts, health, education, and business. They include such traditional disciplines as the visual arts, archery (kyudo), flower arranging (ikebana), and tea ceremony (cha).

At the heart of each Shambhala Center is the meditation hall, which offers an open and protected space for meditation practice, contemplative disciplines, and community gatherings.

Shambhala's residential practice centers offer month-long meditation programs, public weekend programs, solitary retreats, and intensive practice and study programs for all levels of students. One can also live at a meditation center for an extended period of time, participating in the regular practice and contemplative disciplines.

CHAPTER 24

SRI AUROBINDO

The Mother Sri Aurobindo

"True spirituality is not to renounce life, but to make life perfect with a Divine Perfection." The Mother

INTRODUCTION

A dynamic application of spirituality to life and all it's activities is what we are trying to achieve at Sri Aurobindo Society.

Sri Aurobindo Society is a registered society with its chief administrative office at Pondicherry. It has about 300 centers, 50 branches and about 12,000 members in India and outside. The Mother is the founder and the permanent President of the Society.

Sri Aurobindo Society was started by the Mother in 1960. She is its guiding force and its permanent President. She has nurtured the small instrument that was created over 35 years ago and has made it an international organization working in diverse fields of life.

The community of consciousness has kept growing worldwide

CHAPTER 25

SRI CHINMOY

Chinmoy, has established a headquarters in the United Nations where he supervises the bimonthly U.N. meditation program. Born in West Bengal, India, he tries to blend the East and West.

- He claims to have completed 16,000 paintings in one day, and 843 poems in 24 hours.
- Two rock players, Carlos Santana and John McLaughlin, follow the guru in the USA, Canada, Europe and Australia.
- Chinmoy's way to God is by devotion and surrender to one's guru, with the Hindu doctrine of Hatha Yoga, vegetarianism, and meditation.

<u>CHAPTER 26</u>

THE THERAVADA MEDITATION

One of the Pali words gaining popularity in our country nowadays is Theravada. You hear the word in Buddhist meetings and read it in Dhamma magazines. The government and the people alike use it fondly wherever and whenever occasion arises. What then is Theravada? The following is my humble attempt to explain the word grammatically, historically and doctrinally.

1. Grammatically:

The word Theravada is a compound of two members: Thera and Vada; thera means "elder", especially "an elderly Buddhist monk"; here it stands for the inflected form Theranam, "of the Elders"; the second member vada coming from the root vad, "to speak" signifies "speech", "talk", "word", "doctrine" or even "ism". The word Theravada is frequently translated into English "the Doctrine of the Elders"; sporadic translations are "the Way of the Elders" and "the School of the Elders"; even "old Wisdom School" is met with.

Most probably the word first appears as the name of a Buddhist school in the Dipavamsa, the earlier Chronicle of Sri Lanka, dating the 4th century AD. The name is echoed in the Mahavamsa, the later but the better known and more important Chronicle of the 5th century.

But it is the Commentaries and the Sub-commentaries on the Canonical texts that the name is defined and their definitions may be summed up as follows: only the texts (paliyeva) that were formulated at the first two Councils are to be known as Theravada, for they were safeguarded and handed down by such Great Elders as Maha Kassapa and others. They were so named in order to distinguish them from the views of the dissident Mahasanghika School.

2. Historically:

The history of Theravada as a school of Buddhism should begin with a quick survey of the life of Gotama Buddha himself. He was born as a Sakyan prince at a place near the Himalayas about six hundred years BC. Grieved at the ills of life such as old age, sickness and death, he renounced the world at the age of 29 and started seeking the way to Nibbana, "Extinction" of all forms of suffering. At 35 he achieved his goal and became Buddha.

He then carried out his teaching mission for 45 years. At 80 he attained Parinibbana, "Total Extinction" (which is the Buddhist way of expressing his demise). Just before that event he left a message to his cousin and attendant monk, Ananda, part of which being:

When I am gone, the Dhamma (Doctrine) and Vinaya (Discipline) that I have taught and laid down shall be your Teacher!

This implies that the Buddha did not want to appoint any person to succeed him on his demise. The two Great Disciples Sariputta and Moggallana had already passed away; but Maha Kassapa who enjoyed the good reputation of being the Third Disciple was alive. But even a man of his stature would not become the Buddha's successor.

By this injunction the Buddha made it clear that only his Dhamma and Vinaya would adequately and effectively serve as the sole guide to his followers. Dhamma-Vinaya therefore was the designation given by the Master himself to his twofold teaching (pavacana) about the time of his Parinibbana. There was no reason whatever to dub it Theravada.

When the First Council was held at Rajagaha three months after the Buddha's demise with the noble aim of consolidation the Dhamma-Vinaya "before righteousness fades away and before unrighteousness shines forth".

The Council was presided over by Maha Kassapa whose questions on the Vinaya and the Dhamma were answered by Upali and Ananda respectively. The answers were confirmed by 500 monks who recited both in unison and passed on from teacher to pupil orally. The name Theravada remained unheard of, at least publicly. It that Buddhism as one whole body with its original designation of Dhamma Vinaya stood in full bloom all over India.

A century later the Second Council was held at Visalia under the collective leadership of Yasa, Revata and Sabbakami to discuss the "ten points" which in fact were the Buddha's certain disciplinary ruler relaxed and practiced by imprudent Vajjian monks. The Council composed of 700 members decided the points unlawful and condemned the Vajjians who seceded from that Council to convene their own known as Maha sangha or Mahasangiti, the Great Council, since their number 10,000 far exceeded that of the former. It was the open and serious schism that took place in the Sangha, the Buddhist Order, for the first time. And with the schism emerged two factions of Theravadins, followers of Theravada, and Mahasanghikas or Mahasangitikas, those of the secession.

The Third Council in the tradition of Theravada was held in the 3rd century, according to the Chronicles and Commentaries, with Moggaliputta Tissa as its president and Asoka to the Moriyan Dynasty as its supporter. The venue of the Council was the imperial city Pataliputra. The purpose was to purify the religion and to restore peace to the Order, for many heretics who had joined the Sangha for convenient livelihood caused confusion and unfortunate incidents in the Sangha.

At the conclusion of the Council, missionaries were dispatched to nine countries including Sri Lanka and Suvannabhumi; to the former went Asoka's son, Mahinda, leading a group of monks and to the latter, generally taken to be Myanmar, Sona and Uttara.

Scholars are of opinion that Theravada thrived in the country of Magadha in the east and the city of Ujjaini in the west. In his rock and pillar inscriptions, Asoka speaks of compassion, charity, truthfulness, purity and other virtues to be developed which might be common to all the religions prevailing in the country: Buddhism, Brahmanism, Hinduism, Jainism, etc. From the inscriptions, we also know of his tolerance and even gifts to non-Buddhist sects.

But that he was a devout Theravadin in his heart of hearts is evidenced by his famous Bhabru inscription in which he recommends for learning certain Buddhist texts which can be traced in the Pali Canon of the Theravada, the only school which employs that language for recording its scriptures. The inclusion of the Kathavatthu, a work of his time, in the Abhidhamma Pitaka is another piece of evidence, not to speak of his sending of his son Mahinda as a bhikkhu to propagate Theravada Buddhism in the Island as asserted in Buddhist works. In these works, however, the name Theravada is replaced by Vibhajjavada, the "Doctrine of Analysis" or the "Religion of Reason" though the two terms are identical.

The reign of Asoka was however marked by the split of Buddhism into 18 sects which according to one source were Theravada and Mahasanghika plus 10 branching out from the former and 6 from the latter. The misfortune caused by the split was not so great as one might guess, for it was a result of the rapid expansion of Buddhism. Just remember the Buddha's instruction given to his earliest 60 disciples when he sent them to spread the Dhamma for the welfare and happiness of many: "No two persons shall go in the same direction!" The differences between one sect and another were due to the geographical factor rather than to doctrinal except in a few cases. And many of the sects disappeared after existing for some time.

After its heyday during the time of Asoka, Theravada began to wane in northern India. When the mighty Gupta dynasty arose in AD 428, there must be a number of reasons for this sad turning point in the course of Theravada.

One theory says that the decline was brought about by the lack of encouragement of the Gupta kings who as Hindu favored Sanskrit. In fact, it was a time of the revival or even the efflorescence of Sanskrit literature. Their devotion to Hinduism and love for Sanskrit did not help the existence of Theravada let alone its growth, for it is the only school of Buddhism that employs Pali as its language.

It was evident that some of the Guptas showed their interest in Buddhism by making some donations to it, but the recipients were the forms other than Theravada, such as Sarvastivada, an important offshoot of Theravada, and Mahayana, the giant incarnation, as it were, of Mahasanghika, both of which turned to Sanskrit as their sacred language.

Pali Buddhism, Theravada, then moved to the south and settled itself along the east coast form which hailed later such Buddhist commentators as Dhammapala of Kancipura and Buddhadatta of Uragapura.

The establishment of Theravada after its introduction there by Mahinda from Pataliputra long before its journey to the south of India, one knows only too well. Its stronghold was the Mahavihara, "the Great Monastery" at Anuradhapura, to which Buddhaghosa, the greatest of commentators in Theravada tradition belonged. It was also a seat of learning producing a number of other writers in Pali.

The existence of some antagonistic sects was not unknown but the Mahavihara was powerful enough to prevail over the opponents. In times of danger and adversity also Sri Lanka had good friends in Myanmar and Thai Buddhists who went to their rescue. Today she stands out as a land of missionary monks who are not only well versed in Buddhism but also modern educated and efficient enough to spread the Dhamma, especially in the west.

Nowadays Sri Lanka, Myanmar and Thailand are the three stalwart Theravada states with close religious ties. Though Laos and Cambodia have lost much of their religious luster both still deserve to be recognized as Theravada countries. In Vietnam, formerly a land of pure Mahayana, Theravada is somewhat developing. In the hill tracts of Bangladesh many of the Baruas, the Chakmas and the Maghs and their fellow countrymen in the Chittagong area still prove to be staunch Theravadins. So do the Shans in the frontier regions of South China.

As for India, the land of the birth of Buddhism as well as of its death, signs of the revival of the Theravada school have been noticed. Mass conversions of Indians to Buddhism have recently taken place. At the most recent conversion ceremony some Mahatheras from Myanmar played a leading role reciting Pali formulas.

3. Doctrinally:

Now to explain Theravada doctrinally, only a few similarities and differences between Theravada and the three other schools mentioned above -- Mahasanghika, Sarvastivada and Mahayana -- will be touched upon as giving details is impossible here.

Theravada and Mahasanghika: In regard to Vinaya, the code of discipline known as Patimokkha in Theravada contains 227 rules while its counterpart, Pratimoksa, Mahasanghika 119. The formers Bhikkhu-vibhanga and Bhikkhuni-vibhanga probably correspond to the latter's Bhiksu-vinaya and Bhiksuni-vinaya, which are now existent solely in Chinese.

The only surviving work in its original language, Sanskrit, the Mahavastu of the Mahasanghika's Vinaya, has passages that are found parallel to those in the Khuddakapatha, the Vimanavatthu, Buddhavamsa and Dhammapada of the Pali Canon. An important doctrinal difference the two schools is that the Theravadins speak of the human nature of the Buddha where as the Mahasanghikas believe the supramundane nature of Buddhas which is more pronounced in the sect called Lokottaravada and in Mahayana.

Theravada and Sarvastivada: Though the Sarvastivada scriptures are in Sanskrit, they teach the views that are closest to Theravada. Like its patriarch school Theravada, Sarvastivada denies the transcendent powers ascribed to Bodhisattvas. But unlike Theravada, it questions the perfection of Arahats, whom Theravada hold in highest esteem as winners of Nibbana. Its monks observed 155 Vinaya rules.

The school has its own Abhidhamma Pitaka, but the seven books are entirely different from the Theravada's. Two commentaries on the Abhidhamma still exist: Vibhasha and Mahavibhasha, and from this the Sarvastivadins are also known as Vabhashikas, "those belonging to the Vibhashas". They believe that "all is" or "all things exist" (Sarvam asti in Sanskrit and sabbam atthi in Pali). That is to say not only the things in the present exist, but also the things in the past and future which are in continuity with the present. Hence the name of their school Sarvastivada.

Theravada and Mahayana: The name Mahayana along with the other name Hinayana its first appearance between the its century BC and the 1st century AD. Occurring in the Saddharma Pundarika Sutra, the "Discourse on the Lotus of the Good Law", Mahayana -- the "Greater Vehicle" -- is understood today by many as the name the school of Buddhism prevailing in Tibet, China, Korea, Japan and Mongolia, as opposed to the Hinayana until recently represented by Theravada.

Mahayana covers all forms Buddhism prevalent in those countries as it has incorporated many of the view held by the sects that had branched off from Mahasanghika and have disappeared now. The master who gave a clear definition to this school known sometimes as Northern Buddhism was Nagarjuna of the 2nd century A.D. In common with their brethren, the Theravadins, they believe the Four Noble Truths, the Eightfold Noble Path, the Dependent Origination, the Three Characteristics of Existence and a number of other basic tenets.

Above all, both the schools accept Gotama Buddha as their Teacher. Mahayana built on Compassion and Wisdom has its own divergences, of course, of which only the most important one may be stated here, which is expressed by scholars as the Bodhisatva ideal. Every Mahayanist is a Bodhisatva, "a being whose essence is Enlightenment" as one translation goes.

As such he sets his goal not only to attain Nirvana for himself but to provide all sentient beings with the same liberation from the woes of samsara or "life-cycle". Hence their school is greater compared with Hinayana, the school of the "Lesser Vehicle" as its members strive only for their attainment of nirvana as Arahats.

The World Fellowship of Buddhists decided unanimously in Colombo in 1950 that the term Hinayana should be eliminated when referring to the Theravada School of Buddhism. The term Hinayana is now a thing of the past. If the term be used today it should mean any or all of the sects now sunk into oblivion. There exist at present only two schools of Buddhism: Theravada and Mahayana. The two must be friendlier with each other and be more united in contributing their shares to everlasting peace of the world.

<u>CHAPTER 27</u>

TRANSCENDENTAL MEDITATION

Maharishi Mahesh Yogi Founder of the Transcendental Meditation program

Maharishi Mahesh Yogi is widely regarded as the foremost scientist in the field of consciousness, and considered to be the greatest teacher in the world today. Maharishi has completely restored the thousands of years-old scattered Vedic Literature for the total significance of its theory and practice, and has organized it in the form of a complete science of consciousness.

Maharishi's Vedic Science and Technology unfolds the full potential of Natural Law in human consciousness as the basis of improving all areas of life.

The Transcendental Meditation program, the subjective technology of Maharishi's Vedic Science and Technology, is the most widely practiced and extensively researched program of self-development in the world.

Maharishi is now establishing Maharishi Vedic Universities and Maharishi Vedic Schools throughout the world to offer mastery over Natural Law to every individual and to perpetuate life in accordance with Natural Law -- perfection in every profession -- and create Natural Law based problem-free government in every country -- governments with the ability to prevent problems.

Maharishi Mahesh Yogi is widely regarded as the foremost scientist in the field of consciousness, and considered to be the greatest teacher in the world today. Maharishi has completely restored the thousands of years-old scattered Vedic Literature for the total significance of its theory and practice, and has organized it in the form of a complete science of consciousness.

Maharishi's Vedic Science and Technology unfolds the full potential of Natural Law in human consciousness as the basis of improving all areas of life.

The Transcendental Meditation program, the subjective technology of Maharishi's Vedic Science and Technology, is the most widely practiced and extensively researched program of self-development in the world.

Maharishi is now establishing Maharishi Vedic Universities and Maharishi Vedic Schools throughout the world to offer mastery over Natural Law to every individual and to perpetuate life in accordance with Natural Law -- perfection in every profession -- and create Natural Law based problem-free government in every country -- governments with the ability to prevent problems.

"Transcendental Meditation opens the awareness to the infinite reservoir of energy, creativity, and intelligence that lies deep within everyone.

"By enlivening this most basic level of life, Transcendental Meditation is that one simple procedure which can raise the life of every individual and every society to its full dignity, in which problems are absent and perfect health, happiness, and a rapid pace of progress are the natural features of life."

--Maharishi

The Transcendental Meditation (TM) technique is a simple, natural, effortless procedure practiced for 15-20 minutes in the morning and evening, while sitting comfortably with the eyes closed. During this technique, the individual's awareness settles down and experiences a unique state of restful alertness. As the body becomes deeply relaxed, the mind transcends all mental activity to experience the simplest form of awareness, Transcendental Consciousness, where consciousness is open to itself. This is the self-referral state of consciousness.

The experience of Transcendental Consciousness develops the individual's latent creative potential while dissolving accumulated stress and fatigue through the deep rest gained during the practice. This experience enlivens the individual's creativity, dynamism, orderliness, and organizing power, which result in increasing effectiveness and success in daily life.

The Transcendental Meditation technique is scientific, requiring neither specific beliefs nor adoption of a particular lifestyle. The practice does not involve any effort or concentration. It is easy to learn and does not require any special ability. People of all ages, educational backgrounds, cultures, and religions in countries throughout the world practice the technique and enjoy its wide range of benefits.

Research indicates that TM technique Meditators on average have the biological age of a person 5 to 12 years younger, as well as significantly reduced incidence of illness and risk of heart disease. Studies also show that TM technique Meditators have warmer interpersonal relationships, less anxiety, increased self-esteem and self-confidence, increased problem-solving ability and greater creativity. The individual spontaneously radiates a purifying and nourishing influence of positivity and harmony in society as a whole.

What Are Advanced Techniques?

"The purpose of Advanced Techniques is to take the experience to another, higher level. Advanced Techniques are like fertilizers; fertilizers bring better fruit to every tree. To enjoy greater achievement and fulfillment in life, take advantage of this beautiful program of Advanced Techniques to enrich the development of higher states of consciousness." --Maharishi

ADVANCED TECHNIQUES enhance and enrich the benefits of one's daily practice of the Transcendental Meditation program. Through regular practice of the Transcendental Meditation technique, the mind becomes familiar with finer levels of the thinking process and with the source of thought -- Transcendental Consciousness -- the home of all the Laws of Nature. Through the Advanced Techniques of the Transcendental Meditation program, the totality of Natural Law is more quickly and profoundly integrated in the awareness. As the conscious mind becomes more and more infused with pure consciousness, a powerful influence of integration and bliss is created. Every phase of thought and action spontaneously becomes more supported by the evolutionary power of Natural Law, resulting in greater fulfillment of desires in daily life.

The Advanced Techniques hasten one's growth to enlightenment, to that level of unity consciousness which harnesses the full value of Natural Law at every stroke of activity. With the Advanced Techniques, one naturally radiates an influence of fullness and bliss to the environment.

"The practical program to create Heaven on Earth is to develop bliss consciousness, so that no matter where one may be on earth, one will always be in Heaven. To rise quickly in bliss consciousness and prepare the ground for Heaven on Earth, everyone is invited to participate in this beautiful program of Advanced Techniques." Maharishi.

IT IS A GREAT JOY to announce that Advanced Technique teachers from India are now teaching the Advanced Techniques of the Transcendental Meditation program at least once a year at all Maharishi Vedic Universities and Schools.

Advanced Techniques Every Eighteen Months

All those who have been practicing the Transcendental Meditation technique or an Advanced Technique regularly for a minimum of 18 months may apply for instruction in an Advanced

Technique. It is recommended that one continues to receive Advanced Techniques regularly every 18 months. There must be at least six months between learning an Advanced Technique and learning the TM-Siddhi program. The Advanced Techniques course includes three meetings: orientation, personal instruction, and verification and validation of experiences. Each meeting lasts one to two hours.

The TM and TM-Siddhi Techniques

The TM technique is simple mental repetition of a "mantra" or word. The TM movement claims that only specific "words" can be used. They claim that the selection of words is based upon a secret formula. Court documents have shed some light on this "secret" process. It is nothing other than a set of words given out by age, and/or age and sex, depending on the teacher-training course the TM teacher attended.

The TM-Siddhi program is nothing other than a set of sutras (words or phrases), mentally repeated every fifteen seconds after doing a twenty-minute session of TM. Each sutra is repeated twice, with a 15 second pause in between each repetition.

The TM Mantra Tables

1961		1969-Male		1969-Female		1972-Female	
Sex	Mantra	Age	Mantra	Age	Mantra		
Male	Ram	0-15	Ing	0-15	Im	10-11	Ing
Female	Shiriram	15-30	Aing	15-30	Aim	12-13	Im
		30-45	Shring	30-45	Shrim	14-15	Nga
		46 +	Shiam	46 +	Shiama	16-17	Ima
						18-19	Aying
						20-21	Ayim
						22-23	Ayinga
						24-25	Ayima
						25 +	Shiring

1976		1977		1978		Oct. 1978		1987	
Age	Mantra	Age	Mantra	Age	Mantra	Age	Mantra	Age	Mantra
03-10	Eng	03-10	Ing					0-11	Eng
10-12	Em	10-12	In	10-12	Eng	10-12	Eng		
12-14	Enga	12-14	Inga	12-14	Em	12-14	Em	12-13	Em
14-16	Ema	14-16	Ina	14-16	Emga	14-16	Enga	14-15	Enga
16-18	Aeng	16-18	Aing	16-18	Ema	16-18	Ema	16-17	Ema
18-20	Aem	18-20	Aim	18-20	Aeng	18-20	Aing	18-19	Aing
20-22	Aenga	20-22	Ainga	20-22	Aem	20-22	Aim	20-21	Aim
22-24	Aema	22-24	Aima	22-24	Aenga	22-24	Ainga	22-23	Ainga
				24-26	Aema	24-26	Aima	22-25	Aima

24-30	Shiring	24-30	Shiring	26-30	Shiring	26-30	Shiring	26-29	Shiring
30-35	Shirim	30-35	Shirin	30-35	Shirim	30-35	Shirim	30-34	Shirim
35-40	Hiring	35-40	Hiring	35-40	Hiring	35-40	Hiring	35-39	Hiring
40-45	Hirim	40-45	Hirin	40-45	Hirim	40-45	Hirim	40-44	Hirim
45-50	Kiring	45-50	Kiring	45-50	Kiring	45-50	Kiring	45-49	Kiring
50-55	Kirim	50-55	Kirin	50-55	Kirim	50-55	Kirim	50-54	Kirim
55-60	Shiam	55-60	Shiam	55-60	Shyam	55-60	Shiam	55-59	Sham
60 +	Shiama	60 +	Shiama	60 +	Shyama	60 +	Shiama	60 +	Shama

Notes: The year at the top of each column indicates the year the teacher was trained. "Age" is that of the initiate at the time of learning the technique.

Advanced Techniques

First:	AING NAMAH
Second:	SHRI AING NAMAH
Third:	SHRI AING NAMAH NAMAH
Fourth:	SHRI SHRI AING NAMAH NAMAH
Fifth:	SHRI SHRI AING AING NAMAH NAMAH
Sixth:	SHRI SHRI AING AING NAMAH NAMAH (Thought in the heart area)
Seventh:	Age of Enlightenment Technique: A system of putting attention on parts of the body, environment, world and outer space.

Notes: In most cases students were instructed to use their own, previously assigned mantra where AING appears above.

Translation of Advanced Technique Mantras

SHRI	"Oh most beautiful"
AING	"Hindu goddess Saraswati"
NAMAH	"I bow down"

Ayurveda Techniques

Primordial Sound - "AMRITA," used as a mantra

Psycho physiological Technique - Mantra is thought in heart area.

TM-Siddhi Techniques

The names of the sutras used in the TM-Siddhi program are:

Friendliness
Compassion
Happiness
Strength of an elephant
Bronchial tube
Inner light
Sun
Moon
Polestar
Trachea
Navel
Distinction between intellect and transcendence
Transcendence intuition
Transcendence finest hearing
Transcendence finest sight
Transcendence finest taste

Transcendence finest touch
Transcendence finest smell.

The "levitation" or "flying" technique, now known as "Yogic Flying," is used in the same way as all other sutras:

"Relationship of body and akasha - lightness of cotton fiber."

This phrase is mentally repeated every fifteen seconds after doing a twenty minute session of TM. Each sutra is mentally repeated twice (if time allows 4 times), with a 15 second pause in between each repetition.

After doing the flying sutra for 5-30 minutes, the instruction is to rest for 10-30 minutes and then read the Hindu Scriptures for 5 minutes.

An example of the readings (from the Ninth Mandala of Rig Veda):

Flow Soma, in a most sweet and exhilarating stream, effused for Indra to drink. The all-beholding destroyer of Rakshasas has stepped upon his gold-smitten birthplace, united with the wooden cask. Be the lavish giver of wealth, most bounteous, the destroyer of enemies; bestow on us the riches of the affluent. Come with food to the sacrifice of the mighty gods, and bring us strength and sustenance. To thee we come, O dropping (Soma); for thee only is this our worship day by day, our prayers are to thee, none other.

<u>CHAPTER 28</u>

VEDANTA SOCIETY

Formed in New York, in 1895 by Swami Vivekananda, after addressing the Parliament of World Religions in Chicago in 1893. It was the first Hindu organization to be established in the USA; many cults today are but the fruition of this landmark event.

Today, there are 150 Vedanta centers in the world; 124 in India, 13 in the USA with 1,500 members, who influenced Aldoux Huxley, Gertrude Stein, and Gerald Heard.

The Doctrine:

Is taken from Sri Ramakrishna, the teacher of Vivekananda, one of the most famous gurus in India in the 19th century, and teaches that "all religions lead to the same goal, namely, the realization of God: It is like the "water", the Hindus call it "jal", the Muslims call it "pani", but it is all the same... the basic philosophy is "unity among religions", with the believe that every nation has its own unique contribution to bring to the world, and when such is offered up, that nation goes into decline.

- However, "Hinduism" is the basic foundation of the Vedanta Society: To escape from reincarnation, with the Vedas as the authority. Jesus is one of many, but not the only God; the main problem is ignorance, and not sin..... And when it proclaims that "Asia produces giants in spirituality, just as the Occident produces giants in politics and science", it is forgetting the names of Jesus, Mohammed, Moses, St. Therese...

CHAPTER 29

VIPASSNA

We've come here today to do a practice called Vipassana. Vipassana is a word in the Pali language, one of the ancient languages of India along with Sanskrit. Sometimes Vipassana is translated as "insight meditation" because one of the main effects of the practice is that you get deep understandings about the nature of experience, the nature of yourself, the nature of deep issues--universal issues such as how it is that pain turns into suffering, how it is that pleasure either becomes satisfaction or becomes neediness, and how it is that the sense of self arises.

Vipassana meditation is also called "mindfulness meditation" because we are very attentive. The main technique is to become extraordinarily attentive to ordinary experience. Unfortunately the word mindfulness can be a bit misleading if you interpret mindfulness to mean that you are constantly thinking about what you're doing. Mindful in the proper sense of the word means to be attentive and conscious about what's happening. The word "insight" can be a little misleading too because it's not only a word from Buddhism, but also is a word used in psychotherapy. When you do psychotherapy you get insights. Of course those insights are very important, but they are typically insights into your own personality, and the specific issues of your life.

The insights that come as a result of Vipassana are deeper and more general than those that are ordinarily encountered in psychotherapy. They deal with very broad issues that are multiply rather than singularly applicable. In science, a deep theory augurs many specific applications. Out of a single fundamental breakthrough in science you may have dozens--or even thousands--of specific applications. So in the same way, the insights that come from Vipassana practice let us understand the very nature of personality itself, not just things about our own personality. So Vipassana is "insight" in the sense of deep insight and it is "mindfulness" in the sense of extraordinary attentiveness.

The basic premise of this practice can be stated rather simply. Whenever one brings an extraordinary degree of mindfulness and equanimity to ordinary experience this produces insight. And it also produces something called purification. Now, every word I just used is a technical term in Buddhism. Buddhism is a kind of inner science. The West developed an outer science with a technical vocabulary to describe, in a way that no other culture did, the external physical reality.

In the East they have an analogously precise and technical vocabulary, but it is applied to the inner world. That is to say, the world of subjective experience: hearing, seeing, smelling, tasting, the feeling body and the thinking mind. They developed a science of these six senses and it's called Vipassana.

I find in science a very appropriate metaphor for this particular kind of meditation. When you study science you know that you are going to encounter technical terms. When you encounter a technical term you should not project your own meanings onto it. You have to listen very carefully to the exact words that the teacher uses in defining that term. For example, in ordinary colloquial English, force, power, and energy are often used as synonyms, but for a physicist they are defined in specific--and very different--ways.

(Force is proportional to acceleration and mass; energy is force applied over a distance; and power is the rate at which energy is being generated or consumed.) In a similar way, I'm going to give you some technical vocabulary from the Vipassana tradition.

One such term is "equanimity." it does not mean a cooled out, passive or indifferent attitude. Rather, it means an attitude of not interfering with the operation of the six senses. If you have a sensation in your knee and it's painful and it wants to spread, you let it spread. Why? Because you discover that it is precisely the interference with that sensation that causes suffering, not the sensation itself.

Equanimity literally means "balance." It means not to push and pull the flow of the senses. It does not for a moment imply that one would fail to take action with respect to external circumstances, nor does it imply passivity, apathy or anything like that. Equanimity is radical permission to feel. Equanimity is a dropping of internal friction with respect to the flow of these six senses: hearing, seeing, smelling, tasting, the feeling body and the thinking mind. As a state of radical openness, equanimity is intimately linked to love.

Whenever one brings mindfulness and equanimity to ordinary experience, an evolutionary process takes place, consisting of two aspects. One aspect is insight and the other is purification.

Let's talk about what we mean by purification. We all have within us sources of unhappiness.

You notice that very quickly when you sit down to meditate. You'll feel just fine and then there will be something that will make your world less than perfect. You get sleepy, or your mind wanders, or this or that emotion comes up, negative tapes start to come up, traumatic memories appear, you feel angry, you want to jump out of your skin, you're running all sorts of fantasies, doing things to divert yourself, you're aware of inner conflicts. We are chock full of sources of unhappiness which are completely foreign to our being. It is not in the nature of consciousness to suffer. However, we have acquired certain limiting forces: cravings and aversions, painful memories, inappropriate yet habitual behavior patterns, et cetera.

When we sit down and do this practice that's all going to come up. So you don't always feel good while doing Vipassana meditation. In fact you might feel lousy. I know some of you may want to leave the retreat right now having heard that. "I thought meditation is supposed to make a person feel great." Yes, in the long run, but an important aspect of meditation is to sit down and start working through the sources of not feeling great, whatever they may be.

You literally eat your way through them, one after another, after another, after another. How? By just being mindful and having equanimity, that's all. Whatever comes up, you'll observe it and you'll do nothing. You'll be very aware and that's all.

Now that may seem trivial at best, stupid at worst. But it is actually quite powerful. Let's say that one of these blockages to happiness comes up as we meditate--a negative tape, a craving, an aversion, an inner conflict, a congealing. If we reject it and say "I don't want you," we're pushing it away. But in order to reject it we have to "touch" it, by pushing on it.

If on the other hand we identify with it, buy into it and let it pull us away, then again we've "touched" it. As soon as one touches it, one re-charges the energy supply of that negativity. If you try to push it away or pull it to you, any touch whatsoever means that this particular negativity is able to "recharge its battery" as it were, from our general "pool of psychic energy." But if we don't touch it then it has to play itself out on its own power source which is quite finite and if we continue to be alert and simply observe, eventually the intrinsic energy source of that negativity dissipates and it goes away forever. It gets worked through.

This process of observing negativity to death is called purification. As we work through the blockages to happiness, our intrinsic happiness--the nature of our consciousness which is effortless effulgent joy--becomes evident. If the dirt is cleaned away from the window, the sun that was always there is able to shine through. The spiritual reality which is the nature of ordinary experience is able to shine forth.

Most people would affirm such a spiritual reality, but they don't directly experience it. They experience only their own projections, wishful thinking, or beliefs about it, without ever being able to see it directly. Yet everyone has the ability to come into direct contact with the Source.

Through the continued practice of a rigorous liberation oriented meditation, one can work through what's in the way. It takes time, but the time is going to pass anyway, so why not live it to the max?

So the essence of this practice can be stated as a simple formula: ordinary experience plus mindfulness plus equanimity yields insight and purification. In this formula, each term is defined very precisely. Ordinary experience is defined as hearing, seeing, smelling, tasting, the feeling body and the thinking mind. Mindfulness is defined as specificity in awareness, clarity in awareness, continuity in awareness, richness in awareness, precision in awareness. Equanimity is defined as not interfering with the flow of the senses at any level, including the level of preconscious processing.

When sufficient mindfulness and equanimity are brought to bear on ordinary experience, we arrive at purification and insight. And, as a result of the purification and insight, our intrinsic happiness, our true birthright and spiritual reality, gets uncover discover that what we thought was the world of phenomena--the world of time, space, and matter--turns out to really be a world of spiritual energy, and that we have direct contact with it moment by moment.

Because, when the senses become purified, when the inner conflicts--at all levels--have been broken up, the flow of these ordinary senses turns into a prayer, a mantra, a sacred song, and we find that, just by living our life, we are in moment by moment contact with the Source. In the Christian contemplative tradition this is called the "practice of the presence of God." In the Jewish mystical tradition it is called "briah yesh me-ayin"--the experience of things (yesh) being continuously created (briah) from no-thing (ayn), that is, from God.

For most people the senses are "opaque." Do you understand what I mean by the word opaque? A window is opaque if it is covered by soot: light can't come through. The soot is craving, aversion, and ignorance. When that's cleared away, the ordinary senses become literally transparent. It is very hard to describe what this is like. Hearing returns to being part of the effortless flow of nature, seeing returns to being part of the effortless flow of nature, and likewise with smelling, tasting, the body sensations whether they are pleasant, unpleasant, or neutral, they all go back to being part of "God's breath", so to speak.

Even the thinking process returns to being part of this effortless flow. At the beginning stages of meditation one is very concerned with overcoming the wandering thoughts in order to develop enough calm and concentration to be able to practice mindfulness. But when you get further along in the process there will be no necessity whatsoever to have a still mind because the ordinary flow of thought will be experienced as not different from the activity of the Source.

In other words, purification means that in ordinary experience, the operation of these senses becomes transparent and elastic. For most people the senses are opaque and rigid. So no wonder that people think they live in a world of solid matter and fixated space that always exists. But space is generated by the source moment by moment and we become aware of that when the senses become clarified and elastic, no longer rigid. Literally, Vipassana means "to clarify," "to see clearly," or "to perceive clearly"--Vi means "clearly."

Vipassana means that the operation of the senses becomes clarified in the two meanings of the word "clarify." In one meaning of the word, when something is clarified that which was indistinct becomes distinct. The other meaning of the word clarify is that which was opaque becomes transparent. So in Vipassana we do nothing but try to be very distinct. To discern moment by moment what are the components of our experience.

That may seem like a trivial practice. "What's the big deal. I'm sitting here, so now I'm clearly aware of an itch in my thus, or now I know that the sound is calling my attention. So what?" But when all the components of ed and we experience become distinct enough, when there's crystal clarity about exactly what's happening moment by moment, then the senses become literally transparent, i.e., insubstantial.

And as I say, a reality that is beyond time and space can shine through. One is able to contact the Source as a pure "doing" continuously molding time, space, self and world moment by moment. Technically, this is referred to as "insight into impermanence." Well, once you've reached that point you'll never be bored again, I promise you.

Now let's talk a little more about insight. In Vipassana you get understandings into the most fundamental things by observing yourself very carefully. Here we have another analogy from science. When people observe under a microscope they start to discover things they could never see with the naked eye. There's no way to know that our bodies are made up of trillions of little cells. No matter how hard you look at your body, you'll never see them.

But if you look under a microscope you will, and you'll understand something deep and fundamental about the nature of life. It's called the cell theory. It's the basis of modem biology and modem medicine. The microscope is an awareness extending tool that allows us to see something that is always there but not evident to the naked eye. Likewise, the mindfulness practice, the concentration practice that you will be developing here, is to the exploration of your internal world what the microscope is to the exploration of the external world. It's going to allow you to see finer levels of structure that are absolutely invisible to people otherwise, but are very important.

For example, as you are observing, you'll be able to see that pain is one thing, and resistance to the pain is something else, and when the two come together you have an experience of suffering, that is to say, "suffering equals pain multiplied by resistance." You'll be able to see that's true not only for physical pain, but also for emotional pain and it's true not only for little pains but also for big pains. It's true for every kind of pain no matter how big, how small, or what causes it

Whenever there is resistance there is suffering. As soon as you can see that, you gain an insight into the nature of "pain as a problem" and as soon as you gain that insight, you'll begin to have some freedom. You come to realize that as long as we are alive we can't avoid pain. It's built into our nervous system. But we can certainly learn to experience pain without it being a problem. Without it turning into suffering, without it getting in the way, and without it blocking the perfection of the moment.

If you've never meditated you may be completely lost as to what I'm talking about. You may even think I'm talking gibberish. And there's a good reason for that. For most people, by the time they are conscious of a physical or emotional pain they have already turned it into suffering by resisting it. The resistance begins at the preconscious processing level of each moment of experience.

So the idea that you can experience discomfort--be it physical or emotional--and it not be a problem doesn't make sense to most people because for them every time there's discomfort there's suffering. The distinction between pain and suffering and their relationship is invisible to the average person because you have to look with a sort of "microscope"--an awareness extending tool--to observe the pain over and over again with high states of concentration until you can begin to see that the pain is one thing and the resistance is something else and when the two come together you suffer, but when there's just pain you don't suffer. Pain is just a part of nature.

It's just as effortless as ripples spreading on a pond, or as the wind blowing through the trees. Then you'll be in a position to be able to "go on vacation" inside your pain. You don't have to go to the mountains or the seashore. Of course you can also go on vacation inside your pleasure or inside your neutral sensations. This is an example of insight. It's something that you can not see with the naked eye.

I can tell you about it and you'll either believe me or not believe me. On the other hand, if instead you observe long enough and hard enough, you'll see for yourself that it is actually true. And will that be important? How important will that be? Just wait until the next time you suffer in some way and you'll remember.

A spiritual insight is like a many-faceted jewel. One facet is called freedom from suffering. We can't avoid pain, but we certainly can avoid pain as a problem. What are some other facets? Well, look at the other side of the picture, how about pleasure.

Does pleasure bring lasting satisfaction for most people? Does each experience of pleasure transform most people? Does the more pleasure a person has elevate their baseline of satisfaction in life? Usually not. In fact often the opposite. Often pleasure leads to drivenness, neediness, and compulsion.

Does that mean there's something wrong with pleasure? Absolutely not. Just as there is grasping around pain ("resistance"), there is also grasping around pleasure ("craving"). And when one comes to see and is able to observe pleasure arising, one learns a very interesting lesson. Pleasure in and of itself is a very purifying experience, but if pleasure arises and there's any grasping or holding, even the slightest congealing around the flow of that pleasure, then that pleasure does not give satisfaction.

On the other hand, when the grasping is dropped, the pleasure gives really lasting satisfaction, something changes on the inside, and one's level of fulfillment is raised permanently. So pure pain purifies, pure pleasure purifies. What do I mean by pure pain? Pain without resistance. What do I mean by pure pleasure? Pleasure without craving.

Another facet of insights is related to a person's sense of self. There are things that are true and useful to know about how one's sense of self arises moment by moment. We think there is a "thing" inside us called a self, but upon closer investigation we discover that there is an activity called personality that rises and passes as part of the effortless flow of nature. That activity called personality is made up of certain ideas and certain body sensations that moment by moment give us the sense that "I am." When those ideas and body sensations are greeted with complete awareness and zero interference, then we have a wonderful paradoxical experience.

Obviously if you have complete awareness and zero interference with those ideas and body sensations that in this moment give you the sense "I am," then we would have to say that you are allowing your personality to completely express itself. On the other hand, whenever you have any experience and maintain continuous awareness and zero interference, that experience becomes clear in the two senses of the English word as I described before.

It becomes very distinct but it also becomes transparent. So the fully experienced personality is a transparent wave rather than an opaque particle. The fully experienced self is a "doing" rather than a "thing" and hence is sometimes called "no-self." Once you realize that, your sense of self becomes elastic like rubber, and you can expand and contract effortlessly with the flow of events.

You can think of it as an elastic self, which can get as big or as small as the circumstance requires, a bouncy and vibrant pure "doing" called personality. So you can learn how to complete your personality and in learning that you also learn how to sometimes let go of your personality. An elastic self can get as big as the whole universe and therefore can encompass all things and it can get as small as zero and therefore know a state of true rest, real peace and security.

So, with this practice we bring mindfulness (specificity of awareness) and equanimity (non-interfering with awareness) to ordinary experience. As a result we get purification, which is a release of the blockages to happiness, and we get insight, which is deep, many-faceted understanding into the nature of our experience. As a result of this what happens? We become empowered, we become free.

We have a sense of freedom that is not dependent on circumstances; we have a sense of happiness that is not dependent on conditions. This process of developing a sense of happiness independent of circumstances is quite challenging but actually this is only half of the spiritual path: the half relates to how you as an individual become free.

The other half of the path, which is equally important, involves what you "put out" into the world. In addition to Vipassana mindfulness, one also cultivates habitual states of Loving Kindness and Compassion, and translates these subjective states into objective actions that are of benefit to others. One might say that through mindfulness meditation the old dirty paint is scraped off the walls of the soul and through daily loving kindness meditation a new beautiful coat is put on one layer at a time.

There is much to be said about developing Loving Kindness and Compassion and the intimate link between insight and Love on the spiritual path. I will be talking about this later in the retreat. Suffice it for now to say that through mindfulness and equanimity the very substance of the feeling self becomes porous, transparent, elastic, and vibratory.

Being porous it can soak up any flavor, being transparent it can take on any coloration, being elastic and vibratory it can resonate any tone. Through Loving Kindness and related meditations one intentionally imparts to one's feeling core a habitual coloration, flavor and tone of deep human warmth and beneficence. This constantly flows out and subtly but significantly influences the people around. At the level of action it translates into various expressions of effortless service to others.

Mr. Goenka is a teacher of Vipassana meditation in the tradition of the late Sayagyi U Ba Khin of Burma (Myanmar).

Although Indian by descent, Mr. Goenka was born and raised in Burma. While living in Burma he had the good fortune to come into contact with U Ba Khin, and to learn the Vipassana Technique from him. After receiving training from his teacher for fourteen years, Mr. Goenka settled in India and began teaching Vipassana in 1969.

In a country still sharply divided by differences of caste and religion, the courses offered by Mr. Goenka have attracted thousands of people from every part of society. In addition, many people from countries around the world have come to join courses in Vipassana meditation.

Mr. Goenka has taught tens of thousands of people in more than 300 courses in India and in other countries, East and West. In 1982 he began to appoint assistant teachers to help him to meet the growing demand for courses. Meditation centers have been established under his guidance in India, the United States, Australia, New Zealand, France, the United Kingdom, Japan, Sri Lanka, Thailand, Burma, Nepal and other countries.

The technique which S.N. Goenka teaches represents a tradition that is traced back to the Buddha. The Buddha never taught a sectarian religion; he taught Dhamma - the way to liberation - which is universal.

In the same tradition, Mr. Goenka's approach is totally non-sectarian. For this reason, his teaching has a profound appeal to people of all backgrounds, of every religion and no religion, of every part of the world.

SECTION - II

POWER MEDITATION

NOTE: The best way to do each exercise is:

PRECAUTIONARY NOTE:

- It is wisely said, Meditations are done between 3.00 a.m. to 5.30 a.m. or till the sun rises.
- Never sit on the ground, keep a mat or a pillow to sit on (known as "asana")
- Proper erect posture is necessary for a successful meditation.
- Either a lotus, half lotus, easy or a corpse position (padmasana, ardh padmasana, sahaj asana, shav asanas) position should be adopted.
- Always be in the same position.
- Keep phones off the hook.
- As far as possible, keep the same timing for daily meditation.
- Do not try to idle the mind, accept, acknowledge the thought and then come to the present mode, "what I am doing?" answer would be "meditating"
- Be in the present mode, look, what is happening the present.
- This is the instance when no past or future exists.
- Soon you will be in the presence of yourself enjoy this moment.
- Do not discuss about your experiences with anyone, but, your

MASTER, your TEACHER or your GURU.

- Remember, every one has a different experience.
- Try not to entertain yourself by listening to other Meditators experience, as you mind has got the power to accept everything subconsciously, and, run the same anytime and any place.

Wish you Good Luck.

Dr. Mohan Makkar, Ph.D. (A.M.)
Dr. Geeta (Naturopathy)

INDEX Section - II

EXERCISE 1

CANDLE CONCENTRATION

Candle Concentration is an ancient and time-tested exercise. It is not a meditation *per se*; however, it is one of a number of proven methods often used to bring about a very special state of mind that is called "one-pointedness". In "one-pointedness", all your mental faculties are focused or concentrated on one object. When you practice this exercise long enough, you're able to take this "one-pointedness" and apply it to great benefit, not only in various meditations, but also to any activity that requires focus. It is an especially good exercise for beginners.

In a darkened room, place a lit candle approximately three to four feet in front of you. You can do this exercise in any meditative posture or while sitting on a chair with the candle on a table in front of you. Stare at the flame for 2 minutes. While staring at the flame you may notice the different parts of the flame as well as the flame's various colors.

Do not blink. If the eye-lids do flicker, immediately close your eyes, place your palms over your eyes and give this posture at least 60 seconds or one minute (which ever you feel is shorter).

Discomfort distracts your focus. After a short while, you will notice that the flame takes on a "solid" appearance. Continue to concentrate on the flame for an additional two minutes for a total of four minutes in all. At the end of the four minutes, close your eyes and gently cover them with the palms of your hands. You will now notice the image of the flame in your mind's eye surrounded by a rich field of blackness.

While your eyes are closed and covered, notice the various colors of the image; the yellows, greens, reds, purples, etc. Keep the image of the flame focused and centered in your vision. Do NOT force it.

If the image wavers, gently bring your mind back to the image. Should the image begin to rise, and it probably will, you must concentrate and "will" it back down. Should the image blur or in some way go out of focus, you must concentrate and "will" it back into focus. As you continue, you will notice that the colors of the image change.

This is normal. Take note of the various colors as you continue to concentrate on refocusing and recentering the image. Eventually, the image will fade to the point that you think it is gone. When this occurs, concentrate and "will" it back. Continue to do this until you reach the point where the image in gone and cannot be retrieved.

This concentration technique brings about a marked "retraining" of your lower mind. When practiced, it will promote the "one-pointedness" so very necessary to both good meditation and increased awareness.

EXERCISE 2

"JUST SITTING" OR "SHIKAN - TAZA"

This is the ultimate meditation of the samurai and Zen masters. It will go a long way in improving your ability to concentrate and bring you into the perfect state of "nowness" (the zone), a state you must be in so that you can access the totality of your talents and skills. Without it, your efforts may be inconsistent in what you do.

Choose a quiet area, one free of disturbance and interruption. Once your body is physically centered or balanced, lower your eyelids; however, DO NOT CLOSE THEM, and place your gaze on the floor approximately 5' or 6' in front of you.

Now, begin to concentrate on your posture. That's all, just your physical posture. Focus your attention on the physical act of sitting, making sure your head and spine are correctly aligned. When thoughts come to you just let them float by. Do not become "attached" to them or pay any attention to them, just continue concentrating on your posture.

Meditate, at first, this way for a period of ten minutes, twice a day. You can increase the length of time by 5 minutes every two weeks until you are sitting in meditation for 30 minutes a day. It may not seem like you are doing much; however, in reality, you're doing a great deal. You are learning to be in your "moment" or "nowness". You are training yourself to be there and then without thoughts of the future or past. From there you will be able to reach physical and mental relaxation with all the "typical" medical benefits that implies.

NOTE: During any mediation exercise, thoughts are bound to come up. The thoughts are not, in and of themselves, a "problem". The real problem is the nature of the thoughts. If they are random thoughts, just allow them to dissolve, to float by like white clouds in a clear blue sky. The problems begin when random thoughts link together and form narratives or stories.

These can "sweep you away". Recognize them for what they are, distractions of your lower mind because it thinks you "should" be "doing" something. Simply let the pattern go and return to the matter at hand, which is concentrating on your posture. After a while, you'll begin taking dominion over your thoughts and they will dissipate on their own. This will allow you total "control" of whatever you are doing at the time.

EXERCISE 3

MERKABA

Merkaba . . . also spelled Merkabah. . . is the divine light vehicle used by the Masters to connect with and reach those in tune with the higher realms. The Mer-Ka-Ba is the vehicle of Light mentioned in the Bible by Ezekiel.

"Mer" means Light. "Ka" means Spirit. "Ba" means Body.

Mer-Ka-Ba means the Spirit / Body surrounded by counter-rotating fields of Light, (wheels within wheels), spirals of energy as in DNA, which transports Spirit / Body from one dimension to another.

The MER-KA-BA Meditation

The Teaching Of Spherical Breathing: Using 18 Breaths

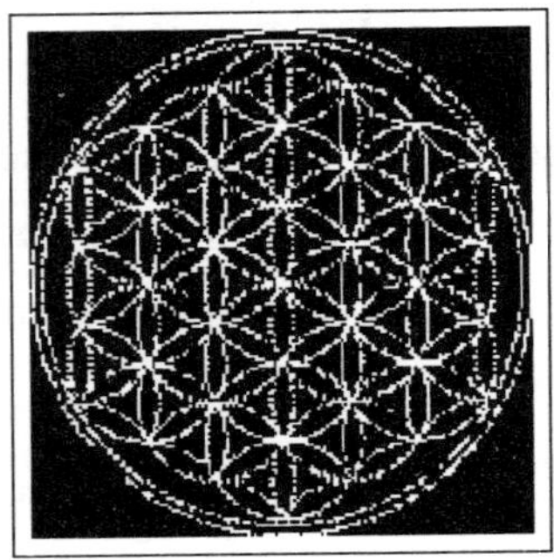

By <u>Drunvalo Melchizedek</u>

There are 17+1 breaths, where the first six are for balancing the polarity, the next seven for proper pranic flow through the entire body. The further breaths are for shifting the consciousness from 3rd to 4th dimension and finally the last three breaths is for re-creating the rotating Merkabah within and around the body. The last breath is not taught.

Once each day, enter into this meditation, until the time comes when you are a conscious breather, remembering with each breath your intimate connection with God.

FIRST BREATH: Inhale

HEART: Open your heart and feel love for all life. If you cannot do this, you must at least open to this love as much as is possible for you. This is the most important instruction of all.

MIND: Become aware of the male tetrahedron (the apex facing up to the sun, the point facing to the front for male, the point to the back for females) filled with the brilliant white light surrounding your body. Visualize it the best you can. If you cannot visualize it, sense or feel it surrounding you.

BODY: At the same moment of inhalation, place your hands in the mudra of your thumb and first finger touching. Remember, lightly touch your fingers, and do not allow your fingers to touch each other or any other object. Keep your palms facing up.

BREATH: At this same moment, with empty lungs, begin to breath in a complete yogic manner. Breath through your nostrils only, except at certain places, which will be described. Simply put, breath from your stomach first, then your diaphragm, and finally your chest. Do this in one movement, not three parts. The exhale is completed either by holding the chest firm and relaxing the stomach, slowly releasing the air, or by holding the stomach firm and relaxing the chest. The most important aspect is that this breathing must be rhythmic. Begin by using seven seconds in and seven seconds out, but as you get familiar with this meditation, find your own rhythm. The following instructions for a complete Yogic Breath are from "the Hindu-Yogi Science of Breath" by Yogi Ramacharake. Perhaps this description will be helpful.

Breathing through the nostrils, inhale steadily, first filling the lower part of the lungs, which is accomplished by bringing into play the diaphragm, which descending exerts a gentle pressure on the abdominal organs, pushing forward the front walls of the abdomen.

Then fill the middle part of the lungs, pushing out the lower ribs, breastbone and chest. Then fill the higher portion of the lungs, protruding the upper chest, thus lifting the chest, including the upper six or even pairs of ribs. At first reading it may appear that this breath consists of three distinct movements.

This, however, is not the correct idea. The inhalation is continuous, the entire chest cavity from the lowered diaphragm to the highest point of the chest in the region of the collar bone, being expanded with a uniform movement. Avoid a jerky series of inhalations, and strive to attain a steady continuous action. Practice will soon overcome the tendency to divide the inhalation into three movements, and will result in a uniform continuous breath. You will be able to complete the inhalation in a few seconds after a little practice.

Exhale quite slowly, holding the chest in a firm position, and drawing the abdomen in a little and lifting it upward as the air leaves the lungs. When the air is entirely exhaled, relax the chest and abdomen. A little practice will render this part of the exercise easy, and the movement once acquired will be afterward performed almost automatically.

<u>FIRST BREATH: Exhale</u>

HEART: Love

MIND: Become aware of the female tetrahedron, (apex pointing to the earth, point facing to the back for males, point facing to the front for females), also filled with the brilliant white light.

BODY: Keep the same mudra.

BREATH: Do NOT hesitate at the top of the inhalation to begin the exhalation. Exhale quite slowly, approximately seven seconds, in the Yogic manner. When the air is out of the lungs, without forcing, relax the chest and abdomen and HOLD the breath. When you feel pressure to breathe again, after about five seconds or so, and then do the following:

MIND: Be aware of the flat equilateral triangle at the top of the female tetrahedron located in the horizontal plane that passes through your chest at the sternum. In a flash, and with a pulse like energy, send that triangular plane down through the female tetrahedron. It gets smaller as it goes down and pushes out the tip or apex of the tetrahedron all the negative energy of the mudra or electrical circuit, a light will shoot out of the apex toward the center of the Earth. The Mind exercise is performed along with the following BODY movements.

BODY: Move your eyes slightly toward each other, or, in other words, slightly cross your eyes. Now bring them up to the top of their sockets, or in other words, look up. Also, this looking up motion should not be extreme. You will feel a tingling feeling between your eyes in the area of your third eye. You can now look down to the lowest point you can, as fast as you can. You should feel an electrical sensation move down your spine. The MIND and BODY must coordinate the above mental exercise e with the eye movements.

The eyes look down from their up position at the same time the mind sees the triangular horizontal plane of the female tetrahedron move down to the apex of the female tetrahedron. This combined exercise will clean out the negative thoughts and feelings that have entered into your electrical system. Specifically, it will clean out the part of your electrical system that is associated with the particular mudra you are using. Immediately upon pulsing the energy down your spine, you change mudras to the next one and begin the entire cycle over again. The next five breaths are a repeat of the first breath with the following mudra changes:

Second breath mudra : Thumb and second finger together

Third breath mudra : Thumb and third finger together

Fourth breath mudra : Thumb and little finger together

Fifth breath mudra : Thumb and first finger together (same as first breath)

Sixth breath mudra : Thumb and second finger together (same as second breath)

The first part, the first six breaths, the balancing of the polarities, and the cleansing of your electrical system is now complete. You are now ready for the next part, the next seven breaths.

Here an entirely new breathing pattern begins. You do not need to visualize the star tetrahedron at this time. Only the tube that runs through the star, from the apex of the male tetrahedron above your head to the apex of the female tetrahedron below your feet, needs to be seen and worked with. This extends one hand length above your head and one hand length below your feet. The diameter of YOUR tube will be the size of the hole formed by YOUR thumb and forefinger touching.

BREATH NUMBER SEVEN: Inhale

HEART: Love. There is another refinement here that can be used after you have perfected this meditation.

MIND: Visualize or sense the tube running through your body. The instant you begin the seventh inhale, see the brilliant white light of the prana moving down the tube from the top and up the tube from the bottom at the same time. This movement is almost instantaneous. The point where these two light beams meet within your body is controlled by the mind and is a vast science known throughout the universe.

In this teaching however, we will only be shown what is necessary, that which will take you from third to fourth dimensional awareness. In this case you will direct the two beams of prana to meet at your navel, or more correct, within your body at navel level, inside the tube. The moment the two beams of prana meet, which is just as the inhale begins, a sphere of white light or prana is formed at the meeting point about the size of a grapefruit centered on the tube. It all happens in an instant. As you continue to take the inhale of the seventh breath, the sphere of prana begins to concentrate and grow slowly.

BODY: For the next seven breaths use the same mudra for both inhale and exhale, the thumb, first and second touching together palms up.

BREATH: Deep rhythmic Yogic breathing, seven seconds in and seven seconds out. There is no holding of the breath from now on. The flow of prana from the two poles will not stop or change in any way when you go from inhale to exhale. It will be a continuous flow that will not stop for a long as you breath in this manner, even after death.

SEVENTH BREATH: Exhale

MIND: The prana sphere centered at the navel continues to grow. By the time of the full exhale; the prana sphere will be approximately eight or nine inches in diameter.

BREATH: Do not force the air out of your lungs. When your lungs are empty naturally, immediately begin the next breath.

EIGHTH BREATH: Inhale

HEART: Love.

MIND: The prana sphere continues to concentrate life force energy and grow in size

EIGHT BREATH: Exhale

MIND: The prana sphere continues to grow in size and will reach maximum size at the end of this breath. This maximum size is different for each person. If you put your longest finger in the center of your navel, the line on your wrist defining your hand will show you the radius of the maximum size of this sphere for YOU. This sphere of prana cannot grow larger.

NINTH BREATH: Inhale

MIND: The prana sphere cannot grow larger, so what happens is the prana begins to concentrate within the sphere. The visual appearance is that the sphere grows BRIGHTER.

BREATH: Sphere grows brighter and brighter as you inhale.

NINTH BREATH: Exhale

BREATH: As you exhale, the sphere continues to grow brighter and brighter.

TENTH BREATH: Inhale

MIND: About half way through this inhale, as the sphere continues to brighter, the prana sphere reaches critical mass. The sphere ignites into a sun, a brilliant blinding ball of white light. You are now ready for the next step.

TENTH BREATH: Exhale

MIND: At the moment of exhale, the small sphere two hand lengths in diameter bulges to expand. In one second, combined with the breath talked about below, the sphere expands quickly out to the sphere of Leonardo, out at your finger tips of your extended arms. Your body is now completely enclosed within a huge sphere of brilliant white light. You have returned to the ancient form of spherical breathing. However, at this point, this sphere is not stable. You MUST breath three more times to keep the sphere stable.

BREATH: At the moment of exhale, make a small hole with your lips and blow out your air with pressure. As you feel the sphere begin to bulge, all within the first second of this exhale, let all of your air out rapidly. The sphere will expand at that moment.

PART3: ELEVENTH, TWELFTH and THIRTEENTH BREATH: Inhale and Exhale

MIND: Relax and just feel the flow of the prana flowing from the two poles and meeting at the navel and then expanding out to the large sphere

BREATH: Breath rhythmically and deeply. At the end of the thirteenth breath you have stabilized the large sphere and are ready for the important 14th breath.

THE FOURTEENTH BREATH

HEART: Love

MIND: On the inhale of the 14th breath, at the very beginning of the breath, move the point where the two beams of prana meet from the navel to the sternum, the fourth dimensional chakra. The entire large sphere, along with the original sphere, which is also still contained within the large sphere, moves up to the new meeting point within the tube. Though this is very easy to do, it is an extremely powerful movement. Breathing from this new point within the tube will inevitably change your awareness from third to fourth dimensional consciousness, or from earth consciousness to Christ consciousness.

BODY: This mudra will be used for the rest of the meditation. Place the left palm on top of the right palm for males and the right palm on top of the left palm for females. It is a mudra that relaxes.

BREATH: Rhythmic breath and deep. However, if you continue to breathe from your Christ center without moving on to the

MER-KA-BA, which is what is recommended until you have made contact with your Higher Self, then shift to a shallow breath. In other words, breath rhythmically but in a comfortable manner where your attention is more on the flow of energy moving up and down the tube meeting at the sternum and expanding out to the large sphere. Just feel the flow. Use your feminine side to just be. At this point don't think, just breath, feel and be. Feel your connection to All Life through the Christ Breath. Remember your intimate connection with God.

The Mer-Ka-Ba, The Vehicle Of Ascension

The Last Three Breaths

You are asked not to attempt this FOURTH PART until you have made contact with your Higher Self, AND your Higher Self has given you permission to proceed. This part is to be taken seriously. The energies that will come into and around your body and spirit are of tremendous power. If you are not ready, you could hurt yourself. If your Higher Self gives you permission to enter into the MER-KA-BA, then don t fear, for you will be ready.

FIFTEENTH BREATH: Inhale:

HEART: Love

MIND: Be aware of the whole star tetrahedron. Realize that there are three whole star tetrahedrons superimposed over each other. One is the body itself, and is locked in place and never, except under certain conditions, moves. It is placed around the body according to maleness or femaleness.

The second whole star tetrahedron is male in nature, it is electrical, is literally the human mind and rotates counter-clockwise relative to your body looking out, or to put it another way, it rotates toward your left side. The third whole star tetrahedron is female in nature, is magnetic, is literally the human emotional body and rotates clockwise relative to your body looking out, or to put it another way, it rotates toward your right side.

To be clear, we are not telling you to rotate the male tetrahedron one way and the female the other way. When we say rotate the whole star tetrahedron, we mean the whole thing.

On the inhale of the fifteenth breath, as you are inhaling, you will say to yourself, in your head, the code words, EQUAL SPEED. This will tell your mind that you want the two rotatable whole star tetrahedrons to begin spinning in opposite directions at equal speeds at the time of the exhale. Meaning that for every complete rotation of the mind tetrahedrons, there will be a complete rotation of the emotional tetrahedrons.

BODY: Continue the mudra of the folded hands from now on.

BREATH: Breath Yogic and rhythmically an deeply again, but only for the next three breaths, after that return to the shallow breathing.

FIFTEENTH BREATH: Exhale

MIND: The two sets of tetrahedrons take off spinning. In an instant, they will be moving at exactly one third the speed of light at their outer tips. You probably will not be able to see this because of their tremendous speed, but you can feel it. What you have just done is to start the MOTOR of the MER-KA-BA. You will not go anywhere, or have an experience. It is just like starting the motor of a car, but having the transmission in neutral.

BREATH: Make a small hole with your lips just like you did for breath Number Ten. Blow out in the same manner, and as you do, feel the two sets of tetrahedrons take off spinning.

SIXTEENTH BREATH: Inhale

MIND: As you let out the breathe, the two sets of tetrahedrons take off from their one third speed of light setting to two third speed of light in an instant. As they approach two thirds speed of light speed a phenomena takes place. A disk about 55 feet in diameter forms around the body at the level of the base of the spine. And the sphere of energy that is centered around the two sets of tetrahedrons forms with the disk to create a shape that looks like a FLYING SAUCER around the body. This energy matrix is called the MER-KA-BA. However, it is not stable. If you see or sense the MER-KA-BA around you at this point, you will know it to be unstable. It will be slowly wobbling. Therefore ~~Breath Number Seventeen is necessary.~~

BREATH: Same as breath 16, make a small hole in your lips, and blow out with pressure. It is at this point that the speeds increases. As you feel the speed increasing, let out all your breath with force. This action will cause the higher speed to be fully obtained and the MER-KA-BA to be formed.

SEVENTEENTH BREATH: Inhale

HEART: Remember, unconditional love for all life must be felt through out all of this meditation or no results will be realized.

MIND: As you breathe in, say to yourself, in your head, the code NINE TENTHS THE SPEED OF LIGHT. This code will tell your mind to increase the speed of the MER-KA-BA to nine tenths the speed of light which will stabilize the rotating field of energy. It will also do something else. This third dimensional universe that we live in is tuned to 9/10 the speed of light. Every electron in your body is rotating around every atom in your body at 9/10 the speed of light. This is the reason this particular speed is selected.

BREATH: Breathe rhythmically and in a Yogic manner.

SEVENTEENTH BREATH: Exhale

MIND: The speed increases to 9/10 the speed of light and stabilizes the MER-KA-BA.

BREATH: Same as breath 15 and 16, make a small hole in your lips, and blow out with pressure. As you feel the speed take off, let all your breath out with force. You are now in your stable and Third dimensionally tuned MER-KA-BA. With the help of your Higher Self, you will understand what this really means.

EIGHTEENTH BREATH:

This very special breath will not be taught here. You must receive it from Your Higher Self. It is the breath that will take you through the speed of light into the fourth dimension. You will disappear from this world and reappear in another one that will be your new home for awhile. This is not the end, but the beginning of an ever expanding consciousness returning you HOME to your FATHER.

EXERCISE 4

THE 'OM' MEDITATION

Each day, just before the session of Reiki comes to an end, a short simple meditation of 30 seconds to one minute is to be carried out.

1. All students stand up and form a close circle
2. All hands are to be put on the shoulders standing on the right and left side of you.
3. Close your eyes.
4. Chant "OM" (Actual sound AHHHHHHH......UHHHHHHHH......OHHHHHH to end in a vibratory MMMMMMMMMM)
5. The chant is to be repeated thrice.

This is the OM Meditation.

EXERCISE 5

OSHO DYNAMIC MEDITATION

Warning: This spectacular meditation method was Rajneesh's trademark and remains a tremendously effective tool for naturally expanding consciousness. Rajneesh never did the technique himself because he didn't need to. He developed the method simply by observing his disciples, who would occasionally go into spontaneous body movements during his early meditation camps. When his judgment started to decline he unfortunately changed the third and fourth stage of the method into a pointless torture test. The correct and most effective version of this meditation technique has four stages, each lasting ten minutes.

Stage -1) Start by standing with your eyes closed and breath deep and fast through your nose for ten minutes. Allow your body to move freely. Jump, sway back and forth, or use any physical motion that helps you pump more oxygen into your lungs.

Stage -2) The second ten minute stage is one of catharsis. Let go totally and be spontaneous. You may dance or roll on the ground. For once in your life screaming is allowed and encouraged. You must act out any anger you feel in a safe way, such as beating the earth with your hands. All the suppressed emotions from your subconscious mind are to be released.

Stage -3) In the third stage you jump up and down yelling Hoo! Hoo! Hoo! continuously for ten minutes. This sounds silly, and is funny, but the loud vibration of your voice travels down to your centers of stored energy and pushes that energy upward. When doing this stage it is important to keep your arms loose and in a natural position. Do not hold your arms over your head as that position can be medically dangerous

Stage #4) The fourth 10 minute stage is complete relaxation and quiet. Flop down on your back, get comfortable, and just let go. Be as a dead man, totally surrendered to the cosmos. Enjoy the tremendous energy you have unleashed in the first three stages and become a silent witness to the ocean as it flows into the drop. Become the ocean.

Rajneesh unwisely changed the third stage of the method to rigidly holding your arms over your head while shouting Hoo! Even worse, he changed the fourth stage to freezing in place like a statue with your arms still awkwardly held over your head. This method is not only uncomfortable to the point of torture; it can also be medically dangerous for those with an underlying heart condition.

When you stand with arms elevated over your head you increase your level of orthostatic stress. This means that your heart must work harder to pump blood that has traveled down to your legs back up to your heart and on to your brain. You could easily pass out in this position or induce a heart attack in individuals with coronary artery disease.

Freezing in place makes deep relaxation impossible as it keeps your mind's controlling functions fully operational. This holds your consciousness on the surface, defeating the purpose of the exercise. The point of the technique was to have three stages of intense action followed by a fourth stage of deep relaxation and complete let go. Rajneesh himself could never have practiced the freeze method even in his youth. Asking his disciples to do it simply showed that he had lost touch with physical reality. Rajneesh was a fallible human being, never a perfect God.

I advise students to only use the enjoyable early version of Dynamic Meditation and not the pointlessly difficult freeze method version. This wonderful technique was intended to grow with the student and change as the student changes.

After a few years of practicing the method vigorously the first three stages of the meditation should drop away spontaneously. You then go into the meditation hall, take a few deep breaths, and immediately go deep into the ecstasy of the fourth stage. Rajneesh intended the method to be fluid, health giving, and fun.

Those new students who wish to experiment with Rajneesh Dynamic Meditation should read the section on Cathartic Dancing Meditation in ***Meditation Handbook*** for further warnings and details before experimenting with this powerful technique.

EXERCISE 6

ZEN MEDITATION

The Benefits of Zen Meditation in Addiction and Recovery

Written by Mary Heath for the Zen Group of Western Australia, 1997.

Foreword by Ross Bolleter Roshi

I warmly recommend Mary Heath's article on *The Benefits of Zen Meditation in Addiction and Recovery.* It shows a sensitive awareness and understanding of the difficulties that people face when they decide to come off drugs and gives a range of strategies for helping this process, ranging from traditional Zen work with the breath and mindfulness and walking meditation, to her own discoveries. Taken together these provide a kit from which people in recovery can choose. Its presentation is vivid and straightforward making it an illuminating, practical, compassionate guide to the path of recovery.

.... Ross Bolleter

About Zen

Zen practice is about having time for yourself in a special way. When you take time off to go for a walk or have coffee with a friend, this is certainly having time for yourself, and is important. But Zen practice goes beyond that. To find out about the deepest parts, the most secret and difficult parts, the parts where beautiful things lie hidden, you may need special training.

One method of training comes down to us from Sakyamuni Buddha, who lived in the sixth century B.C. in Northern India. He taught that although life is basically unsatisfactory and full of pain and suffering, there are still wonderment and joy to be found. To find the wonder you don't have to live a special sort of life by entering a monastery or cutting yourself off from family life and work (although you may do that briefly from time to time).

By noticing and attending to what brings unhappiness you can gradually change your way of looking at things. Why do we suffer? This is the sort of reality most people would like to avoid. But when you give yourself time to look into these deep and secret parts, your lifestyle and relationships will start to work better. Then your life will come alive and blossom right where you are.

Despite its development in very different cultures, the essence of Zen practice remains vital and immediate, since it relies on personal encounter not on scriptures or dogma.

As well as the Zen Group's evening at Palmerston Farm, we run meditation evenings and retreats at our centre in Claremont. Everyone is welcome, but if you have not done meditation with us before it is best to book into an orientation evening. Perth is in the fortunate position of having a resident and fully authorized teacher, Ross Bolleter Roshi, who gives talks and offers regular private interviews.

Where and when to practice Zen

What is overwhelmingly important is that you practice sitting meditation everyday. It is best to do it in a set place, at a set time. All other aspects of Zen grow out of this.

Sitting meditation requires alert attention and concentration. For this reason people avoid the drowsy times after meals. The early morning is an excellent time as the benefits linger all day. Ross wrote a short verse (a haiku), about early morning meditation.

Many people keep their meditation cushions in the bedroom handy to roll out of bed onto for morning zazen. Others sit late in the evening without finding it disturbs their sleep or causes drowsiness.

So find a quiet corner to set up your cushions, and a time you will not be disturbed. This is the ideal. In actual fact many of us cope with early morning toddlers or having the only quiet time in the day after the evening meal. Even this time can be fine. Any time is a good time for zazen. Somehow we manage to spend time on our cushions amidst our daily turmoil. Sitting "amidst", making time "amidst" - this is how it's done, most days in the year.

Apart from sitting, there is mindfulness practice, which can also be called awareness. It's done when you are not doing meditation on a cushion (all the rest of the time) so that gradually over the years you can build up a whole 24 hours of Zen practice. But to start with give yourself islands in the day when you pay attention to how you are. How do you feel? How's your body?

What's your mind chatting about? What's going on for you now -- this moment? People pause and do this at the traffic lights, while washing up or closing doors. Or you can do it at work. Charlotte

Joko Beck, Zen teacher of the San Diego Zen Centre, recommends pausing and doing a few minutes mindfulness during working hours as a definite aid to working concentration.

Together mindfulness and sitting meditation form Zen practice, called zazen.

At a time when you are coming off drugs or alcohol you may find the going hard. Sitting meditation may bring up painful memories -- or allow them to come to your attention. With mindfulness you may become aware of the changes in your body, how hungry you are, how your skin feels. Just bring all of what's happening into your field of awareness by noticing it's there, and this simple exercise will help your efforts towards a new lifestyle without the drugs.

Sitting meditation

Start by sitting for a short time, but make it quality time. Ten minutes daily is a good beginning, and then you can lengthen it.

a) Your back should be straight for meditation. Either sit upright in a chair, kneel astride a cushion or sit cross-legged. You can also buy a low stool to sit on in the kneeling position. These are available from the Zen Group, or you may be able to get one in your local New Age shop.

To sit cross-legged you should have your knees on the mat to give you stability and prevent your back curling up. To do this you'll need a good, fat cushion to raise your bottom and hips, or a rolled up blanket. Providing your knees are on the mat you can fold your legs any way that's comfortable.

b) Wear comfortable clothing. It's mostly belts that cause trouble because you should relax your stomach. Old Zen masters look skinny and thin, but their bellies are round.

c) Your head should be up and your eyes half-closed. Eyes wide open and you can be distracted by sights, or just generally distracted. With eyes shut you easily become dreamy.

d) Your hands should be brought together in front, with your right hand cupping the left and your thumbs just touching, forming an oval. Let your hands rest in your lap and relax your shoulders.

If the above instructions for posture and hand position (mudra) sound rather formidable, they are that way because people have found by experience that a formal way to sit gives discipline and power to meditation. These positions are very solid. They inspire confidence.

Ways to do Zazen (forms of practice)

When you are comfortably seated, take three deep breaths to settle down and place your attention in your solar plexus (the hara) about two fingers width below the navel. Then allow normal breathing to carry on. Each breath just as it is, some are long, some are short. There are two main methods of working with the breath.

EXERCISE 7

USE OF ZEN PRACTICE

What use can you make of Zen Practice?

What's the use of mindfulness?

How can meditation help when you are coming off drugs?

With these questions in mind, members of the Zen Group came down to Palmerston Farm and interviewed some residents who had successfully completed their therapy. We asked questions to pinpoint the really difficult areas for people at Palmerston, so we could offer the best techniques to suit their situation. These techniques come from the many schools of Buddhism. Coming off drugs, stopping drinking, changing your way of life -- it's not easy.

Working with the Zen techniques isn't easy either. If you read through any part of this and feel it all sounds like apple pie, too simple for words or something you already knew anyway, that's because (as an old Zen saying has it) a three-year-old child knows, but an eighty year old man cannot do it. Give the suggestions a try. They've been working successfully for people over thousands of years. But if you think they don't work for you, then trust your own judgment.

EXERCISE 8

ZAZEN, STUDY & POSTURES

Zazen is a particular kind of meditation, unique to Zen, that functions centrally as the very heart of the practice. In fact, Zen Buddhists are generally known as the "meditation Buddhists." Basically, zazen is the study of the self.

The great Master Dogen said, "To study the Buddha Way is to study the self, to study the self is to forget the self, and to forget the self is to be enlightened by the ten thousand things." To be enlightened by the ten thousand things is to recognize the unity of the self and the ten thousand things. Upon his own enlightenment, Buddha was in seated meditation; Zen practice returns to the same seated meditation again and again.

For two thousand five hundred years that meditation has continued, from generation to generation; it's the most important thing that has been passed on. It spread from India to China, to Japan, to other parts of Asia, and then finally to the West. It's a very simple practice. It's very easy to describe and very easy to follow. But like all other practices, it takes doing in order for it to happen.

We tend to see body, breath, and mind separately, but in zazen they come together as one reality. The first thing to pay attention to is the position of the body in zazen. The body has a way of communicating outwardly to the world and inwardly to oneself. How you position your body has a lot to do with what happens with your mind and your breath. Throughout the years of the evolution of Buddhism, the most effective positioning of the body for the practice of zazen has been the pyramid structure of the seated Buddha.

Sitting on the floor is recommended because it is very stable. We use a zafu - a small pillow - to raise the behind just a little, so that the knees can touch the ground. With your bottom on the pillow and two knees touching the ground, you form a tripod base that gives three hundred and sixty-degree stability.

Burmese position

There are several different leg positions that are possible while seated this way. The first and simplest is the *Burmese* position, in which the legs are crossed and both feet rest flat on the floor. The knees should also rest on the floor, though sometimes it takes a bit of exercise to be able to get the legs to drop that far. After awhile the muscles will loosen up and the knees will begin to drop.

To help that happen, sit on the front third of the zafu, shifting your body forward a little bit. By imagining the top of your head pushing upward to the ceiling and by stretching your body that way, get your spine straight - then just let the muscles go soft and relax. With the buttocks up on the zafu and your stomach pushing out a little, there will be a slight curve in the lower region of the back. In this position, it takes very little effort to keep the body upright.

Half Lotus Position

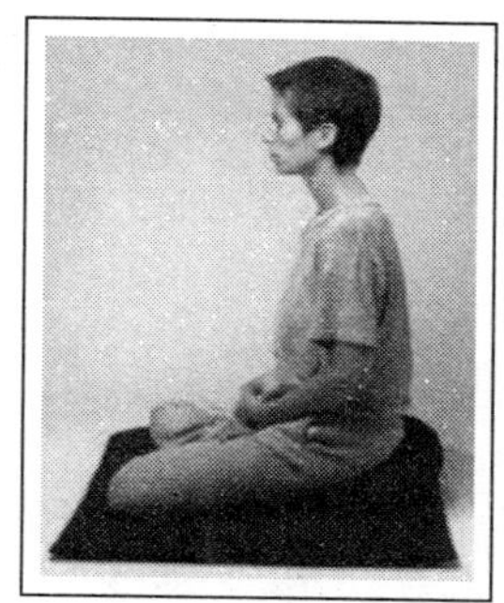

Half Lotus Position

Another position is the *half lotus*, where the left foot is placed up onto the right thigh and the right leg is tucked under. This position is slightly asymmetrical and sometimes the upper body needs to compensate in order to keep itself absolutely straight.

Full Lotus position

By far the most stable of all the positions is the *full lotus*, where each foot is placed up on the opposite thigh. This is perfectly symmetrical and very solid. Stability and efficiency are the important reasons sitting cross-legged on the floor works so well. There is absolutely no esoteric significance to the different positions. What is most important in zazen is what you do with your mind, not what you do with your feet or legs.

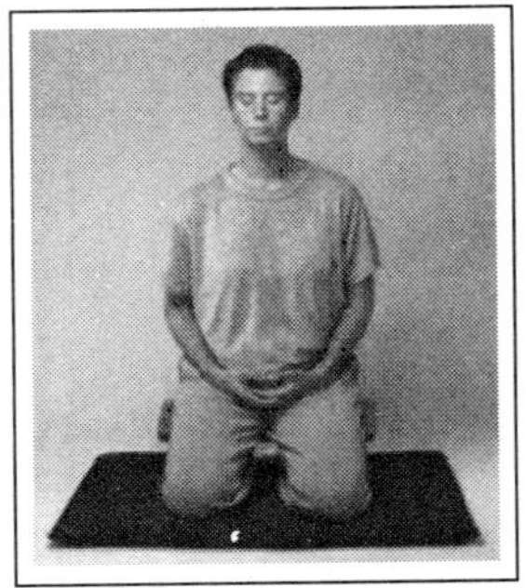
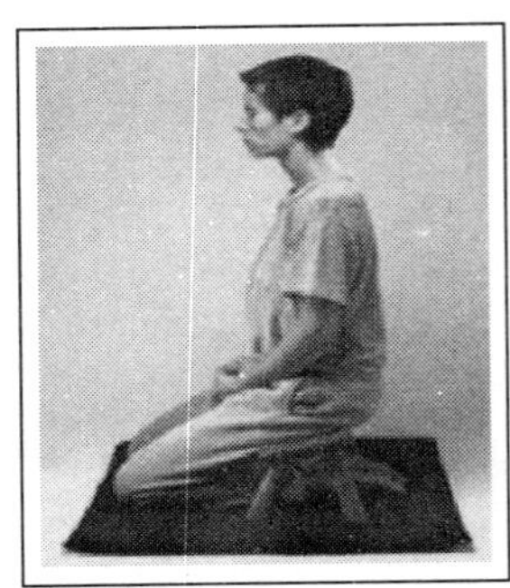

The Seiza Position

There is also the *seiza position*. You can sit seiza without a pillow, kneeling, with the buttocks resting on the upturned feet which form an anatomical cushion. Or you can use a pillow to keep the weight off your ankles. A third way of sitting seiza is to use the seiza bench. It keeps all the weight off your feet and helps to keep your spine straight.

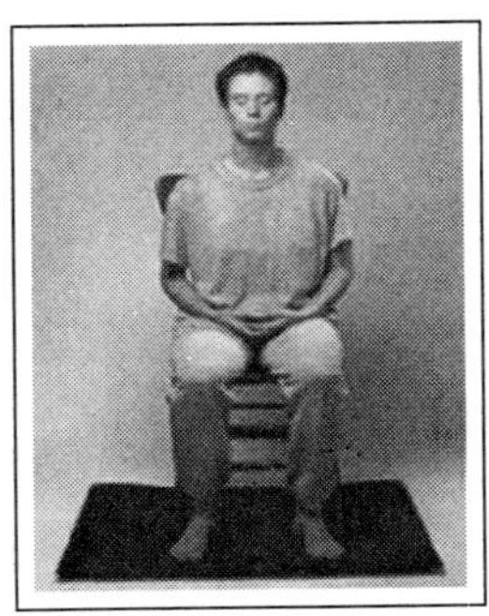

The Chair Position

Finally, it's fine to sit in a chair, though it's important to use a cushion rather than to sit on the hard surface of the chair, and to keep your feet flat on the floor. You use the cushion, or zafu, the same way you would use it on the floor - sitting on the forward third of it. It's very important to keep the spine straight with the lower part of the back curved. All of the aspects of the posture that are important when seated on the floor or in seiza are just as important when sitting in a chair.

The importance of keeping the back straight is to allow the diaphragm to move freely. The breathing you will be doing in zazen becomes very, very deep. Your abdomen will rise and fall much the same way an infant's belly rises and falls. In general, as we mature, our breathing becomes restricted, and less and less complete. We tend to take shallow breaths in the upper part of the chest.

Usually, we've got our belts on very tight or we wear tight clothing around the waist. As a result, deep, complete breathing rarely occurs. In zazen it is important to loosen up anything that is tight around the waist and to wear clothing that is non-binding. For instance, material should not gather behind the knees when you cross the legs, inhibiting circulation.

Allow the diaphragm to move freely so that the breathing can be deep, easy, and natural. You don't have to control it. You don't have to make it happen. It will happen by itself if you assume the right posture and position your body properly.

Once you've positioned yourself, there are a few other things you can check on. The mouth is kept closed. Unless you have some kind of a nasal blockage, breathe through your nose. The tongue is pressed lightly against the upper palate. This reduces the need to salivate and swallow.

The eyes are kept lowered, with your gaze resting on the ground about two or three feet in front of you. Your eyes will be mostly covered by your eyelids, which eliminates the necessity to blink repeatedly.

The chin is slightly tucked in. Although zazen looks very disciplined, the muscles should be soft. There should be no tension in the body. It doesn't take strength to keep the body straight. The nose is centered in line with the navel, the upper torso leaning neither forward nor back.

The hands are folded in the cosmic mudra. The dominant hand is held palm up holding the other hand, also palm up, so that the knuckles of both hands overlap. If you're right-handed, your right hand is holding the left hand; if you're left-handed, your left hand is holding the right hand. The thumbs are lightly touching, thus the hands form an oval, which can rest on the upturned soles of your feet if you're sitting full lotus. If you're sitting Burmese, the mudra can rest on your thighs.

The cosmic mudra tends to turn your attention inward. There are many different ways of focusing the mind. There are visual images called mandalas that are used in some traditions as a point of concentration. There are mantras, or vocal images. There are different kinds of mudras used in various Eastern religions. In zazen, we focus on the breath. The breath is life.

The word "spirit" means breath. The words "ki" in Japanese and "chi" in Chinese, meaning power or energy, both derive from breath. Breath is the vital force; it's the central activity of our bodies. Mind and breath are one reality: when your mind is agitated your breath is agitated; when you're nervous you breathe quickly and shallowly; when your mind is at rest the breath is deep, easy, and effortless.

It is important to center your attention in the hara. The hara is a place within the body, located two inches below the navel. It's the physical and spiritual center of the body. Put your attention there; put your mind there. As you develop your zazen, you'll become more aware of the hara as the center of your attentiveness.

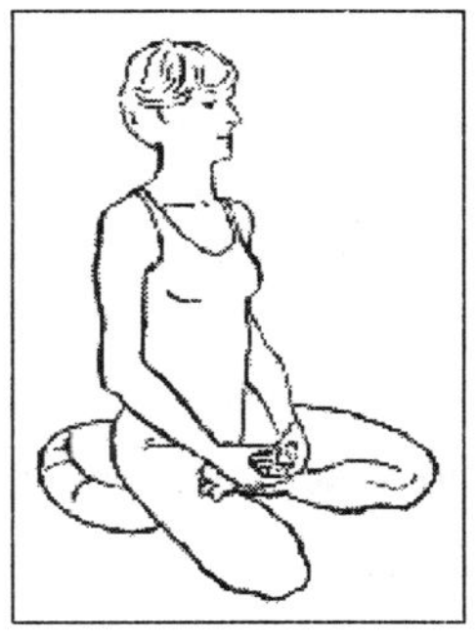

Breathing in Zazen

Begin rocking the body back and forth, slowly, in decreasing arcs, until you settle at your center of gravity. The mind is in the hara, hands are folded in the cosmic mudra, mouth is closed, and tongue pressed on the upper palate. You're breathing through the nose and you're tasting the breath. Keep your attention on the hara and the breath. Imagine the breath coming down into the hara, the viscera, and returning from there. Make it part of the whole cycle of breathing.

We begin working on ourselves by counting the breath, counting each inhalation and each exhalation, beginning with one and counting up to ten. When you get to ten, come back to one and start all over.

The only agreement that you make with yourself in this process is that if your mind begins to wander - if you become aware that what you're doing is chasing thoughts - you will look at the thought, acknowledge it, and then deliberately and consciously let it go and begin the count again at one.

The counting is a feedback to help you know when your mind has drifted off. Each time you return to the breath you are empowering yourself with the ability to put your mind where you want it, when you want it there, for as long as you want it there. That simple fact is extremely important. We call this power of concentration joriki. Joriki manifests itself in many ways. It's the center of the martial and visual arts in Zen. In fact, it's the source of all the activity of our lives.

When you've been practicing this process for a while, your awareness will sharpen. You'll begin to notice things that were always there but escaped your attention. Because of the preoccupation with the internal dialogue, you were too full to be able to see what was happening around you. The process of zazen begins to open that up.

When you're able to stay with the counting and repeatedly get to ten without any effort and without thoughts interfering, it's time to begin counting every cycle of the breath. Inhalation and exhalation will count as one, the next inhalation and exhalation as two. This provides less feedback, but with time you will need less feedback

Eventually, you'll want to just follow the breath and abandon the counting altogether. Just be with the breath. Just be the breath. Let the breath breathe itself. That's the beginning of the falling away of body and mind.

It takes some time and you shouldn't rush it; you shouldn't move too fast from counting every breath to counting every other breath and on to following the breath. If you move ahead prematurely, you'll end up not developing strong joriki. And it's that power of concentration that ultimately leads to what we call samadhi, or single-pointedness of mind.

In the process of working with the breath, the thoughts that come up, for the most part, will be just noise, just random thoughts. Sometimes, however, when you're in a crisis or involved in something important in your life, you'll find that the thought, when you let it go, will recur. You let it go again but it comes back, you let it go and it still comes back. Sometimes that needs to happen.

Don't treat that as a failure; treat it as another way of practicing. This is the time to let the thought happen, engage it, let it run its full course. But watch it, be aware of it. Allow it to do what it's got to do, let it exhaust itself. Then release it, let it go. Come back again to the breath. Start at one and continue the process. Don't use zazen to suppress thoughts or issues that need to come up.

Scattered mental activity and energy keeps us separated from each other, from our environment, and from ourselves. In the process of sitting, the surface activity of our minds begins to slow down. The mind is like the surface of a pond - when the wind is blowing, the surface is disturbed and there are ripples. Nothing can be seen clearly because of the ripples; the reflected image of the sun or the moon is broken up into many fragments.

Out of that stillness, our whole life arises. If we don't get in touch with it at some time in our life, we will never get the opportunity to come to a point of rest. In deep zazen, deep samadhi, a person breathes at a rate of only two or three breaths a minute.

Normally, at rest, a person will breathe about fifteen breaths a minute - even when we're relaxing, we don't quite relax. The more completely your mind is at rest, the more deeply your body is at rest. Respiration, heart rate, circulation, and metabolism slow down in deep zazen.

The whole body comes to a point of stillness that it doesn't reach even in deep sleep. This is a very important and very natural aspect of being human. It is not something particularly unusual. All creatures of the earth have learned this and practice this. It's a very important part of being alive and staying alive: the ability to be completely awake.

Once the counting of the breath has been really learned, and concentration, true one-pointedness of mind, has developed, we usually go on to other practices such as koan study or shikantaza ("just sitting"). This progression should not be thought of in terms of "gain" or "promotion"; that would imply that counting the breath was just a preparation for the "real" thing. Each step is the real thing. Whatever our practice is, the important thing is to put ourselves into it completely. When counting the breath, we just count the breath.

It is also important to be patient and persistent, to not be constantly thinking of a goal, of how the sitting practice may help us. We just put ourselves into it and let go of our thoughts, opinions, positions - everything our minds hold onto. The human mind is basically free, not clinging. In zazen we learn to uncover that mind, to see who we really are.

EXERCISE 9

ZAZEN - ANGER - GIVING IT A PLACE OF HONOR

Anger is difficult to work with, but like many challenges, the rewards are great. Rage sweeps you away, and before you know what's happened you're already upset, and you don't notice what's been going on until hours later. To start with you may only be able to notice your anger when it begins to subside. This is okay. Any noticing is good.

So as you practice mindfulness, notice anger, and name it. You can say "Angry Mind!" Look at your body and see where the anger is. It might be your stomach, or shoulders, the muscles in your neck. Breathe relaxation into that part of your body. With anger, you may notice it first in the body as tension -- a headache, or upset stomach -- or you may pick it up more easily in your mind. It doesn't matter. But do both parts of this exercise. Name the anger and breath into the tense spot.

Thich Nhat Hanh, peace activist and Zen Buddhist, speaks of noticing anger as "taking a little brother by the hand." Reaching out and touching a little brother -- tenderly. Collecting him and holding his hand. It's a beautiful image to work with.

You may be wondering about the moral ground of anger. Isn't it wrong to be angry? But by noticing you are not ignoring it. In fact you are giving it due honor. Usually people leap so quickly to act on anger, or to judge (What should I do? Am I right to be angry?

Whose fault is it? Hers!) that often they forget to notice the simple fact that they *are* angry. Of course it's not good to lose your temper and shout, and mostly it's very counter-productive. There's war, violence, genocide, murder, child-abuse and bodily harm, all of them arising from anger and fear. Australia has law-courts, prisons, and armed forces.

But putting this right can only happen when each person can address personal anger in their own hearts, and acknowledge silently to themselves "I'm angry." Be very tender with yourself, just as you would be with a small child.

Anger and other emotions resurface after drug addiction has ended, and if now you are angry for the first time in many years, consider yourself to be doing well. For self-protection our anger needs to be in good shape. If you are a quiet person coming off amphetamines (which raise self-confidence and self-assertiveness) you should check the health of your anger. To check the health of anger, start by noticing it.

If you are angry a lot of the time, and taking it out on other people, this exercise will help. You should also talk to your counselor about it. If you are not having counseling, then find a wise and sober friend. Name the problem to them, as honestly and openly as you can, including the good bits of the situation. Telling another person is a simple form of naming and acknowledgment. Yoga, dancing and swimming will help the anger in your body.

As you collect anger, you are giving yourself a chance to allow your anger a place in your life, giving it a value. It starts to take its rightful place, to come forward appropriately. You gain a few seconds before you react. Those few seconds heal every war that was ever fought.

EXERCISE 10

ZAZEN - EXPERIENCING THE BREATH

Another method is just to experience the breath. Know that you are breathing. When your mind is no longer on the breath, come back. Re-establish contact and breathe again. Notice everything that's happening. Is the air cold to your nose? Is it still cold in your throat? Is it warmer as you breathe out? Is your in-breath longer than your out-breath? What about your lungs -- does the right move the same way as the left? You don't have to answer all these questions: just take notice of every aspect of breathing.

As you notice and know your breath, move in closer. Everything disappears into your breathing body. Become the breath. Become an atom in the wind of your lungs. Become the wind.

Within a month or so of beginning one of the breathing practices mentioned above you will begin to notice a difference in your attentiveness. Some of the old joys you used to experience before you became addicted will happen again as you start to reclaim your life. At Palmerston Farm we had a girl come to Zen for a few weeks and then she went on camp to the beach, with everybody else at the Farm.

She'd been on heroin for many years, but was doing well with the Palmerston program. She had also begun a meditation schedule, sitting in the early afternoon. So when she came back from camp she told us about the sea water -- cold and wet around her ankles. And the fun of running on wet sand. Not something she had felt for a long time.

The life you reclaim is an undivided life: you will no longer be living two separate existences, shuttling between your highs and the lows you'd rather not have.

EXERCISE 11

ZAZEN - DEPRESSION - A SIGN OF CHANGE

Depression -- one of the symptoms of change, of the old ways no longer working. Boredom and restlessness are sometimes covers for depression. In this section we are not looking at crisis (see *Night Watch,* before this section) so much as those long gloomy days, or even weeks of down time. Those times when normal joys, meeting up with friends, coffee in the morning, fail to raise you even half-way up the happiness chart.

Often this type of deep gloom relates to health. Coming off drugs is an enormous change for your body, a chemical change. Hormonal balance is slowly restored and people become sexually active again. Emotions surface that you suppressed for years by using. Your appetite goes wild, and you find yourself eating enormous meals and then coming back to the kitchen half an hour later for another apple, two pieces of cheese and a tuna sandwich.

Depression is best worked with by walking -- either as formal slow walking in a meditation setting, or just going out for a walk. The movement loosens up that frozen immobility -- you often see it in kids. "I'm bored" they say (meaning depressed) over a noon breakfast. "What's happening today?" Lolling on the couch they wait for stimulation. Another video! You can get very stuck with depression.

Walking meditation can be done formally by holding your right fist on your waist in front of you and clasping the left hand over it. You walk slowly and hold your head up. If balance is difficult for you at this slow speed, try walking with your feet spaced farther apart than you would normally. Just this slow pace is a surprise to many people as they are accustomed always to haste and the need to get from A to B, fast. So slow right down.

As with sitting meditation, you watch your breathing. When you walk, key the steps in to the breath, or notice how this happens naturally. You can continue breath-counting if you wish. This is the ground of the practice -- walking and breathing, and counting if you wish. Your concentration stays with your body in your feet, but in a less intense way than when you sit. With eyes open and senses alert, you notice sounds and sights and let them go, bringing your mind back again to your feet.

Informal walks become mindfulness exercises and for this you can let your hands hang at your sides, but touch the thumb to your index finger on each hand. Curiously this affects the way your arms swing as you walk, and acts as a reminder to return to your body. You take a normal speed and pace: indeed people watching have no idea you are practicing walking meditation.

Apart from walking meditation, any sort of exercise is excellent for depression and will lift your spirits. Just turn it into mindfulness practice by noticing your sweating body, how you feel, which muscles ache and the changing thoughts passing through.

You can also use the naming technique mentioned in *About Zen* to get a better hold on what's happening. For this you will probably need to do seated meditation. Depression is made up of many parts. Maybe some anger that things aren't right, blame for yourself or others, jealousy of those doing better, regrets over what might have been -- a whole mixture. It's like a bowl of soup. How many of the different ingredients can you name?

One of the ingredients that is difficult to spot can be a subtle form of satisfaction, like the pleasure of martyrdom. You might not even suspect that this is one reason your depression lingers. It's like having poor spelling, or badly fitting shoes. It's inconvenient and it causes us trouble or even pain, but we sort of enjoy it. Of course depression can be a serious business, and the hidden satisfaction may cause major family upsets or lifestyle problems like addiction.

But the mechanisms are the same. And this inner satisfaction is extremely common with all negative emotional states of depression, anger, suffering, and grief. So check if you are "wallowing". The word has that wonderful sensuous enjoyment of a hippo in the river mud. Just check and name "Wallowing Mind!" as you notice this ingredient. But don't judge yourself or feel this is shameful -- it is just the way most people's minds work.

Depression is often the dark undertow of the river of success, where the current is sweeping you along and you are going through many changes. Kids are like this, or people handling job stress, relationship problems. You are growing, moving forward making necessary adjustments. The current of development stirs up the river bottom and you get things like "I can't manage to do this because..." in your mind, or "perhaps I should try something easier, where there's less competition." Lots of rubbish on the riverbed.

So by allowing the depression and naming it, working with it, you can integrate the mud rising to the surface. And as you do this the river starts to run more smoothly, faster, with purpose and success.

EXERCISE 12

ZAZEN - HOW TO CHANGE YOUR MOOD

You can use mindfulness and meditation practice to change how you feel -- mood change. Your mood itself will change your mood. Nothing added.

A good way to start with this, is to wait until you feel you need a change. "I must...", "I ought to...", "It's time I...". Of course there are scheduled events everybody has to attend to during the day. But maybe what's really happening is not that you must do the new thing, it's that you are fed up, bored or depressed in your present situation.

This may be one of the reasons you started with drugs or alcohol in the first place. You felt better on drugs. It's nice. You don't have to feel stressed out, upset or angry. After a while it felt normal.

To do this exercise, notice when you are in need of a change. Give yourself five more minutes with what needs changing, and during that time notice EXACTLY how things are. Start with the basic reason you think you should have a change. Let's say you're sitting next to someone who's talking complete rubbish. It's totally opposed to everything you know to be true. You'd like to either straighten them out, or leave. They're unbearable!

So give yourself five minutes to bear the unbearable. (Or as long as you can! You'll get better at this.) Start with your body and see how it feels. Check where the discomfort is. Some particular part will be carrying the strain, where is it? Breathe into that part. Next check and name your emotion. Are you just bored? or would it be better to call it anger? Depression? Use the right word to yourself. Say "I'm depressed", or whatever. Gather up every scrap of depression you can bear. Thoroughly immerse yourself in how you are -- after all it's only for a couple of minutes.

When your five minutes are up you'll find your mood has shifted slightly, maybe quite a bit. But don't try to hold on longer than you feel comfortable. Do your five minutes with the unbearable and then make the change you want to make.

But as you persist with this exercise you'll find you have a little more ease. You are no longer as angry as you were, or at least you can calm down more quickly. Or your tolerance for the other idiots on the road is better. Around the unbearable things in your life you develop a sense of humor, an ability to cope and make the best of difficult situations.

Moving on through the years of meditation practice you'll be able to come back to your moods more often, your constantly changing moods: now depressed, now amused, now exited, now angry.

Always changing. It's a dance. It's like having spent all your life hopping on your right foot only, never knowing that your left foot existed or you could move the weight. Suddenly you've got another way to move -- you are no longer stuck with a one-legged hop!

EXERCISE 13

ZAZEN - NAMING

Naming is a meditation practice that Zen shares with another Buddhist tradition, Vipassana, and is particularly useful at times of stress or when you are in pain. It is also an excellent practice in its own right. You can see if it suits you.

With stress you have pain, emotional pain and sometimes physical pain. Sometimes the physical pain causes stress, or it can be the other way round. But it is overwhelming. It's more than you can handle. Everybody leaving addiction behind will have periods when the craving is intense, depression and restlessness claim the night hours and you don't believe you can ever make it. Or relationship difficulties make your life miserable, or there are problems with money.

You need to name stress in the body, because the body is its home. It creates knots in the stomach, tension in the neck, headache and exhaustion. In a way it's because you aren't noticing how your body feels that your mind becomes so worried and overwhelmed. First of all look to see where the trouble is living in your body and name the worry there. You might notice that your jaw feels like it is cast in iron, and you name "Angry Mind!". Or perhaps one of your children has rung with a problem that you can't help -- and your stomach has tensed up with fear. Just saying "I'm frightened" and noticing the tension means you have taken a moment to look after yourself, a moment to heal your own stress.

Or you might be feeling very sad. Some things are so painful we can't even think about them. They hover, but they won't leave. Naming is very gentle. Just catch hold of the little bit you can manage and see where it lives in your body. Give it a name. "Pain", or "I hurt", or "grieving mind". Simple attention to what's happening will help.

Each time you find yourself worrying again, just do the naming and come back to your body and breath. Something so painful you cannot bear to think about it will take many months to allow your touch, and it is good to have a friend or counselor to encourage you. Someone to listen.

The naming can be done as part of sitting meditation, and you can do it during the rest of your daily life as a part of mindfulness. If you are sitting the procedure is exactly the same as when you are attending to the breath.

But when you notice your mind is wandering, name the thought before you come back to the breathing. "Worrying Mind", "Angry Mind". But don't judge yourself. From the point of view of Zen and naming, it doesn't matter if you are angry, sad, feeling silly or bored. It's just the way you are. Ross teaches that adding the word "mind" gives you less self-judgment, a more neutral view on the situation. If you are worried or upset you will have trouble spending any time with the breath at all. This is when naming is especially useful.

Lastly, don't forget to name the joyous too. "Happy Mind", "Excited Mind". There will be happy moments, probably many more than you noticed before. "I feel great today!" "My partner really has good ideas!" "I love the feel of fur!" Whatever. Feel the joy and happiness... where is it?

EXERCISE 14

ZAZEN - NIGHT WATCH

There are two approaches to the problem of hanging out at night. There's `fix it' techniques, such as making milk drinks, more exercise in the daytime, sex, a better diet. `Fix it' techniques will help you get back to a full eight hours as the effects of drug-taking wear off and you become more healthy. The Turning Point Alcohol and Drug Centre Inc. have excellent booklets on withdrawal, available from some rehabilitation centers and libraries in Perth.

The other approach is to treasure the hours of darkness. We've only got a certain number of hours of life -- let's have them all. On a cell wall in the old Fremantle Prison there's a little sign, said to have been put there by an Aboriginal prisoner: "Life is something that happens while you are planning something else." This is not about how to fix the problem -- it's about how to have it. And since these night hours can be our most desperate, these are crisis techniques.

How shall we have the hours we don't want, the time we feel should not be (h)ours? The waiting time. When we wait between sunset and sunrise -- or we wait outside the operating theatre to hear how a loved one has fared. Those hours of anguish, when our past rises up and devours the future, and our sun is eaten alive.

By coming back to your breathing, you have no waiting hours. You can either sit in meditation to do this, or walk as explained in our section About Zen. Every waiting moment can be breathed through, no matter how painful. You'll be breathing anyway. So as you breathe, breathe with the problems. Name the problems. "Thought of Jan", "jealousy", "despair", "itchy feet", "craving", "sore belly".

Some people get a better grip if they use the word "mind" in their naming. Say "Jealous Mind", or "Despairing Mind". Become aware and name the thoughts and the feelings, and then return to your breathing. As you do that you'll find the dark hours are held, acknowledged. By naming you can move further into your painful spots, bit by bit, and learn about them.

This next suggestion is a crisis technique, one that I learned as a child with bad asthma. Children with asthma in the 1940s just had asthma: there wasn't much in the way of medication. I was fighting for my life. So what you do is to make the naming into a rhyme to fit your breathing. One of my rhymes was "My Teddy can't breathe" on the in-breath, "he's got asthma" on the out-breath.

This is different from a mantra, which some people learn, as it is just created on the spot for your particular situation. You might be having an anxiety attack about your health and your responsibilities as a parent. Let's say it's stomach pain. "My belly is hurting," on the in-breath "and I can't leave my daughter" on the out-breath. That might be too long, but you can get the general idea.

Make up a little rhyme to suit the situation and repeat it silently to yourself as you breathe. Actually make the problem breathe, and give it a voice. When you find your mind has wandered off, just come back to your breath and the words of your rhyme. Keep the rhyme just the same each breath. Gradually your body will begin to relax. You might do it for ten minutes and then be able to return to ordinary naming. If not, make up another rhyme: you'll find your problem has shifted.

Naming gives you a handle on despair, craving, and the sharp edge of pain. Asking someone for their handle in the U.S means you want their name. So by this simple technique you begin to have some grip on the pain.

You are working with it, no longer swamped and immersed, helplessly tumbled. You can begin to handle despair, to touch it with your hands and learn it's shape. Starting on the outside we name and handle each fragment, working gradually towards the centre.

It's hard work. You may find you sit up with the night for many months, doing a little at a time. But after a while the pain and despair will allow you to touch. They no longer cry at the edge of the world, banished to weep in the dark.

EXERCISE 15

ZAZEN - THE RESOLUTION TO 'GIVE UP' AND HOW TO MAKE IT REAL

People ready to leave Palmerston Farm have said that when they decided to give up this time, they knew it was the real thing. When they made the decision, perhaps in prison, perhaps in a car that serves as home, perhaps at a friend's house, they knew this was for real. They were coming off drugs for good.

It's a `resolution' because people who make this transition successfully have a real sense of the difficulties. They may have tried to live without drugs, or alcohol, or perhaps cigarettes, before. So the problems are known. Or if not known, at least sensed and learnt from someone else.

So whether or not it's the first time you've made the resolution, there's a way you can build on that moment so that it does indeed become the turning point in your life. You can use meditation practice and mindfulness to do it.

Each time you return to your breathing, or your present occupation, whenever you return, you affirm yourself. Some people feel the world moves in and confirms them. So when you've made a major change you'll find the return to your body brings you back to the new you.

In the early weeks it may be a miserable you, having sleepless nights and withdrawal cravings. You may be anxious, frightened about the future. But it *is* the new you, the real you. So as well as the pain, you'll be able to see your success so far, and take heart. You've made it so far -- days, weeks, and months of success!

EXERCISE 16

ZAZEN - SMILING - OR WORKING WITH FEAR

The dark shadow of fear rises up. It may be a memory of childhood terror touched into life by an event of today -- a word spoken in a certain tone, the flash of water in a saucepan, and suddenly you remember the buried event. It returns roaring into your mind, and the fear with it. Or it might be something more concrete that frightens you. Your job is threatened, or you are dismissed. How will you support yourself? The family? Or you might just have been told of your partner's car crash, and you put down the phone as if it were a broken body.

So whether you are working with real and frightening events in your life, or the fears could more properly be called hallucinations, or `flashes' from your early life, the feeling is just the same. When you are afraid and people tell you it's imagination, and you are still frightened, then you end up with double trouble. Your heart pulls back and hides like a cowering dog.

How can fear be handled? You need first of all to acknowledge the fear in your heart -- fear and courage live in the heart. This is the country of knights in gleaming Armour riding out fearlessly to face the enemy. Or if you prefer, look at some of the modern computer games. Full of Warlords, Orcs and Maidens of the Seal, riding out to face the Powers of Darkness who are invading our Land of Righteousness and Valor (with accompanying music!). Girls and women can do this too. Be right in there.

Naming the fear. It's like kissing the fear, saying hello. If you have just had a phone call about your partner's car crash, terrible things will be running through your mind. "Bill may have been killed in this car crash." Our minds go into high speed when we are frightened or very angry: our body tenses up in ancient fighting response. Control is not possible. But you can sometimes catch a moment to realize that you are frightened, your body is shaking.

When you realize how frightened you are it's a first step. It allows the fear to be there. If you have time, sit down a moment and breathe with the fear. "I'm very frightened, my legs are shaking." It helps to know. This is the ground of courage as you go forward with your fear. Ross teaches people to say, "I'm going ahead with my fear."

If you think this is a hallucination, or someone says it's your imagination, but it keeps coming back, then treat it as real. If it's real in your mind, then it's real. Otherwise you start the endless merry-go-round of being afraid of being frightened. One fear is enough! Zen is not about how we ought to be -- it's finding out how we are. Work with the fear, name it as best you can, find out where it lives in your body and breathe with it.

Very often you will find just spending a few moments with your fears at the time they come up is enough to make you feel better. Later in the day you can sit in meditation and spend longer attending to yourself. Fear makes of us ghosts, empty shells, withdrawn from life and the heat of blood. If your fear is an old one, it is going to take many months of care before you can breathe the breath of life and courage back into it.

There's a second exercise you can do. This is a crisis technique, but it's good to do at any time as well. Use your heart to smile. This is not a matter of "covering up" or putting on a good face. Allow the fear itself to smile. It's quite a flexible thing, fear, it can smile. Allow it to crack open in a smile.

The smiling is a technique taught by Thich Nhat Hanh and used in his community in Plum Village, France. You can use it with any deep and painful emotion, and it's a good thing to do when things are very bad. Feel the grief, fear, stress in your heart, and allow it to smile. You can do it physically if you like. Just smile. It heals the heart.

EXERCISE 17

ZAZEN - WALKING MEDITATION

When we do meditation in the Zen Group we sit for 25 minutes, and then we walk slowly round the room one after the other for walking meditation, called kinhin -- meditation on the move. This also allows people to stretch their legs or leave the room.

On your own it is a good practice to break up long sittings by getting up for a walk. Keeps you fresh and alert.

Just walk slowly round the room (or you can go outside), and notice your footsteps and breathing as you go. Let sights and sounds pass through, returning your mind to your feet. Feel the good earth beneath your feet. If the weather is warm enough it's better to walk without socks, then you can feel the carpet or the lino.

At Palmerston Farm we walk on a carpet with some coconut fiber mats dotted around, and one soft woolly rug: many different textures. It makes a foot sensation feast! A celebration for your feet. Or you can go outside and feel the pathways, steps and stones near your meditation room.

When you slow down the walking pace and become aware of your feet, your posture will automatically improve as you relax. Bring your head up and let your shoulders fall naturally. Clasp your hands over your navel with the left hand cupping the right fist. If you go outside, or you want to do mindful walking in public -- on your way to work for example -- just touch your thumbs to your index fingers on each hand, and let your arms hang at your sides. This is quite unobtrusive.

Walking meditation is less intensely concentrated than seated meditation. It can act as a sort of half-way house between meditation practice on your cushion and the mindfulness of everyday life.

Mindfulness allows you to move forward with your best aims by including the down side. You travel by way of the down side. Of course there are many times during your withdrawal and rehabilitation when you'll feel good, and this is great. But this is how you can make use of the restless times, the sleepless hours, boredom and depression. The times when you are tempted back into the arms of addiction.

The way it works is like a shortcut. It's a shortcut to the real you, and it goes right through the darkest forest where things are pretty bad. So when you are practicing one of the Zen techniques in this section, and you're working with the down side, this is the shortcut. You aren't kidding yourself. You're working directly with the difficult time, learning its route, mapping the contours, and seeing the boggy patches.

It's a shortcut because it goes straight from your original decision to the success of a drug-free life. Coming back to the present you are connected in again to the real you that made the resolution to come off drugs, the decision-maker who is able clearly to see success ahead. Each time you come back to your mindfulness you step again onto the shortcut, and you make your decision more real by being there. You make yourself real.

EXERCISE 18

ZAZEN - WHAT WILL CHANGE?

Whatever type of life you are living will be enhanced by Zen practice. It's like "The mountains are always high, but they look particularly lofty with clouds flying above." Zen doesn't add anything, but you see the meaning of life more clearly with a practice.

You might think you should wait to begin meditation until you stop shooting up, or come off the bottle. Like not going to the doctor until you know what's wrong with you. But we go to the doctor primarily for the benefit of advice and treatment, and it's best to go with an open mind ready to listen. With Zen practice you need an open mind ready to listen, and what you listen to is yourself.

When you start your practice it doesn't matter what you're like. You don't have to be good, or clean, feeling peaceful or `ready for meditation'. Go to the doctor with an open mind, ready to listen, taking along just how you feel. Wherever you are is fine. Make a start right where you are.

Curiously enough, somebody who has practiced meditation for a long time still feels like a beginner. They still sit down on their cushion with a bunch of worries, addicted to things they think they should give up. It's always an effort. If you aren't making an effort then you aren't at the front edge.

EXERCISE 19

ZAZEN - SO WHAT CHANGES?

There are changes: some you notice yourself and some things are spotted by your family, friends or fellow workers. Your character and identity change.

The practice of Zen puts you in touch. It connects. The results can be seen immediately, and they also grow throughout years of practice.

You will become more sure who you are, more confident, more certain about things. You will be able to weather a crisis better. Your sense of humor will carry you through impossible situations and you learn to laugh at yourself. "Why can angels fly so high? It's because they take themselves so lightly!"

Like that. By learning about yourself and seeing into your own weaknesses you can more easily form relationships with others, because you feel an instant fellow feeling. People will report that you seem more approachable, more willing to listen and love.

Ideas bubble up. When the Zen Group does a 7-day retreat (sesshin) we usually warn people about the uprush of ideas that normally happens in the days immediately afterwards. "Make no rash decisions!" "Wait at least 48 hours before you walk out on your job!" People become creative, or move into different areas of creativity. They paint, or write music or get ideas about interesting things to do with the garden.

They start making delicious meals or learn Chinese cooking. If you go through withdrawal this bubbling flow of creativity will burst forth anyway as your body comes back to health and your emotional life comes alive again. With Zen too we become more in touch with our emotions.

You'll be wondering if Zen will help you come off drugs. There's no guarantee. Some people start a meditation practice because of a particular problem -- to help with their relationship difficulties for example, or because of a major illness -- and the original problem never goes away. But everything else changes so that the problem becomes quite minor. Or your addiction and dependence on the drug will change so that although you are still using, your use becomes more recreational.

We had a heavy smoker in the Zen Group, an older woman with two marriages behind her and a fairly tragic life. This was before Ross became a teacher, during the time John Tarrant Roshi used to visit from California in the 1980s. So she sat for many years, but still smoked, and she asked if she would ever be able to stop. "One day, Sara," John said to her "you'll just stop." She did. No drama at all.

People also develop those gritty character strengths that come from facing hard times. We've put in some meditation techniques to help with hard times in the section What Use is Zen Practice? Certainty about who you are and what you should be doing, courage, faithfulness, steadfastness. In Celtic mythology these characteristics are often symbolized in the character of the dog, our faithful companion. This is a true story from Scotland.

SECTION - III

VISUAL MEDITATION

NOTE: The best way to do each exercise is:

a) Somebody to read the exercise to you while you visualize

b) Record each meditation on a tape and replay.

c) It is your prime object to get the most of these exercises, so,

(i) Put your phones/mobiles/door bell off

(ii) Ensure nobody disturbs you during the exercise

(iii) Lie still for a few minutes after the exercise.

(iv) Select an exercise which is nearest to your heart and you believe it will do the world of good for you.

(v) Let someone read this exercise else tape the same in your own voice and replay during meditation

INDEX Section - III

INDEX Section - III

EXERCISE 1

ACTIVATING YOUR ETHEREAL BODY

- Sit/Lie down in a comfortable position.
- Take a deep breath to the count of 4 filling in your breath to the navel. Stop your breath to the count of 4. Breathe out to the count of 4 from your mouth.
- Repeat till you feel completely relaxed.
- Visualize a white circle over your Crown Chakra.
- Bring this white circle towards your Root Chakra from the spinal column.
- See the White circle being attached to your Root Chakra.
- See the root chakra rotating and emanating Red Light.
- Move the white circle to the sexual chakra and attach the same to it.
- See the sexual chakra rotating and see an orange light flow out of the chakra.
- Move the white circle to the solar plexus chakra and attach the same to it.
- See the solar plexus chakra rotating and throwing out pale yellow light. Now, move this white circle to your heart chakra and attach it.

- See the heart chakra rotating and green light splash in circles.
- Move the white circle to your throat chakra and attach it.
- See the throat chakra rotating. See a light blue light coming out of the throat chakra.
- Move the white circle to your 3rd Eye Chakra and attach the same to it.
- See the 3rd Eye Chakra rotating and emanating an indigo light.
- Bring the white circle of light to the Crown Chakra. Attach this white circle to the Crown Chakra and see the Crown Chakra activated. See a Violet light emerge from the crown chakra.
- Bring the white circle to your front side and attach it to the 3rd Eye Chakra. See the 3rd eye chakra rotating and give out an indigo colored light.
- Slip this white circle into your mouth and from over the soft spot above the tongue into the throat chakra. Attach this circle to your throat chakra. See the throat chakra rotating and giving out a light blue light.
- Bring down the white circle to your heart chakra. Attach the white circle to the heart chakra. Visualize the heart chakra giving out green light.
- Bring the white circle down to the solar plexus chakra. Repeat above and visualize the solar plexus chakra give out a light yellow light.

- Bring the white circle down to your sexual chakra. Repeat above. Visualize an orange color light come out from the sexual chakra.

- Bring the white circle to the center of your root chakra. See the white light evaporate.

- Now, see all the chakras rotating from the root chakra to the crown chakra from your spinal column and from the crown chakra to your root chakra from the front side of your body. You will only see a white color light emanating at a very high speed.

- Increase the speed. As you increase the speed you will see another body, which is attached to your physical body, start to move. Move this body, which is also of white/grayish to your left and right side.

- Move this ethereal body in front of you. You can see yourself now. Let this ethereal body float to the roof. See yourself lying down.

- Slowly, let the ethereal body come back to your body and settle down properly.

- Visualize the white circle slow up its speed and finally stop.

- Put both your palms on your eyes.

- Open your eyes under your palms.

- Relax and open your eyes.

EXERCISE 2

ALPHA / CHAKRAS STIMULATION MEDITATION

This meditation has a twofold purpose: it will bring you into the alpha state and stimulate your chakras simultaneously.

After taking ten deep breaths, visualize yourself standing in a place that is peaceful to you, with your feet on the physical earth. See a bright white ray of light coming from deep within the earth and passing through the soles of your feet into your body. This ray of light rises through your legs to the base of your spine, where it pauses and stimulates your Root Chakra, which is red. See this chakra glow brightly, radiating its red light, growing clear and pure in color. You feel yourself becoming grounded as this happens.

The ray then travels up to your second chakra, the Sacral Chakra, which is orange. See this chakra grow brightly, clear and pure. As this happens, you feel an increase in your vital energies.

The light travels up to your Solar Plexus Chakra, which is yellow. This chakra grows bright, clear and pure. You feel your sense of self and personal power stronger as this happens.

The light then travels up to your Heart Chakra, which is green. It stimulates the chakra, which grows clear, bright and pure. You feel this chakra radiating love as this happens.

The ray then travels up to your Throat Chakra, which is blue. This chakra grows bright, pure and clear. You feel yourself ready to communicate and express your creativity and thoughts as this happens.

The ray of light then travels up to your Third eye Chakra, which is indigo in color, and stimulates it, causing this chakra to grow bright, pure and clear. As this happens, you feel your psychic centers open, and you feel a psychic awareness of those you love.

The ray then travels up to your Crown Chakra, which is purple. The light stimulates this chakra as well and this chakra becomes bright, clear and pure. You feel a strong connection to the higher power as this happens.

The light then passes through the crown chakra and out into the Universe, and you realize that you have become a conduit for the light, which connects the Earth and the Universe. From here, you can follow the chakra balancing meditation below if you wish, (Just skip the first few steps) or move on to any other endeavor you want to.

Employing the Advanced Chakra Meditation to gain greater clarity is a *process of self-education.* Clarity is not a concept Western culture is thoroughly familiar with, and rarely is it a term that is concretely defined. In this system, clarity is defined in terms of the degree of awareness of awareness one possesses. Represented mathematically, this principle of natural law may be shown as A/A=C, whereas, "A" is awareness, (divided by itself) and "C" is the clarity that results.

As greater experiential familiarity with clarity is had, it then becomes a known quality of mind that can be summoned up or enhanced at will, even without the precursor of meditation. Thus it can then be intended into place at a moments' notice, for the purpose of improved mental and even physical function.

In the group meditational setting, it may also be intended into place for oneself as well as others, simultaneously. In other words, awareness of awareness may be psychically projected to others, which aids in their higher establishment of clarity as well. We should not consider this a particularly esoteric act, when remembering that any state of consciousness can be projected. All states of consciousness in fact, automatically radiate from the body/mind as soon as they are gained within, to some degree.

By Intending their projection outward however, we are increasing the potency of rendered psychic effects many times over. In this way too, we are acting on behalf of natural laws, and are thereby gaining the cumulative support of nature in our spiritual practices.

EXERCISE 3

ASTRAL TRAVEL

During the Astral Travels you can perform miracles, which will be known only to you. You can visit friends and relatives.

Our purpose of visiting is to detach the ethereal body from the physical body and request it to visit any place we choose.

Here is what we do:

First we go to our favorite place of relaxation.

1. Relax for some time.

2. Repeat the following words "By the power given to my higher self, I request my Ethereal body to some in front of me"

3. (Here you may see a grayish/bluish substance in front of you - at this stage you will be unable to move any of your body parts, clinically you may be dead at this time, the pulse rate may have dropped to 3 to 5 beats / minutes)

4. When you see your Ethereal Body in front of you, request this body to visit any of your relatives, friends any one you wish.

5. Within seconds you will feel you are there - in the house you wished to be.

6. (Two things are very important here - (a) Try to see the calendar and time in that house - make a mental note of date

and time)

7. Take a note of all surroundings. You will be unable to touch anything. Everything you see may be opposite of what you may have seen in the physical body. For example, when you are facing the kitchen the bathroom door may be on the right hand side (physical), but, in the Astral level the bathroom door will appear on the left hand side. See the bed sheets, the table covers, the mats, cutlery, people, their clothes, colors on the walls every possible detail you can gather.

8. Request your ethereal body to come back to your physical body. It should be back within seconds.

9. Be careful, not to get up immediately.

10. Lie down still, relaxed.

11. After a few minutes, slowly open your eyes assess how you are feeling. If you are feeling fresh get up, if not, close your eyes again and relax for a few more minutes, it may be due to the ethereal body not coming back to the physical body completely.

12. When you are up and about, try to recollect what had happened and what you had seen. Jot everything down. Do not rely on your memory. These thoughts sooner or later disappear.

13. Write a letter to the person whose house you have visited giving descriptions, be vague and brief, just say you had a dream and you saw....

14. DO NOT BE SURPRISED IF YOUR FRIEND ANSWERS WHAT YOU SAW WAS 100% CORRECT.

EXERCISE 4

CHAKRA MEDITATION

Sit or lie comfortably, and immediately begin focusing on the feelings throughout the body. Those new to this practice may begin by focusing upon a very small area of the body, such as the tip of the right index finger. Be carefully aware of every subtle detail of feeling in this area. Allow awareness to spread to the entire finger, then the hand, arm, both arms, chest, torso, head, legs and feet, (not necessarily in that order).

Do not avoid any pain, fear or other unpleasantness found anywhere in the body. [Such feelings are usually the result of Intentions which inhibit personal growth, and these can be "reprogrammed". Fear can be replaced by love, confusion by clarity, and pain by vibrant energy/positivity.]

As thoughts inevitably run though the mind, simply relax, and return again and again to a feeling-awareness focus, even if this means doing so a hundred times every minute. Chronic, rampant, seemingly unstoppable thoughts in the mind, are a symptom of stored stress in ones' being. As the practice of meditation proceeds, stress is released, and the tendency of thoughts to intrude upon this process will gradually diminish. Be patient and don't let the simplicity of this method of meditation deceive you.

Let your awareness travel freely from one area of the body to the next, as it will be inclined to do. Feel every subtle inner detail. Areas of particular stress or activity will attract your awareness, and hold it for longer periods than the rest of the body. Allow this to happen, as it is a function of natural self-healing processes and energy body activity. Don't be concerned or irritated by intruding thoughts, just continue to return to a feeling/awareness-oriented focus within the body, in a relaxed manner.

One particularly notable value of the above meditational practice, is that is can be done any time during the day, at work, at home or in conjunction with any other activity. It can be done for as little as 5-30 seconds at a time, (as daily inner awareness) and it will still render cumulative benefits, though these are usually more pronounced when the eyes are closed, and the body still.

It is recommended that the Chakra Meditation, (or others like it) be performed daily just before going to sleep at night, and before arising in the morning, for 20-30 minutes at a time. Daily inner awareness and meditation compliment each others' effectiveness, acting to improve health, reduce stress, increase psychic sensitivity, clarity and the capacity for love, manifest intelligence and wisdom.

As the meditator becomes increasingly aware of their own inner state of being through meditation, they are also enabled to take greater notice of their psychic environment. The "mood" or "atmosphere" of the workplace is made clearly perceptible to them. The underlying motives and feelings of persons as well as groups, become more and more obvious. Even more importantly, the meditator gains greater awareness of their own patterns of feeling and thought, as well as the Intentions which underlie them.

That which is known can be easily addressed, whereas that which is unknown is difficult to change. Self knowledge implies the capacity for self change. The self-aware individual discovers that the task of building a more evolved self, is often easier than expected. They are thus enabled to build a more evolved world with others in the process.

By applying the Chakra Meditation daily, (or others like it) we become increasingly aware of the subtle feelings/Intents in the body, as they exist in each cubic inch of our physiology. This practice then allows the meditator to begin to transform the Intentions held in the body as a residue of past experiences, to ones that are progressively more evolved.

Long held fear anywhere in the body, such as in the stomach, (third chakra) or the heart, (fourth chakra) can be transformed to love. Confusion and a scattered focus in the region of the forehead, (sixth chakra) can be turned into greater and greater clarity. A lack of energy in the hips/lower spine, (first chakra) can be made into a state of high vitality. All of these changes of cellular memory and Intent can be transformed in such a manner. The meditator may do this by Intending changes to come about, by employing the following four steps.

<u>EXERCISE 5</u>

ADVANCED CHAKRA MEDITATION

Sit or lie comfortably, and immediately begin focusing on the feelings centered in the area of the forehead, or sixth chakra. Those new to this practice may begin by tapping the tip of their right index finger upon what is known as the "third eye", or exact center of the forehead, with the eyes closed.

Tapping increases awareness in that region, which is useful for the beginner. Be aware of every subtle detail of feeling in this area. Allow awareness to spread to the entire region of the frontal lobe of the brain, (the front third of the head, directly behind the forehead), through the middle of the brain, and inclusive of the occipital region, (back of head). FEEL all the subtleties. Do not avoid any pain, fear or other unpleasantness found anywhere in these areas, but instead relax them, and continue the meditation.

As thoughts inevitably run though the mind, simply relax, and return again and again to a feeling focus, even if this means doing so a hundred times every minute. Chronic, rampant, seemingly unstoppable thoughts in the mind, are a symptom of stored stress in ones' being. As the practice of meditation proceeds, stress is released, and the tendency of thoughts to intrude upon the process of meditation will gradually diminish.

Be patient and don't let the simplicity of this method of meditation deceive you. Maintain your awareness on the area of the front of the head, with particular emphasis paid to the third eye, and the temples at the side of each physical eye.

Areas of particular stress or activity in this region, will attract your awareness and hold it for longer periods. Allow this to happen, as it is a function of natural self-healing processes and energy body activity. Don't be concerned or irritated by intruding thoughts, just continue to return to a feeling-oriented focus.

After maintaining this feeling focus in the third eye region for about 5 minutes, shift your focus to one of awareness only. In other words, don't just be aware of feelings in this area, be aware of that in you, which is being aware. This statement may at first sound a little cryptic, but it is actually quite simple. In the basic Chakra Meditation we use awareness to focus on feelings in the body, as a replacement for continuous thoughts in the mind.

In the Advanced Chakra Meditation we start with a feeling focus, and then soon shift to a "focus upon the focuser", or to one of having, "awareness of awareness". So while focused upon the third eye region, the meditator engages in "awareness of awareness", particularly in the frontal lobe of the brain. This act "recycles" awareness back upon itself, thereby increasing its intensity.

This is a primary means to gain greater clarity. Contemplate this concept to comprehend its profound simplicity and value. It is recommended that you perform this meditation twice daily as a temporary replacement for the basic Chakra Meditation, before arising from bed and just before going to sleep at night. Each session should last at least 20-30 minutes.

EXERCISE 6

THE DEEP COVE

Make sure you are as comfortable as possible, and then gently close your eyes.

Begin by taking a couple of deep, full, breaths and let the out breath be a real "letting go" kind of breath.

As you begin breathing slowly, comfortably and easily, invite your body to relax and to let go of any unnecessary tension.

Take the time to bring your attention to each part of your body, and invite it to release and relax, letting go, easily, comfortably.

You can feel the muscles in your face relaxing.

Your shoulders are relaxing.

The muscles of your back are relaxing.

Your legs are relaxing.

Your hands and feet are relaxing.

You're letting all the tensions go.

And your whole body is becoming more and more relaxed.

Just let it happen, releasing, letting go, relaxing even more, now feeling a warm wave of pure relaxation rolling down your body, from the top of your head, to the tips of your toes.

Now, as you are becoming fully centered, feeling in harmony with the entire world, and completely at peace, in your mind's eye, see yourself at the top of an open staircase that leads down to a beautiful beach by the ocean.

You look out towards the sea and before you, as far as you can see, are the glistening waters. The sea breeze blows through your hair, and you breathe it in, savoring the wonderfully clean, invigorating salty smell.

Feel the caress of the warm breeze on your skin. The beach below looks so inviting, that you grasp the wooden handrail and start descending the sturdy hand-hewn steps of the stairs. As you take the steps, you can feel yourself becoming even more relaxed, even more at peace.

And now you are on the beach. The warm sand is beneath your feet. You take off your shoes and leave them at the bottom of the stairs. The sand feels warm beneath your bare feet. You sink into it, and it feels good as your toes curl into the grains of sand. You start walking towards the water's edge, you are so relaxed ... you feel so safe ... you see strips of kelp, bits of abandoned driftwood, seashells.

Now you are there, where the water and the dry beach meet. You walk along the edge of the shore.

The surf is pounding against some rocks somewhere off in the distance. On one side of you the waves rush in and little bubbly foam plays with your bare toes before rushing back to sea.

You are so relaxed...A sea gull flies above you and calls. You follow it with your eyes as it whirls and swoops in the air over the ocean. You look about you and you see a cluster of moss-laden rocks. there is a narrow path between them, and you find yourself in a small quiet cove.

You look around. The cove is shaped like a horseshoe. You still see the ocean dappled with sunshine and small, white crests. There is a ship passing in the distance, and perhaps you can hear the deep-throated call of its horn as it signals to another ship further away.

You breathe in deeply of the moist salt air and smell the ocean's fragrance. You are on your own private beach now, safe from the entire world. You find a nice inviting spot and sit down, feeling so relaxed, so much at peace...just listening to the music, and the ocean in the background.

In the quiet of you mind, you make affirmations to your self:

Today, I willingly release all anger, guilt and judgment that I have directed toward myself or toward others.

I realize that it is now time for me to move past and beyond all negative and limited thinking.

I realize that I can now use the healing power of unconditional love for myself and for others.

I allow my thoughts to be free now, as I become one with the infinite force "within."

I am totally at peace "within."

The sun is starting slowly to sink toward the horizon now. It is time to come back to the here and now. So you get up, and leave the cove through the narrow path between the rocks covered with seaweed, and then walk along the shoreline to the foot of the stairs, picking up your shoes where you left them, clapping them together to knock off the sand, and brushing the sand off yourself. You put on your shoes and now climb back up the steps. With each step you find yourself more and more refreshed and energized, feeling more and more prepared to meet the challenges waiting for you in the coming days.

I will now count from one to five, at the count of three you will open your eyes, at the count of five, you will be wide awake, feeling fine, fully rested and in perfect good health.

One - two - three, your eyes are opening.

Four - you are becoming wide-awake again.

Five - you are now back in your chair, fully awake and aware of your surroundings, feeling fine and in perfect good health. In fact, you feel terrific!!

EXERCISE 7

DEEP RELAXATION

Begin to relax by taking a comfortable position and gently closing your eyes.

Take a couple of deep, slow breaths and let the "out" breaths be real "letting go" kinds of breaths.

You are beginning to release any tension or discomfort in your body.

Now that you have learned to relax, you will find your body and mind relax more quickly and more easily than ever before.

As you focus your attention on each part of your body, you can invite it to release and relax any tension that may be there, and then merely allow it to release in its own way.

Focus your awareness on your left foot, and invite your left foot to release and relax any tension it may be holding.

Notice the beginning sensations of relaxation in that foot.

In the same way, invite your right foot to release and relax any tension that might be there.

Invite the muscles of your left calf and shin to release.

And your right calf and shin.

Just notice and allow your lower legs to relax in their own way, becoming more comfortable and at ease all the while.

Remember, as each part of you relaxes, all of you relaxes more deeply, and as you relax more deeply, each part can relax even more easily.

Invite your left thigh and hamstrings to release and relax, and your right thigh and hamstrings.

Allow your hips and pelvis to join in this letting go and releasing of tension.

Allow your entire lower body to release and relax and notice the relaxing sensations.

Allow it to be a comfortable and pleasant experience.

Invite your lower back and buttocks to join in releasing and relaxing any tension that may be there.

And in your lower pelvic area.

Invite your abdomen to relax and the muscles of your abdomen and your midback to join in this deeper, more comfortable state of relaxation.

Invite the organs in your abdominal cavity to also join in this letting go, releasing and relaxing.

Just allow that whole lower half of your body to let go and become even more deeply comfortable and at ease.

Invite your chest muscles and the muscles between your shoulder blades to release and relax becoming soft and at ease.

The organs in your chest joining in this deeper, more comfortable state.

Imagine your shoulders and neck muscles becoming soft, releasing any tension that may be there.

Allowing them to take a well-deserved rest.

And this relaxation flowing down over your shoulders into your upper arms, elbows, forearms, wrists, and hands.

Invite all the small muscles of your hands

In between the fingers, to release and relax and become very comfortable and deeply relaxed.

Your index fingers, middle fingers, ring fingers, little fingers, and your thumbs deeply relaxed, all the way to the very tips.

Allow your scalp and forehead to release and relax, any tension that may be there becoming soft and smooth and at ease.

The muscles of your face soft and at ease.

And allowing a very pleasant sense of relaxation to come into the small muscles all around your eyes.

Inviting those muscles to release any tension and to feel that sense of letting go flowing through your face and jaws, neck and shoulders, and all the way down.

And as your body relaxes more deeply, your mind becomes quiet and peaceful as well.

You have released all the tension of the day.

Now whatever thoughts are wandering around in the mind, let them go.

For just this moment, here and now, relax from all fear, guilt, worry, and doubt.

This is *your* time, a time for healing and inner reflection.

Take a few moments now, to listen to the music, while you visualize yourself in your favorite restful scene.

Now, as you slowly start

To come back again to the here and now,

You feel completely refreshed,

Physically, and emotionally.

You feel you are now ready

To meet the challenges to come in the days ahead.

In a moment or two,

I will slowly count from one to five,

You will open your eyes at the count of three, and at the count of five, You will be wide-awake,

Feeling totally refreshed,

Physically and mentally restored.

One, two, three, your eyes are now open,

Four, five, you are now wide-awake,

Feeling perfectly healthy,

Completely refreshed, and re-energized.

In fact, you feel terrific!

<u>EXERCISE 8</u>

THE EGYPTIAN SUN MEDITATION - FOR RESTORING ENERGY

This meditation is for those times during your waking hours that you feel low on vital energy. It is a quick, easy way to feel more lively and vibrant. All you need to do is get comfortable, whether in a chair or on a bench, etc. Go into Alpha and visualize a bright golden-white orb of light very much like a miniature Sun about six feet above your head.

This orb emits an intense, vitalizing energy. Feel it flowing down into you through the top of your head and settling into your body, filling every cell and neuron, charging your body with energy. Bask in it, feel it working, and after a few minutes you'll be raring to go!

EXERCISE 9

FOREST MEDITATION

Begin the relaxation process by gently closing your eyes, and allowing your body to relax.

Give yourself permission to relax, affirming to yourself that this is your time, your space; in this moment it is the right thing to do, to release, to let go, to re-lax!

You can feel a beautiful flow of peace, starting at the top of your head, letting the muscles of your scalp relax, then the forehead, the cheeks, the muscles around the jaw and the neck, all relaxing, feeling the wonderful warm feeling of relaxation spreading down through your body, from your shoulders down through the arms and hands, down through the trunk, the thighs, the legs, and finally the feet...you can feel the restful warmth of physical relaxation all through your body now, from the top of your head, to the very tips of your toes.

Sense the flow of peace entering into your mind, giving you a sense of serenity, a sense of trust, and a beautiful sense of oneness with all that is, within and without.

Come along now to the edge of the forest, pause and ask permission to enter, and then take your first steps along the path.

Take a moment to breathe in the aroma of the earth's richness beneath your feet.

Slowly, take in long deep breaths of the refreshing tranquility you have longed for.

As you listen to the music, take a few moments now to fill your lungs with the vitality of the moist scents of pine and cedar and visualize the beauty all around you.

As you begin to relax even more, acknowledge the inner peace you experience as you nourish your body with the fresh, clean air.

Now look around you. Enjoy the canopy of protection above you formed by the towering trees ... shielding you and offering strength as you begin to settle into this temple of beauty built by nature for all its creatures to enjoy.

Feel the security of being alone yet knowing that there is a warmth of love all around you.

Observe the scurrying of birds in dry leaves searching for food; hear the rustle of small animals and insects, accepting your presence. Be thankful for this moment in time and enjoy the happiness of birds fluttering above as though they were angels of protection hovering over you.

Observe the growth in plants and vines and shrubs; see that growing process as it happens. Know that your inner growth develops as surely and steadily, each depending on nourishment from the earth's energy. Notice the strength that seeps into your veins as you marvel at the power in this forest and you begin to sense that this is where you belong.

As you continue to look about, take time to absorb the spirit of the forest and begin to listen.

Hear the sounds of nature's woodland, and let your body acknowledge the rhythm of movement that surrounds you ... allow it to become a part of your heartbeat. As you feel the blood pumping through your body, you sense the energy that rushes through you, giving force to your very being. Know that the higher vibration which you feel is your connection to spirit.

Lift your face to the dewdrops falling from lush greenness and accept this healing power. Feel peace in the bird's songs and happiness in your heart as their music resounds magically through the woods.

With your hand touch the dampness of the leaves, and feel the textures of the rough barks.

Rest for a moment on the cool rock that appears just before you and take in its energy as you observe the happiness of clean water winding its way in the little creek near your feet.

Sit here for a moment and absorb the beauty of this place and this time in your life.

It is time now to retrace your footsteps on the path out of the forest. As you reach the clearing, you feel the warmth of the bright sun on your cheeks; you see the blue of the sky, and the lush green of the grass around you.

As you prepare to return to the here and now, you know that you can return to the sanctuary of the forest at any time you wish. Recalling the thought of this environment will help you during any time of stress or difficulty.

Now I am going to count to five, at the count of three, you will open your eyes, and at the count of five, you will be wide-awake, feeling fine and in perfect health.

One, two, three, your eyes are now open.

Four, five, your are now wide awake, feeling fine and in perfect health; in fact you feel terrific!

EXERCISE 10

THE GLASS TECHNIQUE

(As explained in Silva Mind Control Classes)

The Glass of Water technique is a mental technique that can be used for problem solving and goal achievement. This technique is mostly taught in the Silva Mind Control Classes.

As being a graduate in the Silva Mind Control, I have personally studied and practiced this technique and can promise you one thing - IT WORKS.

Whenever, you come across a hurdle, a problem, that cannot be crossed or solved, do the following:

"At night just before retiring fill a glass of water and take it to the bed. When you are about to go off to sleep, cup the glass in your palms and look for 30 seconds into the water in the glass and repeat 'I know I have (state the problem)' - then close your eyes, look towards the ceiling of the room, and repeat mentally 'This is all I need to do to find the solution to the problem I have in my life'"

Drink away half the water.

The other half can be covered and kept aside.

In the morning when you wake up, before going into your routine chores, taking the half filled glass in your hands, repeat your problem mentally, and say "Today, I will find the solution to my hurdle/problem" Drink away the balance half of the water.

EXERCISE 11

THE GOLDEN WATERFALL

Begin by getting comfortable in your seats, and then gently closing your eyes.

Begin breathing slowly and gently from your abdomen and feel yourself becoming wonderfully relaxed, as tension begins to fall away.

Feel your feet becoming relaxed, then your legs, your thighs and buttocks, all perfectly relaxed.

are now becoming completely relaxed from the top of your head to the tip of your toes.

All the physical tension is drained away, and with it has gone any emotional distress you may have been feeling.

You are feeling at ease, calm, and totally at peace, within and without.

Take a moment now to enjoy this wonderful feeling of being completely at ease.

Now begin to imagine yourself surrounded on all sides by a soft golden light.

Imagine a waterfall of this warm golden light a few feet above your head.

Feel it's gentle, loving, warmth as it cascades around you

And begin to feel it flowing into you through the crown chakra at the top of your head.

All the physical tension is drained away, and with it has gone any emotional distress you may have been feeling.

You are feeling at ease, calm, and totally at peace, within and without.

Take a moment now to enjoy this wonderful feeling of being completely at ease.

As it flows into you, feel its healing golden light pour through you, into your face and neck...into your arms and chest...into your heart...pouring down through your stomach and legs and feet until your whole body becomes part of the waterfall of golden light.

Once again, you find yourself back in your easy chair, basking in the warmth of the fireplace. And as you again listen to the music, take a few moments to reflect on your own personal connection with the Infinite, and how you can make that connection a part of your everyday life.

Bathe in this light for a few moments.

Feel it's healing warmth flowing through every part of you. Feel it flow from the top of your head, down through your body, out through the bottom of your feet and into the ground far below.

Know that in experiencing this golden light pouring into you, you allow the loving, healing forces of the universe into you, to help you be whole, physically, mentally and emotionally.

Feel the beauty, and the peacefulness, and the health that is in you, and know that at all times you can be at one with yourself, with god, and with the universe.

Take a few moments now to rest in the flow of golden light, and in the sound of the music.

Now slowly, gently, as you begin to return to the here and now, you realize you really are feeling rested, renewed, re-energized, and ready to meet the challenges of the coming days.

And you know that in the future when you begin to feel tired, or challenged beyond your capacity, you can call back to mind this wonderful experience of the healing, energizing golden light, and you will once again be restored to full health and vigor.

In a few moments I am going to count from one to five.

Upon the number three, your eyes will open, and on the count of five, you will once again be wide-awake, feeling fine and in perfect health.

One, two, three, your eyes are now opening.

Four, five, you are now wide-awake, feeling fine and in perfect health, much better than before, in fact you feel terrific!

EXERCISE 12

INFINITY MEDITATION

Let us start by getting comfortable in your chairs, gently closing your eyes.

And relaxing, letting go of all the tenseness, wherever it may be in your body.

Become aware of your total body, from the top of your head, to the tips of your toes, and then relaxing any areas of tension that you may encounter.

Now take a few, slo-o-o-w breaths, inhaling deeply each time, and exhaling slowly and completely.

Then resume breathing normally again.

Let all the stresses and concerns of your daily life flow away, for just these few minutes while you are here, in the sanctuary of your favorite place of relaxation.

Feel how much more relaxed you are becoming with each breath, how much more at ease you are becoming.

And enjoy for a moment the sensation of that relaxation and ease, the pleasure of the peace, and security, that surrounds you, here in this haven of serenity.

And as you become more and more centered, accept any stray thoughts that enter into your consciousness; acknowledge them, and release them, letting them float gently away...

Let your mind travel now, to a place I will describe, but only you can envision for yourself.

You find yourself sitting in a very comfortable easy chair. Its high-backed, made of soft leather, with plenty of support for your head and arms. Just across from you in your chair is a fireplace with a couple of small logs burning brightly. You can feel the warmth from the fire; you can smell the resins burning from the pine logs. You watch the little sparks being thrown off by the fire.

You look around you now in the dim light of the fireplace, and you can see you are in a kind of den. There are books on the shelves lining the walls, and deep, rich rugs on the floor. You feel completely at ease in these surroundings, warm, safe, secure, at peace.

And you let your mind focus inward. Until finally you find yourself deep within, at the very centre of your being, that very secret place within, where you become at one with Spirit.

You may greet your spirit friends now, be they angels, guides or counselors, and feel the loving warmth of their presence, and acknowledge their gentle, caring support in all you do. You know that they are there for you always, you need only ask, and accept.

In a moment, I am going to slowly count from one to five. At the count of three, you will open your eyes, and at the count of five, you will become wide-awake, feeling fine and in perfect health, much better than before.

One, two, three, your eyes are opening now, Four, five, you are now wide awake, feeling fine, completely refreshed as if you had just woke up from a good hour's nap. And you feel terrific!

And now, with a silent word of thanks to the Almighty in gratitude for these few moments of serenity and peace, you prepare to return to the here and now with a renewed sense of commitment to your path of spiritual enlightenment, and a feeling of being refreshed physically, mentally and emotionally, ready to face the coming days of the week, with renewed vigor and determination.

EXERCISE 13

INNER HEALING MEDITATION

Let's begin by getting comfortable in your chairs, And gently closing your eyes.

Allow you self to begin by drawing in one...Full... Deep and easy breath.

As the air flows into your body, imagine that it contains soothing, Healing, properties.

As you draw in another full...Deep... Breath, You imagine that the healing breath.

Is flowing throughout your body, healing, soothing.

Then as you release each breath, The air that flows from your body.

Carries away any tension, That you may have been feeling when you began.

Let it go... See it moving out and away from your body.

And when you bring in the next breath, Feel it moving to an even deeper place.

Within you, soothing and relaxing, Even more of your body.

And bringing up even more tension, Even more toxins, Releasing even more tightness...With each succeeding breath it is going a little deeper.

Until your breath is reaching into every part, Every extremity of your body, Soothing... Releasing... Relaxing... Healing.

Just for a moment, Be aware of any place in your body.

That feels uncomfortable.

Say the word to yourself, Like "head" or "neck" or "foot."

Then as you take your next breath, Send the air to those parts of your body, allowing them to be soothed and healed.

See in that vivid imagination of yours, Your toes uncurling, Knots untying, Stiffness being soothed, Like wrinkles being ironed out of a shirt.

Now that you are relaxing

More and more deeply in your body, You feel a growing sense of ease.

Moving into your mind, Just like a fine mist...See that mist now, In any color that you find soothing.

Continue to breathe it in; And watch it curl around your thoughts, Gently embracing them.

And reminding them.

That this is your time to be at peace, Your time to be at ease, Regardless of whatever else.

Is happening in your life.

And once again, Give yourself permission to relax.

All that is real at this moment is the here and now, So just... Let... It...be, And let go, and relax.

If troubling thoughts arise, That's all right ... Let them be, And send the mist to surround them.

And waft them away, As though on a gentle wisp of wind.

Now that you are relaxing.

Deeper and deeper into, A state of peace and ease, You are beginning to focus on, That secret place deep within you, You can see a small white light shining softly, beckoning you toward it, With it's gentle glow.

You start to draw near to it, Attracted by it's soft warm illumination, And as you come closer, You find that your entire being.

Is getting bathed in this gentle, embracing, loving light.

Just as the warm sun energizes your physical body, So is this light cleansing.

And re-vitalizing your spirit.

The soft light is cleansing your inner self.

Of those negative emotions.

That are so hard to get rid of entirely.

Those lingering feelings of resentment, From whatever source, And from whatever time, Some of them may even go back.

To your early childhood.

You can feel that the glow, Of the soft white light is, Replacing those negative feelings, Leaving in their place.

More compassionate feelings, And emotions for all of those, That may have contributed.

To the resentment you have harboured up to this time.

Take a moment now.

To shed yourself of any negative feelings.

You may have toward others, And repeat quietly to your self, In your inner self, "I forgive everyone.

That may have treated me.

Unfairly in the past, And I'm now ready to move on.

Down the path of my life.

Toward the glorious future.

I know is waiting for me."

"I forgive everyone.

That may have treated me

Unfairly in the past

And I'm now moving on

Down the path of my life

Toward the glorious future

I know is waiting for me."

Now just let those thoughts of forgiveness

Float away, Knowing that the great spirit

Will direct them to Wherever they may be most needed. Again, take a moment. And notice how much lighter.You feel because you have rid yourself, Of a burden and have taken on. An uplifting feeling of joyful expectation. In its place.

Where there was resentment, Now there is compassion, Where there was ill will, Now there are good intentions.

And you know you have taken, A big step forward, On your path toward true enlightenment.

You are still feeling relaxed and at ease, You are feeling warm and comfortable, As you continue to bathe, In the soft glow of the healing, Soothing white light.

Your are centered, You are at peace.

Take a few moments now, Listening to the music, Enjoying these moments of inner serenity and tranquility, And I will join you again in a minute or so.

Now, as you slowly start .

To come back again to the here and now, You feel completely refreshed, Physically, and emotionally.

You feel you are now ready, To meet the challenges to come in the days ahead.

In a moment or two, I will slowly count from one to five, You will open your eyes at the count of three, and at the count of five, You will be wide awake, Feeling totally refreshed, Physically and mentally restored.

One, two, three, your eyes are now open, Four, five, you are now wide awake, Feeling perfectly healthy, Completely refreshed, and re-energized. In fact, you feel terrific!

EXERCISE 14

THE LILY POND

- Relax.
- Do the centralizing exercise.
- Good.
- Now close your eyes.
- Relax.
- No thoughts are coming to you. You are totally comfortable and relaxed. Relax...Relax....Relax.
- Visualize yourself outside a building, which looks exactly like the White House. See yourself outside this building. You can see a sign on the top of the building, which reads THE LILY POND.
- You make an immediate decision to visit the LILY POND.
- You start climbing the steps. 1.... 2.... 3...4...5...6...7...8...9....10. Now, you are in front of the main door. Visualize yourself raising your hand and pushing the door inwards. Now, you are stepping into the Lily Pond.
- You are in the main hall where the Lily Pond is.
- What you see now before you are a number of steps, which are going downwards.

- At the bottom it is semi-darkness. You are feeling relaxed. A certain peace, calm is touching you and for some unknown reasons you are feeling internally happy, you are feeling happy.... Happy...very happy.

- You start descending the steps. One, go slow, go with peace, for this is a magical world. Step two, now slowly, Step Three.

- As you set your foot on step three, suddenly dim lights are turned on. You continue descending, step four, now you can hear a soft music in the background.

- Step five; the hall is lit up, everything is clear. Visualize a big lily in front of you, in the center of a pond. See its colors and the strong green petals, surrounded by the background of the sky with it's Red, Orange, blue, violet, Indigo colors because of the rising sun. See the rainbow beyond the lily. Look at the serene atmosphere in and above the hall.

- See yourself taking off your clothes and stepping into the pond. Swim if you may. Talk to the fish; ride on the back of the big tortoise in the pond.

- If you wish to fly towards the sky do so. Relax. You are free of worries. Now, visualize coming downwards and resting in the center of the Lily. Relax. Relax.

- Take a deep breath. Relax. Visualize yourself in the pond swimming lazily; take a dip into the water. See yourself come out of the water. Look around you; what you see is the water turning blackish in color. See the water turn back to its natural color. Take a dip again. Again you see the blackened water surrounding you. This blackishness is the negativity inside you, which is coming out of your system. Continue taking dips, till you see that the water is clear.

- Visualize yourself coming out of the lily pond. Wear your clothes. You need not dry yourself. As you can see your body has already dried as you stepped out of the lily pond.

- Leave the building.

- Relax - try to feel the sensations in your body.

- Open your eyes whenever you feel like it.

(NOTE: Most of the students who have done this exercise in my classroom have had different experiences. Some of them feel giddy, some of them feel elated, and some feel completely positive)

From: Dr. Mohan Makkar's Ph.D. (A.M.) Reiki Magic / Reiki Magic Revised.

What will happen is this:

Anytime during the day that follows, a message may be conveyed to you by anyone, either your favorite TV soap opera; conversation with a friend, a taught from yonder; a remark passed by a friend. Anything. Just be on the look out.

Just in case, nothing follows, repeat the exercise again the next night - it works like magic.

Good luck.

This visual meditation is also given in Dr. Mohan Makkar's Ph.D. (A.M.) Reiki Magic & Reiki Magic Revised.

<u>EXERCISE 15</u>

THE MOUNTAIN PATH

Make sure you are as comfortable as possible, and then gently close your eyes.

Begin by taking a couple of deep, full, breaths and let the out breath be a real "letting go" kind of breath.

As you begin breathing slowly, comfortably and easily, invite your body to relax and to let go of any unnecessary tension.

Take the time to bring your attention to each part of your body, and invite it to release and relax, letting go, easily, comfortably.

You can feel the muscles in your face relaxing.

Your shoulders are relaxing.

The muscles of your back are relaxing.

Your legs are relaxing.

Your hands and feet are relaxing.

You're letting all the tensions go.

And your whole body is becoming more and more relaxed.

Just let it happen, releasing, letting go, relaxing even more, now feeling a warm wave of pure relaxation rolling down your body, from the top of your head, to the tips of your toes.

To deepen this relaxation, imagine yourself now on a path leading alongside an alpine meadow. Towering behind you are the snowcapped peaks of the surrounding mountains. The air is clean and fresh. It is late afternoon on a sunny summer's day. The sky is a beautiful light blue with a few tall fluffy white clouds moving majestically from the horizon.

The pine trees stand tall and stately to your right, and you pick up on the strong scent of the evergreens.

To your left you can hear the rustle of an aspen grove.

Your eye catches the shimmering of the leaves in the soft breeze.

The path slopes downward. It has recently been cleared; the pine needles are brushed to the side. You feel sure-footed and secure as you walk the path leading in the direction of a meadow ahead.

As you reach the edge of the line of trees, you see a comfortable looking bench beside the path between two big pine trees. You sit down and lean back. The bench is made of rough wood, but you find it very comfortable and relaxing to sit on.

As you look around, you can see the meadow below you with its carpet of wild flowers spread out..., blue, red, white, yellow, coral, splashes of green, sunlit, bees humming, a dragonfly flits by.

You look up through the canopy of trees and see the blue sky with the tall white clouds going by.

It is serene, beautiful, and peaceful.

You are conscious for just a moment of inhaling the energy, the life force, that's in the fresh mountain air, and you're exhaling all your tensions, all your worries and concerns are flowing away.

There is just the air, the rustling leaves, the drifting clouds, the scent of pine, the rough texture of the bench all bringing a special calm, a sense of peace, a sense of inner nourishment.

An owl flies up and lights on a branch above you. It doesn't frighten you. Rather you feel a sense of curiosity. You continue to study the owl, as it looks back at you. It ruffles its feathers before settling comfortably on the branch.

Something passes between you, some unspoken communication. You have a feeling of oneness with everything around you.. Your feeling of relaxation is even deeper. Allow yourself the time now to relax for a few moments, drawing on the beauty of the scene as you envision it, taking in the energy to re-energize and revitalize yourself.

Let this be a time of renewal for your inner spirit as you listen to the music.

The owl flies away now. You watch the clouds drifting in larger and darker formations, pushing one another more rapidly than before.

The soft touch of the moist air is on your cheeks. You know it's going to rain, in fact, you can already hear the first drops falling on the leaves nearby.

You leave the comfortable bench and start walking up the

mountain path, in the direction you came from. As you leave, you know that this is a place that you can come back to whenever you wish..., to sit, to relax, to heal, to just watch the clouds roll by.

It is a place where rest and peace and inner healing take place.

You go up the path and with the next five steps, you become more and more awake and aware of your surroundings.

One, going up the path.

Two, feeling better than before, coming awake now, bringing back with you a sense of relaxation and inner healing.

Three, feeling refreshed, as though you had just had a nice invigorating nap.

Four, energizing, eyes opening now.

Five, your eyes fully open now, you are alert and wide awake, now stretch, and smile, because you feel terrific.

<u>EXERCISE 16</u>

THE PINK STAR MEDITATION - FOR SELF - ESTEEM

Sit or lie down, relax and go into Alpha. Visualize a beam of brilliant white light *entering your body through the soles of your feet and traveling through the rest of* your body, exiting through the top of your head. See yourself exiting your body from the top of your head as a passenger on the petals of a silver lotus blossom that is headed for outer space. See yourself going far into space, leaving our solar system, traveling very fast. Take note of other planets and asteroids as you pass by.

Feel the solar wind as you travel through a binary star system. It should feel real. Soon, far in the distance, you will see a tiny, bright pink star. As you get closer to it, you can feel waves of self-esteem wash over you. The lotus blossom takes you directly into the core of the now large star and stops. You are inundated with healing, loving energy. It restores your self worth, confidence and self-respect. You take it into yourself and it fills you to the point of manifesting itself as large, flowing wings.

Bask in this for as long as you like. Once you feel you have been restored, take a double handful of the pink energy and see the lotus blossom taking you back to your body. You will see the planets and asteroids you observed earlier in reverse. See yourself re-entering your body through the top of your head. Before you come out of Alpha, think o f two people who you think could use some self-esteem. Visualize yourself placing the pink energy you took from the star on their Solar Plexus, and see their body/mind absorbing that energy. Then come out of Alpha or choose another task.

I find that this meditation can be modified to bring different results. For example, you could substitute a green star, which would be for balance. You would feel yourself totally grounded when you are done. While you are within the star, you would feel yourself being inundated by peace and calm. You could use a blue star for communication, a purple star for healing, an indigo star for intuition, a yellow star for happiness, a white star for positive energy, a red star for dynamic energy, and a gold or orange star for prosperity.

Employing the Advanced Chakra Meditation to gain greater clarity is a *process of self-education.* Clarity is not a concept Western culture is thoroughly familiar with, and rarely is it a term that is concretely defined. In this system, clarity is defined in terms of the degree of awareness of awareness one possesses. Represented mathematically, this principle of natural law may be shown as A/A=C, whereas, "A" is awareness, (divided by itself) and "C" is the clarity that results. As greater experiential familiarity with clarity is had, it then becomes a known quality of mind that can be summoned up or enhanced at will, even without the precursor of meditation. Thus it can then be intended into place at a moments' notice, for the purpose of improved mental and even physical function.

In the group meditational setting, it may also be intended into place for oneself as well as others, simultaneously. In other words, awareness of awareness may be psychically projected to others, which aids in their higher establishment of clarity as well. We should not consider this a particularly esoteric act, when remembering that any state of consciousness can be projected. All states of consciousness in fact, automatically radiate from the body/mind as soon as they are gained within, to some degree.

By Intending their projection outward however, we are increasing the potency of rendered psychic effects many times over. In this way too, we are acting on behalf of natural laws, and are thereby gaining the cumulative support of nature in our spiritual practices.

EXERCISE 17

THE POWER OF 7TH HEAVEN MEDITATION

Close your eyes for just a momentary expanse and relax into the etheric web of Christ Pure Essence and allow that to embrace your fears, until you are breathing, feeling love. A new door opens today you have no longer to observe the past or integrate duality, for you may have had to understand density, but you certainly don't have to experience it again.

Dynamics in your energy field will change, as everything starts flowing your way including your unique universal God-Cel. As it unravels you eliminate the Gemini essence and house the door of El-Lunia both the masculine and feminine blend. You have intelligence riding the wave of brain activation beyond earth measure opening up with circulation of the crown center.

You may have a moment or two of electronics sparking and that is quite normal. You will have the continual circulation of the I AM Presence enter upon the crown, and it will blend with the heart centers circulation system. It is but another avenue created to merge heaven/earth in the human body. As it deepens its connection the mind will begin to unleash the evolving diamond of light we call your Merkivah.

As it does you will call forth the modern day Temple of Light. There will be 13 manifested on earth with the first one opening in Thailand. They are an important show of unity with master trainers on earth and a support system built on trust of the divine.

The Emerald Way opens up purified Aquarian light, and as it does the body is asked to listen to its yearning for physical biological perfection. Make that commitment to change old patterns and listen as your source carries the final say.

You may stop eating animal products, find yourself juicing and cleansing the colon, but it is the Liver we connect through the mighty throat of change. A tube of light from the back of the throat slides down into the liver and deposits a generator of SOURCE LIGHT. It will take some set up work with your source first, to eliminate old throat patterns.

The liver does not process earth density in a light body, that is why it will no longer be appropriate to run dense energies through the body, as the cells will not accept soul level or higher self living at this point. The God-Cel expands its vision and it will feel as if you are changing a light bulb in the body from the higher self light into God/I AM/Source. The protein/strength synthesis of the human body is best generated from source light, and that carries into the lymph nodes and spreads the source throughout humanity. Heart essence will spread its wings as love for self carries into love of humanity, love of God, love of Source, love of all that has no-conditions.

You are connecting directly with source, as I AM Presence dances to the harmony of Self-reliant behavior in joy. A quality of service assignment connects the power of 7-earth chakra station into the Sacral Center. As you have been given the tools to eliminate the subconscious, deep subconscious and collective unconscious all animal behaviors of survival leave as balance restores its faith into the thinking, feeling and nurturing of a higher nature.

You have every capable creative endeavor at your command, for that is the path of human mastery. The consciousness of earth elements opens up the telepathic assistance and you no longer see fairies, devas that is for higher self, you speak direct with the elements as each earth essence carries source generated light. In this you come alive with clear communications throughout the universe.

You are grounded in human growth and development, yet not beholden to its dense nature, for you can let go of your own density, which goes back to the origination of duality. You know the true feeling of love, passion, commitment, sacred male/female relations of every sort. You remember there is one sacred partner of universal proportions come to rejoin with physical light earth. How grand the illusion, how simple the equation of manifestation.

We ask all components of your physical body, energy field, and universal essence come together, and with that in one instant moment everything changes, as your God-Brain/Mind and Body enters quickly forever changing your waking conscious light. You have the tools to complete and manifest your greatest desires, you are the command of Christ Pure essence and in that will you find the greatest sensation of all, inner Peace.

I love you all in the heart of the Lion's Gate, it will roar with the triumphant return of truth, knowledge and physical sensations of spirit, enjoy dear hearts, you have stepped into a new beginning, Sananda (Ark Angel Zachary, Universal God-Spark and Clarity)

EXERCISE 18

RAINBOW LIGHT MEDITATION

At the heart-level in the center of our chest, now appears a tiny rainbow light. Gradually it expands through our body, totally filling it and dissolving all diseases and obstacles on its way. When we can stay with this awareness, our body shines like a lamp and light streams in all directions, filling space. It dissolves the suffering of beings everywhere and the world now shines with great meaning and joy. All are in a pure land, full of limitless possibilities. Everything is self-liberating. We emanate this light as long as it feels natural. "

EXERCISE 19

YOUR SANCTUARY

In every human life, there comes a day when you are frustrated, disillusioned, finding that you are in the lowest ebb of your life, you are frantic …

And in this state you want one thing … TO GET AWAY FROM IT ALL.

To have a place, where you are alone with yourself. You do not want any outside force to ever see you again. You wish to be just alone, in a SECRET PLACE only which you know of.

But, is there such a place???

Let's approach this from a different angle. But, before we do so, let me ask you a question. Okay?

- Which is the fastest mode of transport?

Think before you can answer.

I will answer this one for you: The fastest mode of transportation is your "IMAGINATION".

In the beginning of the book, I have mentioned that the inner self is much more bigger than the outside world. Comparatively, the outside world is smaller than the inside world.

So, why look to hide on the outside. Why do we not take our imagination, our visualization on the inside?

We create our own hiding spot, in the mountains, on any planet in the Solar System, under the earth, above the earth, anywhere. But, this world of ours will be inside us. Nobody can find us there.

We know how we expose ourselves to the world, clean, pious, caring for others, but we also know what is inside us, don't we?

So, let's make a hiding place inside us. The ideas of the snow clad mountains, forests, ponds, rivers, forests, can be taken from the outside, but this world will be our world in the inside of us.

- Do your breathing exercise, breathe in to the count of 4, hold your breath to the count of 4, breathe out to the count of 4.
- Continue with deep intakes of breath, till you feel a little dizzy or till you feel relaxed.
- Visualize yourself in your favorite place of relaxation.
- Visualize you are taking a stroll in your favorite place of relaxation, where no other human being, animal or bird is allowed to enter without your permission.
- As you are strolling, visualize that there is a cloud following you.
- Look up at the cloud. This cloud looks great.
- Visualize that as you are looking at the cloud, the cloud bursts open and a force of white light descends on you.
- Feel as if millions of bulbs have been lighted up.

- Visualize the colors of the rainbow, the violet, indigo, blue, green, yellow, orange, red, lilac, white.
- Feel the tingling sensations in your body.
- Feel as if you are being carried away on the wings of a big bird.
- You are feeling light, very light.
- All your worries, negativities, fears have been washed away by the light from the cloud.
- Mentally bow down and whisper "I thank you lord for the mercy shown to me, for giving me the power to fight back and rise up, thank you, thank you, thank you my lord"
- Look up at the cloud again, it has vanished.
- Keep strolling in your favorite place of relaxation.
- You do feel relaxed - isn't it??

Come back to the room as and when you feel you are ready to fight back and rise again.

This exercise is also included in Dr. Mohan Makkar's Ph.D. (A.M.) Reiki Magic & Reiki Magic Revised.

EXERCISE 20

THE UNIVERSAL BANK

- Do the breathing technique and reach the Alpha Level
- Go to your favorite place of relaxation (Your Sanctuary)
- Relax for a few minutes - fly if you wish, go visiting your relatives/friends
- Just relax
- After you have relaxed, close your eyes and repeat the following words "By the power given to me by my higher self, I wish to go to THE UNIVERSAL BANK"
- Feel yourself traveling.
- Open your eyes (visualize) and you will find yourself in front of a building on which is written "THE UNIVERSAL BANK"
- Climb the steps.
- Start walking towards the doors.
- Do everything at a leisurely pace.
- Push the door inwards
- You come across a single counter, which is being attended by a beautiful female (always visualize the opposite gender).

- See her looking at you and smiling.
- "Good Morning, Sir" she says
- Reply in sweet tones "Good Morning to you"
- "Can I help you?" she asks you.
- Repeat the following words "Yes, I want to withdraw US$1,000,000.00 (or any figure you wish to withdraw)"
- "One minute Sir" she says and opens up a drawer to give you a blank banker's cheque. "Can you fill this in?" she asks
- Fill in the amount you wish to withdraw. Be confident. Be assured. This is the Universal Bank - you ask and it shall be yours. After filling in the cheque and signing it, hand it over the counter to the lady.
- Visualize her reading and requesting you to hold on.
- Visualize her enter the cabin on the other side of the room.
- Visualize her bringing in a leather suitcase with the cash.
- Visualize her handing over the same to you.
- Visualize you accepting the suitcase with the case and checking for authencity.
- Visualize yourself thanking the lady and wishing her a good day and leaving the bank.

Come out of the Universal Bank and thank the bank for making your realization come true.

Repeat the following words - "By the power given to me by my higher self, I wish to return to my favorite place of relaxation."

Visualize yourself in your favorite place of relaxation.

Come back to your physical self whenever you want to do so.

EXERCISE 21

THE WHITE LIGHT MEDITATION

In every Reiki Class, we do a Meditation known as the "White Light Meditation". During this Meditation, we heal the world by sending a flow of positive energy to make our world a better place to live in.

- Do your breathing exercise as taught to you. (4 breaths in, 4 hold, 4 out & 4 hold - repeat) - only 3 or maximum 4 sets. We will call this CENTRALISING for future records.

- Now, on an out breath, with your mental power create a white ball, the size of a tennis ball. Make this ball spin with your mental power of visualization. Visualize it; see it with your mental eyes in front of your third eye Chakra, the center of your eyebrows. See it spin, slow....slow....slow, now it is picking up speed fast...fast....faster...faster.

- As the speed is increasing, visualize a white light emitting from the ball, this white light is like a mist, a fog. See the white light cover the ball. The amazing thing you notice is that this white light is floating and covering you and the furniture in the room. Repeat see it like a haze, a mist. See it cover the room.

- Let this light float into the other rooms, the kitchen, the bathroom, the storeroom, the bedroom and all the other rooms in your apartment. Now, extend your vision, see it seep out of the balcony doors, the windows, the main door and visualize it going out into the street. Visualize the white light covering your building.

- The speed of the white light is increasing. The white light is now covering the area in which you live. See the white light cover the town, the city you live in.

- See the white light cover the other surrounding cities.

- See the white light cover the entire nation. The white light is now covering surrounding nations and the full world.

- Visualize the white light cover all the mentally handicapped children. See the children improving under the influence of this WHITE LIGHT. See them becoming better and better and better. See the white light cover all the pregnant women. Visualize the pregnant women delivering healthy children normally. Visualize the white light cover the people with terminal diseases like Cancer and Aids. See these people recovering. Visualize the white light cover all the undernourished children on this planet. Visualize these children eating lavishly. See them recovering gradually and learning to smile. Visualize the while light covers all the prisons in this world Visualize the prisoners' turn into better humans.

- Visualize the world leaders signing a peace treaty under the white light.

- Visualize the terrorists' throw up their arms and surrender themselves.

- Visualize brotherhood and love floating in every heart in every being. Visualize all politicians turning to new leaves and working for the benefit of mankind. Keep this visualization in the level of your 3rd eye chakra.

Slowly come back to the room and open your eyes whenever you feel like it.

From Dr. Mohan Makkar's Ph.D. (A.M.) Reiki Magic / Reiki Magic Revised.

EXERCISE 22

THE TREE OF LIFE ASTRAL TRAVEL

Clear your mind, close your eyes, and picture yourself in a darkened place. Picture a pure, radiant white light descending from above your head, and speak the name Eheiah (AHIH).

Let this light enter the crown of your head and descend to your throat, and picturing it radiating a mauve light, speak the name Adonai Alohim. (IHVH ALHIM notes that the Tetragrammaton is used, but you may speak the word Adonai instead, or pause, but generally the IHVH is not pronounced for fear of blasphemy.)

Let that light descend to reach the level of the Heart and Solar Plexus where it radiates a golden yellow, speak the name Adonai Al Va Da'ath (IHVH AL VDYTh)

Let this light descend to the genitals and picture it turning a rich deep purple. Speak the name Shaddai al Chai (ShDI AL ChI)

Let this light reach your feet, and picture it turning a russet, citrine, black and olive color. Speak the name Adonai Ha Aretz (IHVH HARTz)

You will now have a stream of light from above your head to your feet on your left-hand side, under your feet, and up the right hand side. Another similar band of light travels down the front of your body, under your feet, and up the back. This will form the container of your consciousness.

Imagine this container filling up from above, with a liquid that sends your body to sleep as it fills up from the feet. This will displace your consciousness and let it travel freely. It is however still attached to your body with a silver cord, generally from the navel, like an umbilical cord, or from the feet or head. When you have finished your travels, you need only follow the cord to your container, and slowly ease you body back into the container, displacing the liquid as you go. The light can then be reversed as with the drawing down.

EXERCISE 23

THE TREE OF LIFE SPHERES MALKUTH

In any situation, although alone may be more suited, there is a very easy exercise one can perform to realize the sphere of Malkuth. Simply clap your hands and feel the tingling sensation that occurs. Hold them to the air and feel the sensation. This sensation is the realization of the first sphere.

However, you may feel other thoughts as you perform this. You may wonder what relevance this exercise has; you may feel ridiculous doing what you have just done, as well as many other things. These are not associated with this sphere, but with other higher spheres, and should be cleared from your mind.

By doing this, you experience each sphere as an individual, which you can later mesh into a whole divine plan without being confused as to what things are, and how they link together. It is not wrong or bad to have these feelings and associations, but for this sphere, the start, they will confuse your reading of it.

Clasp your hands together in whatever way you wish. Feel the sensation of one hand against the other. Again, you may experience feelings of being in prayer (which you may relate to this pose), but pay no attention to these.

Look at a picture, be it in a magazine, photograph or anything. Direct your mind to see only what is there. Do not begin to associate the picture with a subject, or an emotional response, just with the fact that it is a picture, not a picture of something that does something for you.

Finally, say any words out loud, and listen to them. It is best not to make a special effort to choose these words wisely. They are just words, devoid of meaning for this sphere. Say them out loud, listen to them, but do not react to them. This is the sphere of Malkuth.

EXERCISE 24

THE TREE OF LIFE SPHERES - YESOD

Prepare yourself by making yourself comfortable in a space where you won't be disturbed, close your eyes and take a few deep, cleansing breaths. Be aware that you are a unique individual, choosing to utilize your energy in a realm of magickal consciousness.

Picture yourself standing in a field at the bottom of a hill. Be aware of everything that is around you, creating a clear picture of your surroundings, including all of the senses.

Walk across this field and to a path which slopes upwards toward the hill. Take your time to feel your feet on the ground, always being aware of what is around you. Start waking up this path, still noticing everything that is around you, using all of your senses.

About half way up the slope, stop for a rest. Look back down the path you have taken, into the field where you have come from, taking in all of the feelings of being alone in the beauty of nature.

Before you recommence your journey, you are aware of something hidden in something nearby, be it in a bush, under a rock etc. It is wrapped in a shiny golden cloth. Clean everything off of this, and unwrap the cover, noticing beneath it a book with a beautiful cover. Lift it up to the light, feeling excited and alive by doing this. The book seems to be filled with energy. Clearly form a picture of this book in your mind with every little facet of its appearance.

When you have done this, open the book to find that the pages are pure white and completely blank. You now realize that this is a book in which you can keep all of your magickal discoveries, this is your Magickal Diary.

When you have done this, recommence your journey to the top of the hill, whereat you find a large stone, waist high. Place your newfound book on top of this stone, and feel the energy of the sun radiating down, and the energy of the earth seeping up through the rock. Allow you book to change shape, design, or simply radiate, being aware of what it has become.

Pick the book up once again, and hold it to your heart. Affirm that you will keep an honest record of all your workings in it. Let the energy of the book through your heart to the deepest depths of your being, realizing that the energy from these depths can also fill your book with your own unique truth.

When you have done this, thank the sun and stone, and briskly walk back down the path to the field. Bring the book with you. When you return to the meadow, be sure to feel the sensation of your feet being on the ground. Open your eyes, bringing the book into reality with you.

Be sure to create a clear picture of this diary in some way when you return to reality, so that you can actually create it, to act as a diary for all of your workings. This will ground whatever knowledge you have gained, into the sphere of Malkuth, an important thing to remember with all Kabbalistic workings.

EXERCISE 25

THE TREE OF LIFE SPHERES - HOD

For this exercise, simply consider the following attributions related to the ten spheres of the Tree of Life. These represent the energies attainable when we contact the spheres through traveling the appropriate paths. As you meditate upon the spheres, be aware of the Tree of Life diagram, and how they have been put together on it.

Malkuth: Discovering the mysteries of the physical universe; the ability to discriminate; physical healing and overcoming inertia and sloth.

Yesod: Discovering the mysteries of the astral levels and lunar energies; to realize the workings of the universal energies; to connect with the divine plan.

Hod: Discovering the mysteries of information systems and Mercurial energies; truthfulness; greater ability to communicate clearly.

Netzakh: Discovering the mysteries of loving sexuality and Venusian energies; unselfishness; increasing artistic creativity.

Tipareth: Discovering the mysteries of beauty and harmony, and the solar energies; centered consciousness; stimulating the energy of soul manifesting in life.

Geburah: Discovering the mysteries of power and the use of Martian energies; purposeful change; awakening inner and outer strength.

Hesed: Discovering the mysteries of love and the use of Jupiterian energies; peace and love awakened; stimulating the force of abundance.

(Da'ath): Discovering the mysteries of the shadow side of existence; inner depths explored; knowledge of the rainbow bridge.

Binah: Discovering the mysteries of silence and secrecy; increasing understanding; realizing that all things are united.

Hickman: Discovering the mysteries of purpose and initiative; increasing wisdom; realizing the universal plan as manifest throughout the world.

Ether: Discovering the mysteries of unity and union; the inner quest; amplification of spiritual energy and the revelation of divine inspiration.

Thoughts on these can be recorded in your Magickal Diary, grounding them in the sphere of Malkuth.

EXERCISE 26

THE TREE OF LIFE SPHERES - NETZAKH

In the first exercise, all feelings and thoughts were disregarded because they were of another sphere. Hod is the sphere of thought, as in the last exercise when you thought about correspondences. Netzakh is the sphere of feelings. It is often associated with a chalice or 'holy grail'. In this exercise you will be using these, but will also be using the sphere of Hod in the fact that you will need to think to create them in your mind. A clear distinction should be made between them during this exercise.

Prepare yourself once again in a place where you will not be disturbed. Think of a chalice or Holy Grail. Imagine that you were supplied with all of the materials and skills to make this, and create a chalice of any kind. Gain a clear picture of it in your mind. When you have done this, create a representation of it in the real world by either drawing it or writing a description of it. Be sure to go in depth with this, not leaving out any small detail.

Sit in a comfortable position, relax and close your eyes. Picture yourself in a wood, surrounded by light young trees. Smell the fresh air and allow yourself to really 'be' in this place. Feel your feet on the ground, imagine the sun shining down on you, and listen for any sounds that you might hear. Picture the chalice being there with you.

As you tune in to this place, imagine the sound of a spring bubbling up somewhere nearby, and start to walk in that direction. Do not hurry; take notice of everything which occurs around you.

You come to a clearing or grove and find the spring.

In your own time, walk to the spring and fill your chalice with the clear water. Drink from your chalice and notice the feelings which occur, such as the taste, and what effect the water has on you.

When you have fully realized these feelings, come back to reality, and be sure to retain how you are feeling, what the experience was like for you.

It is now time to attempt to express what you have felt in the real world, grounding it in Malkuth. How can you do this?

EXERCISE 27

THE TREE OF LIFE SPHERES - TIPARETH

Prepare yourself by sitting comfortably, relax and focus on your breathing. Do not attempt to alter your breathing pattern, but instead, follow the air as it enters your lungs and is released. If there are any tensions within your body, release them in your out breath, relaxing your whole body.

Picture yourself wearing a dark, heavy black cloak with the hood up, covering your whole head and face. Spend some time imagining this cloak, feeling its presence all around your physical form. This is the cloak of your negativity, fears and the negative thoughts, emotions and sensations from your everyday life. Be aware of the heaviness of the cloak.

Become aware of the cloak lifting from you, taking all of the negativity with it. Really feel the cloak loosening, lifting and becoming lighter on your physical form. Then, imagine the cloak slowly vanishing.

When the cloak has completely gone, you will be free to clothe yourself in a cloak of your choice. A cloak of love, beauty, happiness, or anything that you wish. Really picture yourself wearing this cloak of light and positive energy. See its color and feel its strength and quality all around you. This cloak is a symbol of your soul, and you as a soul can choose to wear any cloak you wish. Choose this cloak wisely, and when you return to reality, remember to bring it with you, and use the cloak in your everyday life.

EXERCISE 28

THE TREE OF LIFE SPHERES - GEBURAH

Prepare yourself by making yourself comfortable and relaxing. Take deep breaths, and as you breathe out, release your tensions, and as you breathe in, realize that you are breathing in life-giving energy. Close your eyes and imagine yourself out in a windswept field. Take the time to clearly picture this in your mind, filling in as much detail as possible, not forgetting to use all of your senses. Include your clothing, emotions etc., really imagine yourself alone in this field.

As you look around you, you see a single stone standing in the field. Start walking toward this stone, still staying connected to the feeling of being alone in the field. As you reach the stone, there is a small opening in the clouds above. A ray of light penetrates the field and illuminates the stone. You can now see that lying atop the stone is a small object, a gift left there for you by an angel. Don't try and work out what the gift may be, but without judgment and censorship, see what the gift actually is. In your own time, pick up the gift, hold it tightly in your hands and thank the angel for giving it to you.

Return to the real world, bringing this gift back with you. Spend a little time (as much as possible!) writing about this experience and describing the gift, or draw a picture of it. Make sure that you go into great detail concerning the gift; leave no small part of it out for any reason. At this point, you may not know what the gift is, or even understand why it was given to you. Trust in the fact that it was right for you, and the meaning of it will become clearer.

It is now time for you to ground this gift in Malkuth. There are many ways of doing this, and it all depends on what the gift is. If it is a symbol that you understand, then concentrate on using its meaning. For example, if you received a red heart, you may need to express love in the real world. Other symbols may need more researching, and things that are real objects make take longer to decipher. What is important is that you take this gift and begin to use it in Malkuth, the real world.

EXERCISE 29

THE TREE OF LIFE SPHERES - HESED

In order to feel comfortable in your inner world, it is a good idea to construct an outer world where you also feel comfortable. This is your Sacred Space. To do this, the first thing you need to do is consecrate the room to your intention.

You can do this by lighting candles and/or incense, sprinkling water or by simply walking around the room, stating your intentions out loud. Once you have done this you are ready to find your power spot in the room.

Focus on your heart and start walking around the room with your eyes closed enough to not see any of the objects in the room clearly, but not so much as you start bumping into things. It is important, as with most of these meditations, to not attempt to work out where the power spot is. This will force you to make one, and it will most likely not be the true one. Allow yourself to be open to the experiences non-judgmentally, and let it find you. By doing this, you will find a spot in the room where you feel better than you do anywhere else in the room. This is your power spot.

You may wish to do a small ritual now to 'mark your territory' as many animals do. It may be as small as turning around a few times, just like dogs do before lying down, or even more complex. Your body has the same animal instincts as animals do, and you will know what is sufficient for this little ritual. This little 'dance' or ritual may be accompanied by music of your choice.

Drumming has often been used in ritual, but any sort of music will do if it feels right. This has created an outer temple, and the Sacred Space will be complete with an inner temple.

To create an inner temple, centre yourself in any way you know and pay attention to your breathing. At first keep it deep and slow but without forcing it in any way. Then, consecrate your space with a ritual that expresses your intention. You can use any movements or sounds or smells etc. which expresses your intent in a way which you devise. (it should be noted that at this point of development, one should be able to know the right things to do and sue without anyone telling you what to do.)

Remain centered, focus on your heart once more and make a series of at least three ritual prostrations. Each time you prostrate yourself, give yourself permission to go right down to the floor, lying on your belly, feeling the ground beneath you. The first prostration is to thank 'Mother Earth' for supporting you. Inwardly voice this thanks. Your second prostration is to affirm awareness and choice in embarking upon whatever work you do. On the third (and later) prostration, be aware of the specific intention for the work at hand. Be aware that in prostrating yourself to the earth, you can affirm not only the sanctity of your work, but also the sanctity of all life on earth.

Finally, silently meditate in your power spot, aware of the sacred energies in both your inner and outer temples. The process you have just undertaken will have affirmed your place in Malkuth. You are now ready to commence your ritual dance or any other ritual work you wish to undertake.

EXERCISE 30

THE TREE OF LIFE SPHERES - BINAH

This is an exercise for inner peace and certainty, which will help you balance yourself, particularly in times of disturbance or low energy. This meditation is very powerful, but can never be over used.

Relax yourself, but not so relaxed that you are liable to fall asleep. Pay attention to your breathing, watching the unforced, natural flow of air and energies in and out of your body. After several minutes of this, still focusing on your breathing, silently affirm to yourself: 'My body is at peace'.

Be aware of any sensations in your body- do not try to suppress them in any way, but also do not become attached to them. Simply watch them pass through your consciousness.

Then silently affirm to yourself: 'My emotions and feelings are at peace.'

Let any thoughts that arise be noted, but do not become attached to them. Spend a few minutes now watching sensations, emotions, feelings, thoughts, images, insights or anything else that come into your consciousness. Observe these events without getting caught up in them.

Visualize your being as perfectly silent and at peace in a silent and peaceful world.

Affirm silently to yourself: 'I have sensations, emotions, feelings, thoughts, but I, as an individual spark of the Self, am eternally at peace and at one with the universal rhythm.'

Realize the truth of this statement.

EXERCISE 31

THE TREE OF LIFE SPHERES - HOCKMAH

Prepare yourself as you have in the previous exercises with relaxation and natural breathing. Slightly alter your breath by breathing a little deeper, and connecting you in-breath with your out-breath. This means the when you have finished your in breath, immediately begin breathing out and the same with your out-breath. This results in a series of continuous breaths, with no pauses in between.

Focus on yourself as a Tree of Life, overlaying the image on your body. Concentrate on the central spheres of Kether, Tipareth, Yesod and Malkuth, with Kether at the top of your head, Tipareth at your heart, Yesod at your lower belly, and Malkuth at your lower spine.

As you breathe in, focus your attention on energy rising up the Middle Pillar, up the back of your body. As you breathe out, focus your energy on this energy coming down the front of your body. Keeping your breath connected as before let this energy cycle build up within you.

Determine where energy is needed within you to restore balance. Give yourself over to this place in your body, visualizing energy there. On your in breath, imagine the energy there becomes stronger and more balanced, and on your out breath, let out all of the disease and unbalance. Allow yourself to relax in this place within your body and let go of all of the tension.

See if there is a color or image that will aid your balance, and simply imagine this color or image sinking into this part of your body. Keep this up, letting the part of your body, which you are working with to be filled with this color or image.

Focus on your breathing again, directing your attention from this place in your body and returning to the image of the Middle Pillar of the Tree of Life, then the whole tree.

Take time to be aware of your whole body, relaxed, feeling well and healed.

Return to the real world and thank the forces in whatever way you see fit, and affirm that your healing is the healing of yourself, and also the healing of the whole planet.

[This exercise contains a method that is similar to the rising of Kundalini in yoga philosophy. Although not strictly akin to this same situation, it would be negligent of me to at this point leave out my knowledge of the effects of this. It is said that to raise the Kundalini energy without having naturally pierced all of the etheric blocks (or webs), one can create great mental anguish for one's self. I see this similarly to attempting to deal with the powers of the higher spheres without having dealt with the lower ones.

This exercise was designed for someone who has reached the point of spiritual development where these etheric webs would have been pierced and so would not do any damage to one's self. I am not saying that you may go insane if you just leap into this exercise, but it is expected that you undertake it as a fully developed individual. I.e. don't play with powers you don't understand!]

EXERCISE 32

THE TREE OF LIFE SPHERES - KETHER

At this point in time, there are very few exercises to adequately connect with Kether. Kether is a very high sphere, which many people never connect with during their physical lives, and hence, I shall not enter into any exercise for it.

This ends The Tree of Life Meditations

EXERCISE 33

REBIRTHING

A simple breathing rhythm that helps connect to deep unconscious levels. Past memories may be experienced and emotional blockages cleared. It can be a powerful technique for restoring a physical, emotional and spiritual balance. Rebirthing is simple and powerful; yet gentle healing process, which dissolves tension and stress in the body, while integrating the body and mind into a new aliveness and wholeness.

It is a journey into an unfolding of our soul's potential. It takes us to an awareness of our passions, desires, choices and goals in life - the soul's purpose, which is often obscured behind negativity and self-doubt.

It uses a combination of skilled counseling and body-orientated therapy involving a particular mode of circular breathing. From conception, birth childhood, adolescence, and beyond we have continued to form a deep sense of self. Much of this self-concept is formed within the family dynamic, which is made up of long-standing traditions of behavior and experience. This pool of family structures, as much as giving us a sense of identity, can also contribute to limiting our true growth. The rebirthing process takes us beyond this reality of the family-molded 'self' into a realization of a truer, deeper self - a spiritual self where innocence and beauty stand above guilt and pain.

It is from this realization of self where we derive the true power for creating the life we choose. Without this movement, we can remain trapped in patterns of addiction, dependency, betrayal and powerlessness as we go on clinging to our familiar stable structures. The ties that bind us here are often compounded by unresolved anger and resentment residing in family issues.

The process of rebirthing brings this suppressed material to the surface from the unconscious, reducing its power to sabotage our lives and giving us the opportunity to forgive and let go of hurt from the past. In the session, focus is given to the world of the "inner child".

The connected breathing cycle softens the diaphragm and bridges the heart to the belly, contacting and integrating feelings and memories of the child. Bringing this "inner child" into consciousness helps to reduce its needs being unconsciously projected onto present relationships. It helps us see where we may remain in fear of "parental disapproval" as we struggle to be free and self-motivated.

Indeed the environment of our birth may be where our "original sin" of guilt and shame stems from - the feeling of being pushed out or rejected from the "heaven" of the womb and, in the panic and fear, not being able to feel the "fingers of love" holding our inner security as we make this important journey. Rebirthing may heal the effect of the presence of fear or the absence of love at our birth. Rebirthing is safe and gentle.

It allows the body to remember and integrate "disowned" states, it purifies and cleanses the chakra system of the body, it relaxes, and nourishes -and most importantly it can birth one into a new spiritual reality - a place of deeper trust and security. On wider level it may enhance an understanding of our place in this present quantum leap in consciousness on our planet. It is true, that, as we heal our "victim consciousness", we empower ourselves to become a more open and clear channel for the creation of a new world from the truth within

Note:

Here is what you do..

You have done too many visual exercises. Read, re-read and grasp the idea of the above.

Then make a rebirthing exercise from the above note and record on a tape.

Start, (giving minimum 3 minutes of blank tape, the time for you to sit, relax and go into alpha level).

See what happens.

Good luck.

SECTION - IV

MANTRA MEDITATION

The Maha Mantras:

GAYATRI MANTAS DIFFERENT TYPES

Gayatri Mantra is known to be the greatest mantra. The Rishis of the yore composed different Mantras on the same meter as that of Gayatri on different manifestations of God. Twenty of them are given below. These twenty are a part from the Vaidika Gayatri "Om Tat Savitur Varenyam Bhargo Devasya Dhimahi Dhiyo Yo Nah Pracodayat."

Though the complete import of the mantras cannot be given, the implied and closest translations are given against each mantra.

- ***Ganesa Gayatri***

Om Ekadantaya vidhmahe
Vakratundaya dhimahi
Tanno dantih pracodayat

May we realize Lord Ganesa. Let us meditate on that elephant-headed god who removes the hurdles. May that one-tusked god enlighten us.

- ***Narasimha Gayatri***

Om Vajranakhaya vidmahe
Tiksnadamstraya dhimahi
Tanno Narasimhah pracodayat

May we realize Narasimha, the man-lion god, with his diamond nails that pierce the veil of ignorance. Let us meditate on that sharp-toothed one that destroys the demon of darkness. May that Lord Narasimha illuminate us.

- ***Mahayana Gayatri***

Om Narayanaya vidhmahe
Vasudevya dhimahi
Tanno Vishnu pracodayat

May we realize Lord Narayana, the Heavenly Father. Let us meditate on his Vasudeva aspect (indwelling spirit in all). May that Lord Vishnu illumine us.

- ***Mahalakshmi Gayatri***

Om Mahalakshimi ca vidhmahe
Vishnupatni ca dhimahi
Tanno Lakshmi pracodayat

May we realize Mahalakshmi. Let us meditate on that spouse of Lord Vishnu and may Goddess Lakshmi illumine us.

- ***Ali or Devi Gayatri***

Om Adyayai vidhmahe
Paramesvaryai dhimahi
Tanno Kali pracodayat

May we realize the Primordial Energy. Let us meditate on that Paramesvari, the spouse of Siva. May that Goddess Kali illuminate us.

- ***Brahma Gayatri***

Om Paramesvaraya vidhmahe
Paratattvaya dhimahi
Tanno Brahma pracodayat

May we realize the Supreme Brahma. Let us meditate on that transcendental principle, and may that God Brahma illumine us.

- ***Hamsa Gayatri***

Om Hamsaya vidhmahe
Paramahamsaya dhimahi
Tanno Hamsa pracodayat

May we realize Hamsa that is our own Self as swan Let us meditate on that Paramahansa, the Supreme Self. May Hamsa illumine us.

- ***Agni Gayatri***

Om Vaisvanaraya vidhmahe
Lalelaya dhimahi

Tanno Agnih pracodayat

May we realize Vaisvanara, the fire-god. Let us meditate on that seven-tongued, mystic fire and may that Agni, the fire-god illumine us.

- ***Surya Gayatri***

Om Baskaraya vidhmahe
Divakaraya dhimahi
Tanno Suryah pracodayat

May we realize Bhaskara, the shining one. Let us meditate on that Divakara, the presiding deity over the day, and may that Surya, the sun god, illumine us.

- ***Durga Gayatri***

Om Katyayanyai ca vidhmahe
Kanyakumari ca dhimahi
Tanno Durga pracodayat

May we realize Katyayani, the Sakti. Let us meditate on Kanyakumari, the virgin goddess. And may that Durga, illumine us.

The Description of Gayatri Mantra

Om	The word that is God
Om Bhuh	God who is eternal
Om Bhuvaha	God who is the creator
Om Svah	God who is independent
Om Mahah	God who is worshipful

Om Janah	God who has no beginning
Om Tapah	God who is the light of wisdom
Om Satyam	God who is the truth
Om Tat	That Eternal God
Savitur	The creative principle of light manifesting through the sun
Varenyam	That Supreme God propitiated by the highest Gods
Bhargo	The light that bestows wisdom, bliss and everlasting life
Devasya	The light of that effulgent God
Dhimahi	We meditate
Dhiyo	Intellect
Yo	Who
Nah	Our
Pracodayat	May lead towards illumination
Om Apo	Om (one who protects us from) the waters (of karma)
Jyotih	(One who is) the Light (of all the Lights)
Raso	(One who is) quintessence (in everything)
Amrtam	(One who blesses us with) immortality
Brahma	That Almighty God
Bhur Bhuva Svar	(Who is pervading in earth), atmosphere and heaven
Om	(May he bless us with enlightenment)

- ***Maha Mrityunjaya Mantra***

This Mahamritunjaya mantra is from the Rig-Veda and needs initiation for attaining Siddhi. Anybody can recite this mantra and attain good health, release from bondage and other problems. This is the greatest reliever from all evils and can be recited at any time like any other Maha-mantra. It should be recited preferably for forty days both in the morning and evening, after lighting a jyoti and sitting on a woolen asana while facing east.

Recite the Maha-mantra 108 times (one rosary) or its multiples in each sitting. This is the greatest work of Maharishi Vashistha. Before commencing the Mahamrityunjaya mantra recite the following small prayer to the everlasting spirit of the Maharishi for his blessings and guidance.

OM SUCHIRMARKAIR BRIHASPATIM ADHVARESHU NAMASYATAH (21 Times)

We pray to Brihaspati (the Lord of this Universe and the teacher of this Vedic Knowledge), whose wishes are inviolable, for good thoughts (that will lead to good speech and actions that cannot be violated as it will be the truth).

Vyam Vashishthaya Mamah (21 times)

This is the prayer to Maharishi Vashistha (whose Holy Spirit is Omnipresent).

The initiated should practice the Pranayama ten times with the Beejakshara Mantra "OM HOUM JUM SAH". Others can skip this and go to the Maha-mantra directly.

This is to be followed by the Dhyana Mantra (Meditation) of Sri Tryambakeswara (One of the twelve Jyotirlinga) and then meditate on Sri Tryambakeshwara (Lord Shiva) and Sri Amriteshwari (Gouri or Parvati Shakti) with the relevant beejakshara and Rudra Pooja. Meditate for at least 15 Minutes before starting the Japa (Recitation of Mantra).

Then repeat the following Mahamrityunjaya mantra 108 times or multiples of this number. The Mahamrityunjaya Mantra reads:

OM TRYAMBAKKAM YAJAMAHE SUGANDHIM PUSTIVARDHANAM URVAROOKAMEVA BANDANAAN MRITYORMOKSHEEYA MAAMRITAAT.

What is the meaning of this Mahamantra

It is important to understand the meaning of the words as this makes the repetition meaningful and brings forth the results.

OM is not spelt out in the Rig-Veda, but has to be added to the beginning of all Mantras as given in an earlier Mantra of the Rig-Veda addressed to Ganapati.

TRYAMBAKKAM refers to the three eyes of Lord Shiva. 'Trya' means 'Three' and Ambakam' means eyes. These three eyes or sources of enlightenment are the Trimurti or three primary deities, namely Brahma, Vishnu and Shiva and the three 'AMBA' (also meaning Mother or Shakti' are Saraswati, Lakshmi and Gouri. Thus in this word, we are referring to God as Omniscient (Brahma), Omnipresent (Vishnu) and Omnipotent (Shiva). This is the wisdom of Brihaspati and is referred to as Sri Duttatreya having three heads of Brahma, Vishnu and Shiva.

YAJAMAHE : means, "We sing Thy praise".

SUGANDHIM : refers to His fragrance (of knowledge, presence and strength i.e. three aspects) as being the best and always spreading around. Fragrance refers to the joy that we get on knowing, seeing or feeling His virtuous deeds.

PUSTIVARDHANAM : Pooshan refers to Him as the sustainer of this world and in this manner, He is the Father (Pater) of all. Pooshan is also the inner impeller of all knowledge and is thus Savitur or the Sun and also symbolizes Brahma the Omniscient Creator. In this manner He is also the Father (Genitor) of all.

URVAAROKAMEVA : 'URVA' means "VISHAL" or big and powerful . 'AAROOKAM' means 'Disease'. Thus URVAROOKA means deadly and overpowering diseases. The diseases are also of three kinds caused by the influence (in the negative) of the three Guna's and are ignorance (Avidya etc), falsehood (Asat etc as even though Vishnu is everywhere, we fail to perceive Him and are guided by our sight and other senses) and weaknesses (Shadripu etc. a constraint of this physical body and Shiva is all powerful).

BANDANAAM : means bound down. Thus read with URVAROOKAMEVA, it means 'I am bound down by deadly and overpowering diseases'.

MRITYORMOOKSHEYA : means to deliver us from death (both premature deaths in this Physical world and from the never-ending cycle of deaths due to re-birth) for the sake of Mokshya (Nirvana or final emancipation from re-birth).

MAAMRITAAT means 'please give me some Amritam (life rejuvenating nectar). Read with the previous word, it means that we are praying for some 'Amrit' to get out of the death inflicting diseases as well as the cycle of re-birth.

SUN / SURYA MANTRA

The Sun is the Creator, Preserver and destroyer and takes the three forms of "BRAMHA", "VISHNU", and "RUDRA". Hence the Sun symbolizing godhead is said to be Omniscient (all seeing / knowing Brahma), Omnipresent (Present everywhere and preserving Shri Vishnu) and Omnipotent (all-powerful like Lord Shiva). Thus the Sun becomes the "Ayana" (direction) of the Nara (humans) and is called "Narayana" (God).

Depending upon the direction of one's chief activity in life, the human beings can be classified as :

- ***Brahamins*** (Seeking knowledge i.e. Teachers, Priests etc.)
- ***Kshatriyas*** (Protectors i.e. Police, Military)
- ***Vaishayas*** (Preservers i.e. Businessmen,)
- ***Shudras*** (Involved in Labor)

Since the 10th house governs "Karma" the "DasAkshari" (10 lettered) Mantra of the Sun God helps one to achieve success in his career / profession and in one's endeavor.

The three mantras for BRAHMINS / KSHTRIYAS / VAISHAYAS are as follows:Mantras for:

Brahmins OM HRIM GHRINI SURYAADITYA OM

Kshatriyas OM HRIM GHRINI SURYAADITYA AIM

Vaishyas OM HRIM GHRINI SURYAADITYA AIM

For Others OM GHRINI SURYAADITYA

SUN Surya

Om jabaakusuma sankaasham kaashyapayam
mahaadyutim Tamorim sarvapaapaghnam
pranato-smi divaakaram Om suryaaya namah

Translation:

Om, I bow down with devotion to the shining light that is shining red like a hibiscus flower, shining onto the earth, removing all the darkness and removing sin.

Om, I bow to the Sun.

MOON - Chandrama

Dadhi sankha tushaaraabham kshiirodaarnasambhavam Namaami shashinam somam shambhormukuta bhushanam Om candraaya namah

Translation:

I bow down to the Moon, who is creamy white like a container of yogurt (dahi) and most pleasing, born from the churning ocean of milk, the effulgent emblem of devotion, which adorns the head of Lord Shiva

Om, I bow to the Moon.

MARS Mangal

Dharaniigarbhasambhutam vidyutkaanti samaprabham
Kumaaram shaktihastam ca tam mangalam pranamaamyaham
Om mangalaaya namah

Translation:

I bow down to Mars, the auspicious one, who supports the womb of all creation, shines forth with the radiance of beauty enhanced by love, and wields power in his hand.

Om, I bow down to Mars.

MERCURY Buddha

Priyangukalikashyaamam ruupenaa-pratimam budham
Saumyam saumyamgunopetam tam budham pranamaamyaham
Om budhaaya namah

Translation:

I bow down to Mercury, whose beloved body is dark like the night, the symbol of intelligence, and whose qualities are most beautiful. Om, I bow down to Mercury.

JUPITER Guru

Devaanaanca rishinaanca gurum kaancana sannibham

Buddhi bhutam trilokesham tam namaami brihaaspatim Om gurave namah

Translation:

I bow down to Jupiter, teacher of gods and sages, the greatest treasure, and the most intelligent of all creation. Om, I bow down to Jupiter.

VENUS Shukra

Hima kunda mrinaalaabham daityaanaam paramam gurum Sarvashaastrapravaktaaram bhaargavam pranamaamyaham Om Shukraaya namah

Translation:

I bow down to Venus, who is fragrant like crushed sandal and jasmine, the great guru of the demons, expounding all scriptures, and the descendant of sage Brigu. Om, I bow down to Venus.

SATURN Shani

Niilaambujasamaabhaasam raviputram yamaagrajam Chaayaamaartandasambhuutam tam namaami shanaishacaram Om Shaanaishcaraaya namah

Translation:

I bow down to Saturn, who is blue like a storm cloud, the son of the Sun and the brother of Death, who can cast his shadow even over the Sun. Om, I bow down to Saturn.

RAHU

Arddhakaayam mahaaviiryam candraadityavimardanam Simhikaagarbha sambhuutam tam Raahu pranamaamyaham Om Raahave namah

Translation:

I bow down to Rahu, the great warrior who divides even the Sun and Moon in half, born from the womb of Simhikaa. Om, I bow down to Rahu.

KETU

Paalaashapushpa sankaasham taarakaagrahamastakam Raudram raudraatmakam ghoram tam ketu pranamaamyaham Om Ketave namah

Translation:

I bow down to Ketu, who is red like a paalaasha flower, who makes the star-eyed constellation to set, terrible and awesome to behold. Om, I bow down to Ketu.

"Om Namo Bhagavate Vasudevaya"

The mantra of Lord Vishnu. Any thing in the world is possible by worshipping lord Vishnu, who sustains the life in world. Enchanting this mantra saves a devotee from many troubles. It bestows the devotee with prosperity, peace, wealth etc.

"Om Namah Sivaya"

It is the mantra of Lord Shiva. Many people have become rich from virtually state of starvation by enchanting this mantra. Lord Shiva (Bhole Shanker) is very innocent (Bhole) God and bestows his blessings immediately on the devotee.

"Om Sri Ramaya Namah"

The description of word "Rama" is unlimited. Lord Rama is the incarnation of Vishnu. A devotee can gain overall benefits in all fields of his or her life by enchanting this mantra.

"Om Sri Maha Lakshmyai Namah"

The mantra of Goddess Lakshmi, the goddess of all the wealth and Prosperity in the world.

"Om Sri Durgaya Namah"

This mantra is of Goddess Durga the combined form of the powers of Lakshmi, Saraswati and kali. By enchanting this mantra all the physical, mental, economic problems are solved.

"Om Aim Saraswatyai Namah"

Godess Saraswati bestows the devotee with the memory, Knowledge and the power of speech.

"Om Sri Maha Ganapataye Namah"

The mantra of elephant headed God (Ganeshji). A remover of obstacles and bestower of success.

"Om Kleem Krishnaya Namah"

The mantra of lord Krishna, the incarnation of Lord Vishnu. Solves all the problems of devotee and bestows him with wealth and prosperity.Buddhist Mantras

Om Vajrapaani Huum

Vajrapani doesn't, to many newcomers to Buddhism, look very Buddhist at all. He is a Bodhisattva who represents the energy of the enlightened mind, and his mantra also symbolizes that quality. He's pictured dancing wildly within a halo of flames, which represent transformation. He holds a vajra (thunderbolt) in his right hand, which emphasizes the power to cut through the darkness of delusion. Vajrapani looks wrathful, but as a representation of the enlightened mind, he's completely free from hatred.

His mantra is simply his name, which means "wielder of the thunderbolt", framed between the mystical syllables Om and Huum. This mantra helps us to gain access to the irrepressible energy that Vajrapani symbolizes. A familiarity with Vajrapani does, of course, help here, although the sound of the mantra is itself rather energetic.

Pronunciation notes:

'a' is pronounced as 'u' in 'cut'
'aa' is like 'a' in 'father'
'j' is hard, like 'j' in 'judge'
'uu' is long, like 'oo' in 'book'
'm' in 'hum' is pronounced 'ng', as in 'long'

Buddhist Mantras

WHITE TARA MANTRA

Om Taare Tuttaare Ture Mama Ayuh Punya Jñaanaa Pushtim Kuru Svaahaa

White Tara (Sitatara) is associated with long life. Her mantra is often chanted with a particular person in mind. She's another representation of compassion, and she's pictured as being endowed with seven eyes (look at the palms of the hands, soles of the feet, and her forehead) to symbolize the watchfulness of the compassionate mind.

As a variant form of Green Tara, her mantra begins very similarly. But added to the play on the name of Tara are several words connected with long life. Ayuh is long life (as in *Ayur*vedic medicine). Punya means the merit that comes from living life ethically, and this merit is said to help one to live long and happily.

Jnana is wisdom. Pushtim means wealth or abundance.

Kuru is a mythical land to the north of the Himalayas, which was said to be a land of long life and happiness (it may have been the original northern home of the aryans). Mama means "mine" and indicates that you'd like to possess these qualities of long life, merit, wisdom, happiness, etc. You can of course choose to wish these qualities for someone else -- perhaps a loved one who is ill.

Pronunciation notes:

'a' is pronounced as 'u' in 'cut'
'aa' is like 'a' in 'father'
'jñana' is meant to be pronounced with a hard 'g', but many people pronounce it as "nyaanaa"
'm' in 'pushtim' is pronounced 'ng', as in 'long'

Buddhist Mantras

So Hum: Breath and Mantra Meditation

By Shiva Rea

Mantra, the chanting of sacred words or sounds, is a central part of yogic meditation. Mantra comes from the combination of two syllables: "man," meaning "to reflect" or "be aware," and "tra," meaning "tool for" or "agent of." A mantra is a tool for reflection and the cultivation of awareness, and is used for both concentration and contemplation on the Source.

Within yoga, mantras are based upon sounds that reflect the energy of our divine nature. Om is considered to be the universal, consummate mantra. The following meditation is based upon the mantra "so hum," ("I am that") used within the traditions of Tantra and Vedanta. Since "so hum" also indicates the sound of the breath, it is a mantra that repeats itself effortlessly.

Find a comfortable posture for meditation (seated on a cushion or blanket, in a chair or against a wall). Place your palms facing up in *jnana mudra* (forefinger and thumb touching) with your palms facing up to open your awareness or facing down to calm the mind. Scan your body and relax any tension. Let your spine rise from the ground of the pelvis. Draw your chin slightly down and let the back of your neck lengthen.

Bring your attention to the tidal rhythm of your breath, feeling the rise and fall of your inhalation and exhalation. As your focus settles on your breath, begin to employ the simple mantra "so hum." As you inhale, say "so" silently to yourself, and as you exhale say "hum." Keep your focus on the sensation of your breath while silently repeating the sacred syllables, "so hum." As you drink your inhalation, gently drawing your breath along the base of your throat, listen for the sound of "so." As you exhale, listen for the sound of "hum" as your breath is amplified in the throat.

Let your mind become absorbed in the sound of so hum-in your internal chanting and your actual breath. As if you were watching the waves of the ocean, let your mind be naturally drawn into presence and stillnessno place to go, nothing to do, so hum, so hum. If a thought *(vritti)* arises, come back to the mantra so hum.

In the beginning, it may be helpful to set an external timer for 10, 20, or 30 minutes so you are not distracted. When you are finished, bring your hands together in *anjali mudra* (prayer position) and close with a moment of gratitude, reflection, or prayer to soak up the energy of your meditation into your being and life.

Buddhist Mantras

SHAKYAMUNI MANTRA

Om muni muni mahaamuni shaakyamuni svaahaa

Shakyamuni (the sage of the Shakyan clan) is the historical Buddha, also known as Siddhartha Gautama. He was almost certainly the first enlightened figure to be visualized. There's a beautiful passage in the Sutta Nipata (an early Buddhist text) where Pingiya talks about how he is never separated from the Buddha. He says that at any time he wishes he can see and hear his teacher.

His mantra is a play on his name. 'Muni' means 'sage'. 'Maha' means 'great'. So the mantra reads "Om wise one, wise one, greatly wise one wise one of the Shakyans, Hail!"

Pronunciation notes:

'a' is pronounced as 'u' in 'cut'
'aa' is like 'a' in 'father'
'u' is like the sound in 'put' or 'foot'
'v' is pronounced halfway between English 'v' and 'w'. If in doubt, then a 'w' sound will doBuddhist Mantras

Sabbe sattaa sukhi hontu

Sabbe sattaa sukhi hontu is a Pali phrase meaning "May all beings be well (or happy)". It's not, properly speaking, a mantra. It's a chant that is used in exactly the same way as a mantra. Unlike most mantras, it has a definite grammatical meaning.

Sabbe = all
Sattaa = beings
Sukhi = happy, well
Hontu = may they be

The chant has an attractive tune, and it's lovely to chant this at the end of a period of the *metta bhavana* (development of loving kindness) practice. It makes a beautiful group chant as well. Out side of formal meditation, you can chant this mantra while walking, driving, or while engaged in any other such activity.

Pronunciation notes:

'a' is pronounced as 'u' in 'cut'

'aa' is pronounced as 'a' in 'father'

Buddhist Mantras

Prajnaparamita Mantra

Gate gate paaragate paarasamgate bodhi svaahaa

This mantra represents a class of Mahayana scriptures known as the Prajñaparamita (perfection of Wisdom) Sutras. These include such famous teachings as the Heart Sutra and the Diamond Sutra. These texts were the subject of worship in Mahayana Buddhism, in much the same way that devotional figures were. Prajñaparamita eventually became personified as a goddess, but this is not her mantra. This one is associated with the texts themselves.

The words here do have a literal meaning:

"Gone, gone, gone beyond, gone utterly beyond, Enlightenment hail!"

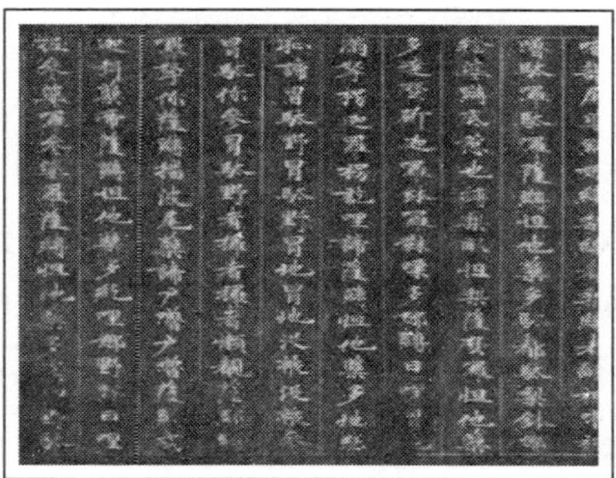

Pronunciation notes:

'o' is pronounced like 'o' in 'ore'
'a' is pronounced as 'u' in 'cut'

'aa' is like 'a' in 'father'
'i' in speech is pronounced like 'i' in 'mill', but in chanting ispronounced like 'ee' in 'bee'
'm' in 'parasamgate' is pronounced like 'ng' in 'long'Buddhist

Mantras

Padmasambhava Mantra

Om Aah Hum Vajra Guru Padma Siddhi Hum

Padmasambhava was a historical teacher, who is said to have finally converted Tibet to Buddhism. He was a renowned scholar, meditator, and magician, and his mantra suggests his rich and diverse nature.

'Om Ah Hum', as we've seen, have no conceptual meaning. Often they're associated with body, speech, and mind respectively (i.e. the whole of one's being. So there's a suggestion that we are saluting the qualities that Padmasambhava represents with all of our hearts (and minds, and bodies).

'Vajra' means 'thunderbolt', and represents the energy of the enlightened mind. 'Guru', of course, means a 'wise teacher'. 'Padma' means 'lotus', calling to mind the loving and compassionate nature of enlightenment. And Siddhi means accomplishment or supernatural powers, suggesting the way in which those who are enlightened can act wisely, but in ways that we can't necessarily understand.

Pronunciation notes:

'a' is pronounced as 'u' in 'cut'
'm' in hum is pronounced 'ng', as in 'long'
'j' is hard, like 'j' in 'judge'
'u' is short, as in 'put'

APPENDIX 1

MANTRA MEDITATION

MALA

Mala in different cultures are known by different names, viz. *Prayer Rope, Rosary, Mala, Tenwa, Komboloi, Trayer Beads, Seb'ha, Power Beads, Dream Beads, Tasbiyye, Fozhu, Ojuzu, chaplet.*

A device for counting prayers or mantras has been used by people of various cultures for thousands of years. It may consist of a notched stick, a simple knotted cord or a leather strap that has rings of metal sewn to it in such a way that one after another can be flipped over when each recitation is completed.

The mala in its most common form consists of a series of beads threaded onto a closed loop that can be worn around the neck or the wrist. It may be inherited, received as a gift, purchased ready-made new or an antique. If you would like one made to order especially for you.

The first criterion in choosing the beads is the substance and color. It should correspond with the color of/or substance associated with, the deity or the practice. For example, for Krishna Meditation, a tulsi mala is used, for Shiva Meditation a Rudraksha mala is used.

It is said that pearl will multiply prayers by 1,000,000. If you can afford precious stones, diamonds might be even more effective.

Coral beads are cherished for their reddish tint that is the result of their growth in seabeds rich in iron off the Italian coast. As a consequence of their rarity in inland countries, the color is often enhanced by special dyeing techniques.

Red symbolizes the blood associated with the essence of female energy. It is a suitable choice for a mala to be used in the practice of Vajrayogini or Dorje Pamo.

Lapis lazuli, the stone native to Afghanistan, has been associated with royalty and wisdom for thousands of years. The Sumerian/Babylonian Great Goddess,

Inanna-Ishtar, divests herself of her lapis ornaments before descending to the land of the dead. After her crucifixion, she resurrects herself, restoring her dark blue and gold ornaments before returning to the land of the living.

In Tibetan Buddhism, lapis is associated with ***Sangye Menla***, the Medicine Buddha. It is the color of Guru Rinpoche's inner garment. In other words, there are archetypal significances to these substances that go beyond color associations.

Beads in the golden and orange range such as are found in amber, tiger's eye, topaz and hessonite are suitable for many practices of

Manjushri.

Even when vegetable (*i.*e. plant) material such as sandalwood (red or white sandal,) or tulsi seed -- what are known as ***bodhi*** seeds -- are used to make a mala, the "guru" [or in some Hindu practices, the Meru] bead which is the larger or terminal bead, and/or any marker beads at the 21st or 27th place, may be of a mineral or other substance. Coral, turquoise, Amber, silver, and bone are some of these. Carnelian and lapis are also used, and they are also characteristic of Islamic amulets and ornaments.

The brown and white 'Buddha-eye' or *dzi* beads are nice if you can find the old, authentic ones, now very expensive. Because of their long shape, they tend to be used alone as amulets. There is a characteristic design of white lines produced by a resist or etching process or by the mix of two materials used in their formation. Few of those on the Internet or for sale in shops today have the true "eye" design.

People have said that dzi [or Zi] beads just manifest from the soil of Tibet; others think that they are the product of a lost Tibetan technology. It was recently shown that their place of origin is south India, although Persia [now, Iran] was also cited as their place of origin.

Rudraksha

Rudra is the Vedic name for Shiva in his capacity as the forces of nature, *aksha* means *tears*, so the name means *Shiva's tears*. These beads consisting of drilled brown knobby seeds (Elaeocarpus ganitrus *roxburgii*) are associated with austerities, penances and Shiva-ritual worship. They are also believed to confer various benefits according to the number of segments in the seed.

Strength & durability are priorities in malas used for *japa* (repetitions of mantra).

The ones made to order are strung on three cords of strong linen or silk; usually white but sometimes black or red. (Each cord is made of three threads twisted together.) As each bead is slid into place, there is a mantra repetition that goes with it, often accompanied by visualization.

The type of guru, or Meru bead (at the 'end') depends on the denomination [or religion] of the practitioner. In some lineages a vase-bead is used through which the ends of the cord are knotted.

When the mala is being worn around the neck, some teachers say the guru bead goes at the nape or back, others say it does not matter, and some say a mala should never be worn like a piece of jewelry. As in other matters, it is best to ask your own guru.

Counters are inserted at bead 21 [or 27] and its opposite number, although some denominations prefer that if two are being used, they both be on the same side, probably because that is less ostentatious.

If you interrupt your *japa* or mala-round and want to keep track, little silver pinch-clips are available for the purpose. (You could use a small safety pin, a brooch, a little tie of cord or even a paper clip.)

Using your beads

In India, -- that is, in the Hindu tradition -- the mala is rarely used in the left hand and the index, thought to be a rude finger, is not used to manipulate beads. It is also the custom not to cross over the Meru or Guru bead, but rather to flip the mala around and then go on again, since it is believed the power of accumulated mantras stored there could be dislodged.

To go back and forth with a short mala, insert your left hand into the ring of beads so that the guru bead is at the top. Flick or draw the beads towards you using the thumb. When you have 'run out of beads' so that they are up against the guru bead at the back of your hand that is away from your body, let the mala drop around the hook formed by the thumb so that you turn it around with a rotation of the wrist 'into the body' so that you have flipped the mala over, as it were.

AS SOON AS YOU GET THE MALA:

1. Have it blessed by a Rishi, Sage or your Guru; you could also bless it yourself if you know the proper way to do it.

2. Store it in a safe and clean place when not used. Some people wear it on their wrist, but that tends to wear it out faster than you might like.

3. Take it out when you start your practice -- Malas are for counting Mantra repetitions -- although it can be used for other purposes such as divination and giving empowerment, which probably does not apply to most of us. Don't fiddle with it; leave it in front of you until you start the Mantra recitation part.

4. As you say each Mantra (e.g., OM MANI PEME HUNG), you use your left thumb to draw one bead toward you. That's to invite the merit and wisdom IN.

5. When you finish the whole Mala (i.e., 108 or 111 times of OM MANI PEME HUNG), you can either keep counting in the same direction or turn the Mala around to count from the other side.

6. When you are done, put the Mala back in its safe and clean storage place. It is neither a toy or a collector's item -- it's not for playing or showing.

May your Malas be the rope that pulls you from the sea of Samsara!

The prayer beads are a traditional accessory. The basic number of beads is 108, which is said to represent the number of earthly desires which common mortals have.

When we use beads during *Gongyo*, [chanting] the end of the figure eight, with the two strands, is place over the third finger of the left hand. The end with the three strands, over the third finger of the right. They lie on the outside of the hands, which are placed together with palms and fingers touching each other.

Although traditional meaning has been assigned to the various parts of the prayer beads, they have no special power and are not an essential part of the Buddhist practice.

The Mala Oracle

A mala may be used as a type of oracular device, too.

To tell the future; that is to predict an outcome, one picks up the mala grasping it between the hands and poses the question. By fingering the beads moving both hands at once towards the mid-point, either *one* (yes) or *no* beads will be left between the hands. A variation is the "he loves me, he loves me not" method by picking up the heaped mala at any bead without looking, and then sliding the beads towards you until the end bead.

What do the numbers mean?

Though we think of Hindu and Buddhist malas as comprising 108 beads, as long as there are around a 100 (in a long or full mala) it is still usable.

108 is a number with numerological [9 x 12] and cosmological significance. Another, Vedic [ancient Hindu] reason, is that there are believed to be 108 channels going from the heart chakra out to the rest of the subtle body.

Buddhist Theravada tradition views the number 108 in this way:

"What are the thirty-six feelings? There are six feelings of gladness based on the household life and six based on renunciation; six feelings of sadness based on the household life and six based on renunciation; six feelings of equanimity based on the household life and six based on renunciation.

"What are the hundred and eight feelings? There are the (above) thirty-six feelings of the past; there are thirty-six of the future and there are thirty-six of the present.

On a more mundane level, the reason for the 8 "extra" beads is to make up for any errors or omissions in the "telling" or for breakage or loss of a bead.

In buying or making a mala, the size of the beads must also be considered, as well as the length of the space of bare thread that will permit the shifting of the beads. These choices depend upon the size of the hands that will be using the mala. Generally one made for a man is composed of beads of at least 10 mm. in diameter but often 12 or greater.

The wrist mala has become quite popular. It usually has 21 or 27 beads, and though some use elasticized cord, if it is to be used not just as a decoration, it is better that it be made of the usual strong cord or string in a length to suit the user. It must allow for being wrapped around the wrist without dangling so loosely that it will get caught on things or slip off too easily.

There does not seem to be any profound significance to holding the mala while doing prostrations, but some prefer it. The knocking of the beads against the floor can be distracting to others.

Basically, a mala is a tool for keeping track of counting. However, many people believe that the energy of accumulated mantras may be stored in the mala, and hence it should be kept in a bag with its drawstring drawn tight, or enclosed in a special box when it is not being used.

A BLESSING FOR THE *MALA*

"om rutsira mani prawa taya hum"

In the *Palace of Vast Jewels*, it says to recite this seven times and blow on the to increase the power of subsequent recitations.

Rosary (or any counters to be used)

The Vishnavite Hindu mala

[*Vishnavite* is the adjective for Vishnu-worshippers; Krishna is one of his avatars or manifestations.]

1. There are 108 beads and the Krishna bead. The 108 beads symbolize the 108 Gopis [dairymaids] who represent *bhakti* (loving devotion to Krishna).

2. The Krishna bead is the starting point and you pay your respects to your Guru Maharaj, to the line of succession and to Krishna to cleanse you of sinful reactions and to protect you if you commit any offenses when chanting that you are not aware of.

3. The beads are made from the tulsi plant [basil] because Tulsi Maharani is a surrendered soul and is always at the Lotus feet of the Lord. Therefore contacting her when chanting also reminds us to surrender to Krishna.

4. There are counters that are separate to mark the rounds that have been completed. Your spiritual master will let you know how many rounds to chant.

5. The reason for chanting is because Krishna is not different from his name and therefore chanting his name means you are in his company. It also means that you are re-establishing your eternal relationship with him. Therefore there is congregational chanting by devotees of his mantra:

Hare Krishna Hare Krishna
Krishna Krishna Hare Hare
Hare Ram Hare Ram
Ram Ram Hare Hare

By this mantra, we ask the Lord [Krishna] to allow us to serve him, and to re-establish our relationship with him. *Bonafide* chanting means:

1. To be sincere and to endeavor to chant attentively.

2. To have faith in the Holy names.

3. To not misuse the Holy names.

"Saying the Rosary"

The device used by Catholics as a tool to aid in counting may have been adapted from the *mala.* But the Christian rosary is in fact, more than that, since it provides the order and the cues for a complete *sadhana* as it were, dedicated to Notre-Dame or Our Lady.

Early Christians used a rosary of 150 beads -- the number derived from the ***Old Testament***'s 150 Psalms. The contemporary rosary consists of various sections; the ten-bead sections are known as *decades*. A chaplet is a short rosary of only a decade (10 beads.)

Sufi and Other Islamic Bead Practices

The so-called worry beads carried by Middle Eastern men number 33 beads. They are used (3x) in Muslim practice to count the 99 Names of God.

For many people, though, when the beads are rolled between thumb and forefinger two at a time, they serve merely as an outlet for anxiety, or to channel nervous energy, so they are often truly *Worry Beads*. Often the number of beads will be few and the beads much larger if it is intended to be used in this way.

God Bless You.

GLOSSARY

DIFFICULF WORDS MADE EASY

SECTION I

Abhidhamma Pitaka — the third and historically the latest of the three "baskets," or collections of texts, that together compose the Pali canon of Theravada Buddhism, the form predominant in Southeast Asia and Sri Lanka (Ceylon). The other two collections are Sutta ("Discourse"; Sanskrit Sutra) and Vinaya ("Discipline") Pitakas. Unlike Sutta and Vinaya, the seven Abhidhamma works are not generally…

Acharns — It is not an exaggeration to say that before the time of Phra Acharn Sao and Phra Acharn Mun, the Northeastern region was predominantly ruled over by ghosts, spirits and demons. People beginning work on a farm or in a garden, anyone building a house or anything else--all having to consult a sorcerer or a soothsayer for the auspicious moment, day, month, or year.

They were then required to make

offerings to propitiate the spirits before beginning their work or whatever it was they planned to do. Otherwise, whatever mishap occurred, however trivial or insignificant, was always attributed to the wrath of these ghosts and demons. Even coughs or sneezes, so commonplace even among dogs, were again regarded as the spirits' work! No function of the body was independent of the control of some demon, and the sorcerers at that time were surprisingly all-knowing and all-powerful.

They always managed to find that the people had angered the spirits and ghosts in doing such-and-such, and so to alleviate this wrong doing on their part, they would be required to propitiate the spirits by making offerings. They would be told that after such a propitiation was made, their cold, cough, sneeze, or whatever, would be cured. And this despite the fact that the symptoms of the disease would still be there!

The people thought that 'as the spirits'

man has spoken, so it shall be done.' And they would feel relieved through auto-suggestion, which was effectively applied by both patients and physicians alike through the so-called spirits' power. Medicines were of little importance in these cases. After both Acharns had instructed and awakened them to the truth of Buddhism, these superstitious beliefs and mystic rites gradually lost their hold over the people's minds. Many a spirits' man was convinced of the truth and came to accept the Triple Gem, instead of ghosts and spirits, as their Refuge.

This is the heritage both Venerable Acharns bequeathed to the people of the Northeast, and, in most parts, is still preserved today. A person wandering in that region today will hardly ever tread on the oblations offered to the spirits, which would have been found to have been scattered profusely in days gone by.

In this respect the Northeast may be said to have been liberated from the spirits' yoke through the kind instruction of both the Venerable Acharns. The grateful people of the Northeast will remember this precious and noble heritage for a long time to come.

Analogously	corresponding in function but not in evolutionary origin; "the wings of a bee and those of a hummingbird are analogous"
Annihilate	kill in large numbers; "the plague wiped out an entire population" eradicate, decimate, wipe out, carry off, eliminate, extinguish
Apathy	an absence of emotion or enthusiasm
Apocalyptic	prophetic of devastation or ultimate doom
Apparitions	a ghostly appearing figure; "we were unprepared for the apparition that confronted us"
Arahat	The Arahat is the "Perfected One" who has overcome The Three Poisons of Desire, Hatred and Ignorance.
Charlaton	Charlatan is a pejorative word which accuses a person of the practice of quackery or some similar in order to

obtain money by false pretenses. In usage, a subtle difference is drawn between the charlatan and other kinds of confidence people. The charlatan does not try to create a personal relationship with his marks, or set up an elaborate hoax using role playing. Rather, the person called a charlatan is being accused of resorting to quackery, pseudoscience or some knowingly employed bogus means of impressing people in order to swindle his victims by selling them worthless nostrums and similar goods or services that will not deliver on the promises made for them. The word calls forth the image of an old time medicine show operator, who has long left town by the time the people who bought his realize that it does not perform as advertised.

Convocation	This word literally signifies called together.
Dakpo Kagyu tradition	It was from Milarepa's disciple, Gampopa (1079-1153) that the tradition received its full name of Dakpo Kagyu.

Dhyana Mantra	'OM' doing meditation on Om with the mind completely engrossed and its meaning fully understoon.
Efflorescence	the period of greatest prosperity or productivity
Frugal	prudence in avoiding waste
Gaudiya Vaisnavas	The Brahma Sampradaya is divided into two schools: the Gaudiya Vaisnavas and the Tattva-vadi Madhavas (the Dvaitas).
Gomti Chakras	Higher chakras above Crown
Guhajasamaja	Highest Bodhisattva-aspect of the water element (Buddha Akshobhya), embraced by his female consort. His seed syllable is the blue HUNG. He embodies all wisdom qualities and magical powers of the six elements, symbolized by the attributes in his hands like vajra (water), wheel (ether), lotos (fire), jewels (earth), wisdom sword (air). His crossed hands holding vajra (male) and gantha (bell/female) symbolize the primordial, nondualistic state of his mind.

Hevajra tantra	The Hevajra tantra belongs to the fourth tantra class, the Annutarayoga (the others being Kriya, Charya and Yoga) and is very important within the KagyuImpetus 1. The act of applying force suddenly; "the impulse knocked him over" 2. a force that moves something along
Inculcates	to fix beliefs or ideas in someone's mind, especially by repeating them often
Intrinsic	essential
Kathavatthu	A group of seven suttas on the topics of discourse-past, future, and present
Khon family	The family known in Tibet as the Khon family, the holders of the Sakya lineage. The origin of the Khon family is in the realm of the gods of clear light ('od gsal). It is from the heaven of the clear light devas that the Khon family descended to our world. Thus they are known as the descendants of the clear light.
Kriya Yoga	A technique for life-force control and

	Self-realization
Kundalini	Salient power placed at your root chakra
Lahiri Mahasaya	Comtemporary of Yogananda Paramhansa, disciple of Maha Avatar Babaji and Guru of Swami sri Yukteshwar
Mahakala	Personal tutelary deity of the Mongol ruler Kublai Khan
Mahasangrika School	It is universally believed that the Mahasanghikas were the earliest seceder and the forerunners of the Mahayana. Around the 3rd century B. C. Mahasanghikas has split up into 7 schools, among them the Caityakas and the Saila schools were the most prominent and had great influence in the south. Both of them paved the way for the growth of Mahayanism.
Maitripa	"Seer of the Esssence". is an important figure both in mahayana and vajra-yana Buddhism.
Monotheist	A Mazdah-worshipper, a Zarathustrian, enemy of the demons, servant of the Lord" (Yasna 12, 1), whereby the believer declared himself

Nada	a monotheist, Chant
Nyingma tradition	The Nyingma tradition (literally, "Old School") is recognized as the most ancient among the Buddhist Schools of Tibet
Paranoia	self-referential,
Paraphernalia	The name given to all such things as a woman has a right to retain as her own property, after her husband's death; they consist generally of her clothing, jewels, and ornaments suitable to her condition, which she used personally during his life.
Patanjali	Maharishi Patanjali who lived before 2500 years is glorious, precise and perfect systematic study for realization of true knowledge of self-body, sense-organs, mind-thoughts, self-sense, self-conscious, soul and pure spiritual knowledge working behind the endless forms in universe, matter elements, subtle elements, subtest and formless inner nature essence and inner most and true essence of nature essence that is working in super conscious mind of

	all living being and non living being of universe and is cause of spiritual evolution and also becomes source of liberation of cycle of birth and death of living being.
Porous	able to absorb fluids;
Rosicrucians	The Rosicrucians are a legendary and secretive order dating from the 15th or 17th century, generally associated with the symbol of the Rose Cross, which is also used in certain rituals of the Freemasons. Several modern societies have been formed for the study of Rosicrucianism and allied subjects, but in no sense are they directly derived from the "Brethren of the Rosy Cross" of the 17th century, though they are keen followers thereof.
Sakya tradition	is closely bound up with the Khon ancestral lineage, which derived from celestial beings. The lineage has descended intact up to the present time from Khon Könchok Gyelpo (1034-1102), founder of the Sakya tradition.
Sarvastivada	The Sarvastivada school of Buddhist

Philosophy is a contraction of the Sanskrit "Sarvam asti", meaning "All of them exist" --a reference to one of the distinguishing doctrines of the school, the existence of dharmas in all of "the three times" (past, present, and future).

The Sarvastivada are one of only two of the "Early Schools" of Buddhism to have their written works survive in substantial, whole books unto the present day. Thus, their importance to modern scholars may be greater than their share of popular adherents had been.

Shabda	Holy verse
Shalivahana dynasty	Satavahan Dynasty 40 BC - 220 AD Simuka founded the Satvahana (also called Andhra and Shalivahan) dynasty (in 230 BC?). They ruled from Paithan on the banks of Godavari. Satavahan Satakarni I, is said to have performed *Ashvamedha Yajnya.*
Sirius	Sirius is the brightest star in the sky, after the Sun.

Solstice	either of the two times of the year when the sun is at its greatest distance from the celestial equator
Theogamy	product of bestiality (man x animal) and of theogamy (god beneath and above their station"
Uddees Tantra	Mrityormaa Nityam Yah Karoti Dine Dine Tasya Rogaah Prannayanti Deerghaayushcha Prajaayate. i.e. The person who chants Dharmaraaj Mantra daily is freed of all pains and afflictions and he attains to longevity. Dharmaraaj is the son of Sun and the brother of Venus.

Hence through the Sadhana of Dharmaraaj the boons of Venus Sadhana are also obtained. It is when all problems are neutralised that happiness in life is attained.

In the present age this Sadhana is very fruitful and divine and it surely produces the desired result. For success in life and in one's tasks one should surely try this Sadhana. If possible daily chant the Mantra before going to sleep each night.

Vajrakilaya	The wrathful heruka Vajrakilaya is a yidam deity who embodies the enlightened activity of all the Buddhas, manifesting in an intensly wrathful yet compassionate form in order to subjugate the delusion and negativity that can arise obstacles to the practice of Dharma. In fact the practice of Vajrakilaya is famous in the Tibetan Budhist world as the most powerfull for removing obstacles, destroying the forces hostile to compassion, and purifyng the spiritual pollution so prevalent in this age.
Vajrayogini	Vajrayogini, the dakini of wisdom. She is joyful, open, and empty embodiment of the most profound.

GLOSSARY

DIFFICULF WORDS MADE EASY

SECTION II

Hormonal	Hormonal comes from the Greek word "hormon" meaning "to rouse or set in motion.".
Matrix	a rectangular array of elements (or entries) set out by rows and columns
Mudra	Posture
Orcs	A Latin word for a demon or a creature of the underworld, the word Orc was revived by J. R. R. Tolkien in his fictional stories of Middle-earth as the name of a race of creatures that are often used by evil forces as soldiers.
Samurai	The samurai (or bushi) were the members of the military class, the Japanese warriors.

GLOSSARY

DIFFICULF WORDS MADE EASY

SECTION III

Devoid	entirely without
Ether	The upper regions of the air
Kabbalistic	A simple spiritualistic wisdom, order people use to improve their lives
Stimulation	cause or provoke a reaction in the body

GLOSSARY

DIFFICULF WORDS MADE EASY

SECTION IV

Narasimha	10th avatar of Lord Vishnu. This incarnation was taken to rescue Bhakt Prahalad from the atrocities of his father Hrinyakashyap. Narasimha is half man, half Lion.
Mystic	someone who believes in the existence of realities beyond human comprehension

Katyayani — Katyayani. Meaning: another name for Goddess Parvathi.

Sakti — Mostly refered as Kundalini. Consciousness as power, the supreme energy, the female counterpart of Siva as Pure Consciousness.

Rahu — The Puranas say that Rahu is instrumental in strengthening one's power and converting even an enemy into a friend. Even the effect of a snakebite could be removed by his grace. Success of effort is a blessing of Rahu as he stands for vigour and valour.

Ketu — Ketu is also an imaginary planet, a node.

Photo Gallery

Maha Avatar Bade Baba, resident in the Northern Hemisphere of the Himalayas. Guru of Lahiri Mahasaya

Highest Bodhisattva-aspect of the water element (Buddha Akshobhya), embraced by his female consort.

LAHIRI MAHASAYA Disciple of Maha Avatar Bade Babaji, Guru of Shri Sri Yukteshwar Maharaj and contemporary Guru of Swami Yogananda Paramhansa.

Photo Gallery

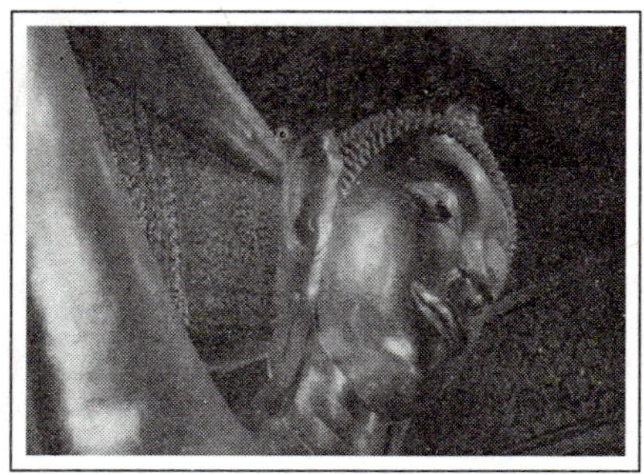

Paranibbana Sitting Buddha

Narasimha Avatar

Vajrakilaya

Rahu